LENNY HENRY

RISING
TO THE
SURFACE

faber

First published in 2022
by Faber & Faber Limited
The Bindery
51 Hatton Garden
London EC1N 8HN

This paperback edition first published in 2023

Typeset by Faber & Faber Limited
Printed and bound by CPI Group (UK) Ltd, Croydon, CR0 4YY

Graphic novel sequences written by Lenny Henry, illustrated by
Mark Buckingham and lettered by Todd Klein.

Extract from *Worstward Ho* by Samuel Beckett
© The Estate of Samuel Beckett

A CIP record for this book
is available from the British Library

ISBN 978-0-571-36879-2

Printed and bound in the UK on FSC® certified paper in line with our continuing
commitment to ethical business practices, sustainability and the environment.
For further information see faber.co.uk/environmental-policy

2 4 6 8 10 9 7 5 3 1

To every single writer.
To the Henrys and the Parkers

CONTENTS

PROLOGUE

Previously on *Who Am I, Again?* . . .

It began with my mum, Mrs Winifred Henry, arriving in the UK in 1957 at the behest of her brother, Clifton, who sent her a letter which said:

Dear Winnie – Come to Dudley in England. There are plenty of jobs here, some of which pay up to 30 shillings a week.
P. S. Bring me a wife.
Love, Clifton.

On arrival in the West Midlands she met a factory worker, Albert 'Bertie' Green, and they soon became soulmates and, not too long afterwards, my co-parents.

This is where I enter the story.

Thereafter, I was raised in a noisy household (especially after my dad, Winston Henry, arrived and found baby Len there) and grew up among school 'mates' who would rub my hair and ask if it was Velcro, or quiz me on which part of Africa I was from, or advise me to scrub myself with Brillo pads to see if 'the black came off'.

To put Dudley into context: don't forget we're not very far from Smethwick, where a Conservative MP called Peter Griffiths was elected under the slogan: 'If you want a n*gger for a neighbour, vote Labour.' This was deemed to be the 'most racist election campaign' ever fought in Britain.

Although I didn't realise it at the time, I was being raised in a toxic environment.

Then one momentous day, my mother stood us kids in the hallway and told us we all had to 'H'integrate with the people of Dudley', which was a predominantly white neighbourhood. So, liking a challenge, I went out and mixed with everyone I met. Eventually, I became fast friends with Greg Stokes, Mac Cooper and Martin 'Tommy' Thomas – buddies for life. They were three white boys from local grammar schools who were older than me, and (the *big* plus!) they had cars!

The moment I met them, the barriers that had kept me trapped within the walls of the hostile environment were smashed apart; we drove to every pub in the area and demanded alcohol, pork scratchings and the nearest jukebox.

We visited a number of drinking establishments that frowned upon the idea of 'intermingling with darkies', but Greg, Mac and Tom paid this nonsense no mind. We were there to try a dozen different types of beer and play Motown, Northern Soul and glam rock.

My role within the group was that of court jester. I would do anything I could to make them laugh and splatter Mild and Vimto from each nostril.

From here, it was a natural progression to performing in discotheques and dancehalls across the Midlands, impersonating Elvis Presley, Tommy Cooper, Muhammad Ali, James Stewart, Dave Allen and Deputy Dawg. Soon, I'd performed at the Queen Mary Ballroom in Dudley Zoo, the Ship and Rainbow in West Bromwich, and the Summerhill House hotel in Kingswinford. I was 'hood' famous.

But when my newly acquired manager, DJ Mike Hollis, wrote to two TV talent shows and asked them if they were interested in a black impressionist from Dudley, he was blown away when *New Faces* agreed to give me a try.

I auditioned in 1974, when I was fifteen, and told no one in my family I was bunking off school that day – it could have meant trouble . . .

The audition was exhilarating and fun. I got a huge round of applause from the audience and almost floated out of there. I was in!

Having passed the audition, Mike Hollis drove me back home and dropped me off at my front door. However, I was shocked when Mum interrogated me about my whereabouts that day, then made me perform the entire act on the front doorstep before she'd let me come in the house for my dinner!

My television debut on Saturday 8 January 1975 was seen by around sixteen million people. Life changed considerably thereafter. I was suddenly 'that black kid off the telly who does impressions'.

I was now nationally famous.

From here I was plunged into an insane thousand-miles-an-hour tidal wave of hard knocks and even harder-won lessons: i.e. always *listen* when Big People are talking through a deal on your behalf, or you might end up acting the fool in a damn minstrel show and then have to cope with the aftermath (i.e. the everlasting shame, smothered in a duvet of depression). I worked with Robert Luff's Black and White Minstrels from 1975 to 1979 on and off. I was eventually brave enough to beard him in his den and tell him that I was quitting. Then I waited to see what would happen next.

This book resumes my story in 1980, when I was booked for a summer season with Cannon and Ball at the North Pier in Blackpool, and also inked in for another season of the anarchic Saturday-morning extravaganza known as *Tiswas*. Life was starting to show promise.

It felt like I'd been well and truly chucked in at the deep end once more and it was up to me to see if I could claw my way to the surface and doggy-paddle to victory. Welcome to *Rising to the Surface* . . .

1

WHAT HAPPENED NEXT

Late 1970s, Early 1980s – Summer Shows and *Tiswas*

I soon realised that the entertainment industry was a reluctant bedfellow at times. Just when you thought you had an equal share of the eiderdown, you'd wake to find yourself with an ice-cold rear end and no cover at all.

My every advance was marked by a resounding KER-THUMP as I flew twelve steps backwards. Just as I thought I was heading for success, I'd do a bad show, or a producer would lose interest, or a series would get cancelled. It's the way of the world of entertainment: sometimes it's just not your turn.

In the early days, I honestly believed that the only reason people were laughing at my routines – and this is hard to admit now – was that a black kid doing impressions of Tommy Cooper, Dave Allen and Max Bygraves was an oddity. Like a dog on a skateboard or a black person reaching the final of UK *MasterChef*, it was something they didn't expect to see or hear. But I persevered, in the hope that this 'potential' that everyone kept talking about would make itself known to me at some point.

It was hard work, though, and 'potential', like the artistic muse, must be wooed diligently, gracefully and persistently. You can't just sit around and expect these things to appear and bestow their many gifts on you; you gotta get up, strip to your long johns, pick up a shovel and dig all the way down till you can't dig no mo'. That's a direct quote from Keats, by the way.

Thankfully, my overzealous work rate, enthusiasm and determination forced that upon me. Throughout this book the word 'potential' is used in its true sense, as in:

'Potential: having or showing the capacity to develop into something in the future.'

And also in my sense, as in: 'When will this "potential" thing happen, then?'

The Last Knockings
of Summer Season, 1980

If you've never experienced a British summer season, the idea is simple. Just like Jewish folk decamping to the Catskills to enjoy the charms of endless food, swimming, boating, camping and relentless stand-up comedy and songs from Broadway shows, the British seaside was a similar destination for middle- and working-class people to let down their hair and go wild for two weeks every year. Usually, as spring rolled around, each resort – whether it was Bournemouth, Blackpool, Bridlington, Torquay, Weston-super-Mare, Morecambe or Great Yarmouth – would prepare its hotels, amusement rides, penny arcades and beaches for a raving onslaught of demanding families looking for an inexpensive good time to be had by all.

In the mid-to-late fifties, at the theatres along Blackpool Pleasure Beach, you might find film, TV and radio stars such as Tommy Trinder, Jewel and Warriss, and George Formby; in the sixties and seventies you might see the cast of the *Carry On* films, Cliff Richard and the Shadows, champion drag queen Danny La Rue or Mike Yarwood, Dick Emery, even Cilla Black! Every British comedian you'd care to name spent some of their apprenticeship treading the boards in the seaside trenches. However, by the time I got to Blackpool – fresh from my TV exposure via *New Faces* – I got the feeling, as I explored the rather old-fashioned local environs, that this was the end of an era, not the beginning.

I had an inkling that the world was moving on from this archaic form of family entertainment. By the time I'd reached Blackpool for the second time, in 1980, there was a wide array of new performers springing up via the club or alternative comedy circuits – not just Cannon and Ball, but Alexei Sayle too.

My manager booked me for Cannon and Ball at the North Pier Theatre in Blackpool, and the experience was akin to being pummelled from all sides by a ton of bricks.

Summer 1980: Comedy Kings!

If you check out the programme displayed overleaf, you'll see
the top of the bill: Tommy Cannon, all suave and debonair, like
a Lancashire version of the crooner Jack Jones; and Bobby Ball,
a Chaplinesque ball of energy in too-short trousers, white socks,
red braces and curly quiff.

My section in the programme is indicative of the time. My
press photograph was a black-and-white shot of me in a dark
blue suit from a tailor in Wall Heath, Dudley, with INSANELY
awful lighting and a big showbiz grin on my face.

Lenny Henry is firmly established as one of our brightest comedy
entertainers. He achieved prominence as the first schoolboy
winner of TV's *New Faces* and has starred in TV series and made
many guest appearances in clubs and the theatre.

His act combines comedy with singing and impressions of
top personalities, including an almost life-like send-up of his idol,
Muhammad Ali.

The repertoire is extensive, and Lenny points out he has the
most natural gimmick in showbiz. 'It's not every day audiences are
treated to coloured versions of Max Bygraves, Tommy Cooper or
Michael Crawford,' he quips.

Did I really *quip* about doing 'coloured versions' of those
people? It's such a long time ago, I can't remember, but, clearly,
I had a very long way to go.

SHOWTIME 80

NORTH PIER BLACKPOOL

Cannon and Ball

Cannon and Ball have unleashed a new catchphrase for the 1980's with "Rock on, Tommy", but more than that they have proved conclusively with their TV series that they are one of the funniest comedy duos in showbusiness.

Tommy Cannon and Bobby Ball were both welders in Oldham when they first met. They became pals and formed a singing duo called the Harper Brothers. This meant a change in their lives; by day they were welders and in the evening entertained in local pubs and clubs. Such was their popularity that they were soon considering becoming professional entertainers, and an engagement in Wales made them reach such a decision. "We'd never worked outside Lancashire," says Tommy, "and suddenly we had a week of work in Wales. It went so well, we came home and handed in our notices.

That was how Tommy and Bobby entered showbusiness — though they were still the singing Harper Brothers. Slowly Bobby's flair for comedy crept into the act, and although their club successes continued, both felt they were getting nowhere.

"We needed a better name," says Bobby, "so we sat down and started throwing names at each other. One of us said Cannon and the other Ball — and that was it."

One of their earliest TV appearances was in Wheeltappers and Shunters Social Club, but their breakthrough came when they were signed by London Weekend Television.

Cannon and Ball have arrived. Both are happily married and live close to each other in Oldham. They off stage interests are similar — Bobby is a fishing fanatic, while Tommy is one of the best sellers in showbiz — and they remain forever ambitious . . . Rock on Tommy, Rock on Bobby!

Lenny Henry

Lenny Henry is firmly established as one of our brightest comedy entertainers. He achieved prominence as the first schoolboy winner of TV's New Faces and has starred in TV series and made many guest appearances in clubs and the theatre.

Since his initial breakthrough as a 16 year old winner on New Faces, Lenny's razor-sharp range of impressions, spontaneous approach to comedy and fine singing voice have delighted audiences.

Still living in his native Dudley, Lenny's credits include two series of The Fosters, in which he showed his abilities as a comedy actor, and guest appearances in Celebrity Squares, Seaside Special and The Ronnie Corbett Show.

His act combines comedy with singing and impressions of top personalities, including an almost life-like send up of his idol Muhammad Ali. The repertoire is extensive, and Lenny points out he has the most natural gimmick in showbiz. "It's not every day audiences are treated to coloured versions of Max Bygraves, Tommy Cooper or Michael Crawford," he quips.

The programme also mentioned that I still lived in Dudley. The actual truth was that I'd moved out of my mum's house and was living mainly out of a suitcase, on the road, or in Wembley with my friend, the actor Joseph Charles.

This separation from my family and close friends caused a deep ache within me. Although necessary, it was at times unbearable. Out of necessity, I was compelled to create new families and friends wherever I went. My childhood days had been all about finding a way to protect myself from bullies, racism and unnecessary heartache. Having friends and being part of a family, no matter how dysfunctional, was a big part of that. Now they were gone.

To all and sundry, I was 'that black kid off the telly' who cracked gags and did *coloured* versions of TV personalities. With hindsight, I can now acknowledge just how unhappy I was about this aspect of celebritydom. Apart from the odd night at the disco and numerous public appearances, I didn't hang out that much in the real world. I had work to do, loads and loads of it – two shows a night, every night. It was exhausting, relentless and, in the down times, as depressing as anything. But I tried to have as much fun as possible – I was still in my teens.

Life with Cannon and Ball –
Summer 1980, Continued

Tommy and Bob had a great act, the embodiment of the art of barnstorming – that feeling of walking on-stage and, through sheer force of personality, taking the entire audience on an exhilarating, laughter-filled journey. Their show was diligently rehearsed, with ample opportunities for ad-libs and messing around.

But as I watched them night after night, I realised something: these weren't ad-libs.

The hilarious bit when Bobby flipped the mic between his legs and then winced, 'Don't worry, Tom, I'm wearin' a box!' . . . the bit when Tom grabbed Bobby by the lapels, released him, and Bobby hissed, 'Tom, you got me piggin' *skin* then!' . . . every single ad-lib had been pre-rehearsed, practised and honed. Nothing was left to chance. And every night they'd get a standing ovation.

I was in awe. How did they *do* it?

In their past lives Tom and Bob had been welders, and they often mentioned this on-stage. The two of them seemed (off-stage) to be men from another era – working-class lads who couldn't believe their luck. I envied them their past work experience. When you're a comedian, your past life is as valuable as gold, grounding you and enriching every performance. What you did for a living, where your mum and dad came from and what they did – all of this is source material and, at any given point, will inform whatever decisions you make in the business, whether on-stage or off. This 'real life/work' stuff can lend the whiff of verisimilitude to your material. Billy Connolly in the shipyards, Tom O'Connor's stint as a teacher, Richard Pryor working in a mob-owned speakeasy – this experience becomes the ever-present reminder of who you were. It's a good thing.

As far as Tom and Bob's stage act was concerned, there was clearly love and respect for each other – the audience could tell that they had each other's backs. And, having slogged their way through the working men's clubs for a pittance, they were now earning crazy money at last.

I remember very clearly Bobby (rather unwisely) purchasing an ENORMOUS gas-guzzling, bootleg-hooch-smuggling Pontiac Trans Am. Early one evening, just before show time, he drove up, beeped his horn and pulled up next to me. He repeatedly pressed several buttons on the dashboard and talked at me in his usual manner:

Bobby: All right, lad?

Zzzzzzzdddddhhhhhh (the windows whirr down and then back up again).

Len: Nice car, Bob.

Bobby: 'Nice?' Just 'nice'? It's crackin', is this!

Zzzzzzzzzcccccchhhhhh (his seat shoots back all the way to horizontal, and then flips up again . . . the headrest pops up).

Len: Yeah, it is, it's beautiful!

Bobby: Aye, chuffin' beautiful, that's what it is!

He flicks a switch (the wipers spray gallons of water all over the windscreen, the roof and me . . .).

Len (now drenched): Ahhh! Lovely motor. Look at the tyres.

Zzzzzzzzzddddddhhhhhhhh (Bobby's seat rises quickly, until his head is touching the ceiling).

Bobby presses more buttons.

Bobby: This motor's a bobby dazzler, son, end of story!

Zzzzzzzddddddhhhhh (his seat returns to its original position).

BUMP! (His seat sinks lower until Bobby can't see over the steering wheel.)

Len: Anyway, Bob, I better get in, the half-hour call's in a minute . . .

Bobby: Yeah, I'm right behind you, just as soon as I can work out how to open this bloody door.

Zzzzzddddddddhhhhhhhh (the boot pops open).

Watching Tommy and Bob light up an audience every night made me jealous. Where was this palpable excitement for my act? Where were my big laughs? At the time, even though I was holding my own up there, it all felt a bit six out of ten.

Obviously, more experience and stage time were the key issues here. But how do you achieve that? It was all about rolling one's sleeves up and grafting. It was also about writers; nothing happens without great ideas and excellent writers. (It was such joy being twenty-two years old.)

Learning My Craft, from 1975
to the Present Day . . .

I watched as many comedians as I could, live and on TV. I listened to all the comedy albums I could get my hands on. Don Maclean gave me *A Wild and Crazy Guy* by Steve Martin and *Wonderfulness* by Bill Cosby. I bought *That N*gg*r's Crazy*, *Bicentennial N*gg*r* and *Is It Something I Said?* by Richard Pryor, *Standup Comic* by Woody Allen, *Class Clown* by George Carlin and *Reality . . . What a Concept* by Robin Williams. I soon discovered that there were more types of comedian than I had at first thought, particularly judging by what was on offer in the UK. There were dozens of types of comedy, and I was only tickling the surface. Richard Pryor's *Bicentennial N*gg*r* contained sketches, riffs, improvs, politics and dramatic set pieces on racism; Steve Martin's *A Wild and Crazy Guy* sounded like he was at a rock concert (it was thrilling to listen to – he throws almost every joke away as if he doesn't care a whit as to whether the audience *like* him or not); Woody Allen's *Standup Comic* is full of crafted and smart, well-structured bits that could almost be short films . . .

I had no idea how to transform the basic template of what I was doing at the time into something that worked consistently:

Opening song
Patter routine: 'Hey, Enoch Powell wants to give people like me a
    thousand pounds to go back to where we come from. Which is
    great for me, because I only live in Dudley!'
World of Sport theme

Eddie Waring

Muhammad Ali: 'Joe Frazier's so ugly, when he was a baby they
had to tie two pork chops round his neck to get the dog to play
with him.'

Henry Cooper

Dave Allen at Large theme

Dave Allen jokes

Max Bygraves joke: 'I took my dog to the vet. My dog was poorly,
ladies and gentlemen. Everybody say, "Ahhhh."'

Audience: 'Ahhhhh.'

Max: 'Anyway, the vet said, "I'm gonna have to put your dog down."
I said, "Why?" He said, "'Cos he's really heavy."'

Little song

Trevor McDoughnut newsflash: 'Owing to cut backs at
the BBC the TV shows *Crackerjack*, *Wacky Races* and
Jackanory are to be combined. The new show is to be called:
Crackerwackyjackanackynory.'

Clement Freud impression

David Bellamy impression

'Gwapple me Gwapenuts' (ad infinitum)

'The Bellamy Rap' (this was a parody of 'Rapper's Delight' by
the Sugarhill Gang, as performed by the TV botanist David
Bellamy. Only the diehard *Tiswas* fans got this – when it was
performed at the Royal Variety Show there were many blank
faces in the audience. Sigh)

Play off

That was it: twelve minutes, usually, but on a bad night it could
take anything up to half an hour to get off. Usually to the accompaniment of tinned fruit banging against the curtains.

I would do this twice nightly for twenty-two weeks at a time (including Sunday concerts), never changing, always doing the same thing over and over again.

By the early eighties things had started to improve material-wise, because Don Maclean had introduced me to a writer called Howard Imber, who started to funnel jokes by post all the way from Grantham in Lincolnshire. He charged a fair price per joke, and I'd get five pages of jokes from him each time. Result.

However, Howard wrote for everybody, so if you used his jokes, you stood the chance of sounding like everybody else for whom he was writing.

But – or so I thought at the time – 'the hell with it!': at least I had someone to talk to regarding the act. It was frustrating, though. Although there were non-stop requests for me to be on this or that show, I lacked a support network regarding jokes or bits I might do on them. It takes a while to figure out what you need . . .

The Delightful David McKellar

About a quarter of the way through the season, I started seeing a long-haired guy with dark glasses watching the show from the wings. Not every show, but definitely a couple of times a week. His name was David McKellar and he was a comedy writer. I found out later that he'd been working with Bruce Forsyth when ITV had basically given Forsyth all Saturday nights to host a sequence of shows, featuring anyone he wanted. But the reason David was in Blackpool watching Tom and Bob repeatedly was because they were about to get their own sketch show, and he was their head writer.

I befriended him. I was watching from the wings every night, too, so we were hanging out anyway. We'd go out for curries, drink together and laugh a lot. McKellar was funny and seemingly knew *everything* about comedy – from Peter Cook and Dudley Moore to Tommy Cooper, the Pythons and Dick Emery. He told me that the key to a lot of these people wasn't the rate of ideas, but the consistency. If you invent a small pool of sketch characters and repeat them, the punters love it because they just want characters they know every week – which means you can concentrate on the material rather than constantly having to invent new voices and catchphrases for each show.

It was the first of many eureka moments in my young life. It made sense! Why spend every hour of the working day coming up with new characters and voices when you could just perfect a few and keep feeding them with new material? You could continually please your audience without having to keep explaining who you were all the time.

I was hooked. I loved this behind-the-sparkly-curtain inside talk about comedy methodology. David spoke about comedy in terms of texture and tone, not just the binary 'got a laugh/didn't get a laugh'. He was about more than jokes. I asked him, very tentatively, if he'd write for me, and he said, 'Yeah, of course. What do you wanna do?'

My primary concern was *Tiswas*.

The Last Knockings of *Tiswas*
(Just Starting to Get It Right)

The blessing of all blessings by the end of the seventies was that I hadn't been dismissed from the *Tiswas* gig. But I was quick to realise that without a regular series on TV, my newfound fame might slip from my fingers, like an oyster smeared in Vaseline. So, I tried a variety of ways to hold onto my position amid all the chaos.

Luckily for me, Trevor McDonald, Britain's first black newsreader, had begun burrowing his way into the public consciousness. I was able to do a silly, halfway-decent impression of Trev, so newsflashes became my forte on the show.

Also, there was an eccentric TV botanist called David Bellamy, who had a way of rolling his Rs and speaking in a delicious, saliva-laden, fruity way. Soon Len as Dr David Bellamy, with the rolling Rs and a stupendous ginger stick-on beard, Hawaiian shirt, baggy shorts, boots and a handful of pig manure (or was it?), became a regular on *Tiswas* too. During a recurring segment called 'Compost Corner', Chris Tarrant would quiz me about growing unusual plants in the *Tiswas* allotment. As David, I would say: 'Well, Chwis, here we are in the bwilliant *Tiswas* garden and, as you can see, there is a mywiad of pewennials for us to pwesent, pewuse and pwactise our gardening skills on.' To which Chris would reply, 'Well, that's easy for you to say.' Then I'd rub pig manure under my armpits and say, 'Splash it all over, yeah, yeah, yeah,' like Henry Cooper in his recent Brut aftershave commercials. Then Chris would belt buckets of water over me and the fifteen firemen stuck in the cage! There's no business like it, folks.

These were different times – I was twenty-two and didn't understand the hurt an impression like this might cause. It would take me a long time to learn that . . .

Though I had developed in terms of providing content for the show, there was something missing. People like Bob Carolgees (of Spit the Dog fame) and John Gorman (the Scaffold, the Masked Poet) had limitless confidence in their abilities, no matter if things went wrong or they forgot what they were doing. It didn't matter to them; they'd just laugh and crack on. Tarrant could keep his cool in the midst of a hurricane, while being chased by zombies and reciting his seventeen times table backwards. Sally James was a seasoned broadcaster; Frank Carson, whenever he was on, just seemed to open his mouth and be funny. I felt as though I was the only one who, as the floor manager counted us down from ten to one, was panicking like Tom Daley running out of wool during the Olympics. It wasn't just a fear of failure, though. It was also the knowledge that I was still a kid, who hadn't served his time yet. I was vastly inexperienced, and the next few years would bear that out. I couldn't just keep doing a three-minute set – it was not what Chris or the viewers wanted.

David suggested I start thinking of my role on the show in terms of comedy bits, some live, some pre-recorded. We would come up with material on that basis. I'd work on it and rehearse with him, then I'd perform it for Chris on the phone and see how it went. Well, it only bloody worked. Having pitched several ideas to Chris, he laughed, told me I was an idiot and then asked me if I could pre-record stuff while I was in Blackpool for the upcoming summer season.

Woo hoo! David and I proffered me as Tommy Cooper performing stupid magic tricks in the street; some Trevor McDoughnut sketches (newsflashes from interesting locations, i.e. the sea) and a new character called Algernon Winston Spencer Churchill Gladstone Disraeli Palmerston Pitt the Elder, Pitt the Younger Razamatazz, a Rastafarian with a penchant for condensed-milk sandwiches who kept saying the word 'OOOOOOOKAAAAAY'. These were simpler times . . .

Luckily for me, these pre-recorded pieces seemed to go down really well, and it was the beginning of me actually fulfilling some of that missing 'potential' that everyone kept talking about. I did longer Trevor McDonald sketches called 'Pulsebeat'. I did quizzes where the rules were so complicated that, by the time I got to the end of the set-up, the programme was over. I did more structured David Bellamy bits. Algernon did routines and sang songs. Everything changed for the better that season because of David McKellar. Howard Imber also provided gags for *Tiswas*, so it was a win–win for all of us.

Thankfully, this improvement coincided with *Tiswas* being broadcast nationwide (it had only been shown in some regions before 1979; the plan was to increase the budget for this season), providing 'water cooler' TV at a time when no one in the UK even had a water cooler. There were legendary moments when we (the *Tiswas* presenters) would be walking down the street or eating in a restaurant, and people would rock up and say/yell/ drool: 'Now THAT bit was classic.' They'd be referring to things like four-year-old Matthew Butler dressed in a rabbit suit and singing 'Bright Eyes' spectacularly out of tune, or the day we blew up the spherical racist northern comic Bernard Manning on the I Speak Your Weight machine, or the time we all dressed as rabbits and did a routine with Chas and Dave, singing their hit song 'Rabbit', or the time we did 'Compost Corner' with Genesis, and I smeared Phil Collins with a mixture of shaving foam, horse manure and fuller's earth. There were stand-out moments every week, and (thank the gods!) I was a team regular by this time. *Tiswas* mania was growing.

The Cheapest Show on the Telly, 1979 into 1980

At the same time, my mentor, Don Maclean, and I did a TV sketch show called *The Cheapest Show on the Telly* for BBC Birmingham. They called it a 'regional opt-out programme', meaning that people in the Midlands could watch us instead of whatever mainstream BBC fare was on at the time. The show did surprisingly well in the region, considering we had no money for costumes, make-up, sets, music or jokes. We treated it like a radio show. Don's house was mission control – I'd show up there and go through material with him and our producer, John. There would be lots of laughing and messing around, and Toni (Don's lovely wife) would make vegetarian pizza, while their kids, Rory and Rachel, would hang around and listen to everything. It wasn't a bad life.

There were two series, and the response was pretty good, although some of the material had whiskers. Don and I enjoyed ourselves so much we even did a double act on *Seaside Special*. However – no offence to Don – I knew I wasn't a double-act type of guy. I couldn't imagine being on the road constantly with another person, although, as my career continued to gather momentum, company was the thing I'd end up craving more than anything.

A Mercifully Brief Explanation
of *Six of a Kind* . . .

Don and I were asked to participate in a show called *Six of a Kind*. It coincided with a massive strike at the BBC's Television Centre; everyone downed tools and walked out. No one dared to cross a picket line, so that was that for *that* show. *Six of a Kind* was intended to be a Saturday-night light entertainment vehicle for new talent, but its basic problem was that it lacked an original premise. Also, there were too many of us: six cast members, none of whom were allowed to contribute to the content, and none of us brave enough to broach the subject with our producer, the legendary creative juggernaut behind the later series of *Morecambe and Wise*, Ernest Maxin.

Ernest had dreamed up an idea for a big show with three singers (Leah Bell, Pearly Gates and Karen Kay) and three comics (Don Maclean, me and David Copperfield). It was going to be glamorous, bursting with song, with a little sketch comedy as a welcome buffer between musical numbers. We all hoped it would be the next big thing, but, unfortunately for us comedy performers, Ernest's enthusiasm and preference for the musical set pieces took the number-one spot in his hierarchy of things to nail. We rehearsed the big numbers endlessly. The sketches were farmed out to the usual suspects and, when they arrived, we had to like them or lump them.

David, Don and I would rehearse our comedy routines for each other, but that was all the attention we got. The most enjoyable part of the experience was being in that little family, the recurring jokes, all of us rehearsing as though we were on an early-sixties TV variety show with guests like Lucille Ball, Jack Benny, Frank Gorshin and Gene Kelly!

A Word on David Copperfield

David Copperfield was Doncaster born and bred. He and I were kindred spirits from the get-go. He just had that comedy-jokes spark: not only a gifted musician with a lovely singing voice, but also genuinely funny.

David had a great physical presence and could perform pitch-perfect pratfalls that echoed Buster Keaton, but with a modern twist. He would wrestle *himself*, pretending to be both opponents. He could do a somersault from a standing position. He'd deliberately walk into things *and* make the sound effect: '*Bam!* Sorry . . . bit pissed.' I found him hilarious, and we got on well. I guess when the bods at the BBC saw the tapes of *Six of a Kind*, the conversation must have gone: 'Well, Copperfield's like Freddie Starr but for a quarter of the price.' God knows what they said about me, but whatever that was, David and I were fished out of the mire and chosen to be in a new show: *Three of a Kind*. They'd done a show like this before with impressionist Mike Yarwood, comic Ray Fell and the magnificent Lulu, and they thought they could reboot it with some new blood. And they were right – eventually.

While all this was going on, I'd taken my final *Tiswas* pie in the face, my final bucket of water down the pants. We were an enormous, dysfunctional but loving family who ate, drank, rocked and created chaos together. The show would continue with Sally James at the helm, along with new cast members. Meanwhile, Tarrant, Gorman, Carolgees and I would continue with a brand-new thing. For Central Television, which was a new network and therefore a clean slate for us. Central gave Tarrant a bit more money, a late(ish) time slot and creative freedom. This could be brilliant, right? What could go wrong?

Moving from *Tiswas* to *OTT*

It all started very well. Chris and I had had a few meals where we'd talked about Lorne Michaels's highly original *Saturday Night Live*, which featured returning characters, topical sketches, special guest stars and up-to-the-minute music. We saw this format as a kind of template. We weren't trying to copy them but, in my mind, the more *SNL*-like we were, the better. We got the green light from Central's boss, Charles Denton, and *OTT* was born.

We auditioned for new cast members and found Helen Atkinson-Wood, from BBC Radio 4's *Radio Active*, who performed a very funny monologue and had us all howling with laughter. There was also Bob Carolgees, John Gorman, Tarrant and myself – all hardened veterans of Saturday-morning telly (this was how we saw ourselves in our minds . . .) – along with our secret weapon: Alexei Sayle, the killer compère and lead comedian from the Comic Strip posse.

A Bit About the Comic Strip

They were a motley crew consisting of Peter Richardson and Nigel Planer, who, as the Outer Limits, were a slick double act who used music and parody to send up whatever they felt like. Whether it was Space Invaders or rock stars, they were physical and could move in sync. Nigel sang well and played guitar and was good at being gormless (particularly when he did this hippy-dippy character called Neil, who just happened to be a hippy-dippy hippy). It was Peter's idea to form a production company called the Comic Strip and make everyone shareholders. No fool he.

Arnold Brown wasn't an official member of the company (Rik Mayall and Alexei didn't sign up either), but he played a role in the live shows, providing a droll Glaswegian counterpoint to some of the more insane goings-on. Arnold told jokes about having pictures of the royal family on his mantelpiece when he was growing up and thinking for years that he must be related to them. His catchphrase 'And why not?' became something that was muttered by almost everyone who worked with him. He was a genteel Scottish one-liner merchant. When Frank Sinatra came and performed in Glasgow, Arnold opened for him.

Rik Mayall and Ade Edmondson had been to Manchester University together and had an act called 20th Century Coyote. I remember seeing them on the yoof-centric *Oxford Road Show* and not quite understanding what they were up to. They were inspired by Samuel Beckett and were also trying out Brechtian alienation techniques to see how those could work. History has proven that they were right to abandon that stuff and just concentrate on being kick-ass hilarious. Adrian was an explosive performer who was incredibly physical and seemingly unhinged – nothing like his off-stage persona. Off-stage, Ade is quietly intelligent, funny, and also plays various instruments and has a great singing voice. On-stage he was LOUD and willing to have his meat and two veg grabbed on many an occasion for the glory of comedy. He and Rik performed twisted and illogical double-act-type routines; one was about a gooseberry entering a lift – they made it work.

With Peter Richardson

Rik was naturally charismatic. It wasn't just that he was funny, skinny, supple and could move; he could also swing his pants like a mofo – and he could make the word 'pants' seem hilarious. The repetition of the word during his version of Wilson Pickett's 'Land of 1000 Dances' that went *'Pants, pantsitty pants, pantsitty pants pantsy pants pantsy pants – pantsitty PANTS!'* (Rik channelling Wilson) was keel-over-and-bite-yourself-on-the-thigh laugh-out-loud high-goddam–larious. Rik could make you laugh without saying *anything* (just like Tommy Cooper or Richard Pryor could). He'd come on as a daft student poet and glare at the audience, snort, then say, in an incredulous, effete middle-class voice, 'What? What is it?' and get massive laughs. Rik would do a trick with his ear: when he did Redditch's premier investigative reporter Kevin Turvey, he'd start by bending his ear in on itself, before scrunching up his face until the ear b'doinged out once more! It was genius.

I loved watching him, and he (well, all of them, eventually) appeared in the eighties iteration of *The Lenny Henry Show*. Rik was a comedy god – we all loved and respected his skills. He is greatly missed since his death in 2014.

I was lucky to see him perform on many occasions. Even when something wasn't working, he was always funny. Watching Rik's realisation and eventual regret while wearing a huge, boiling-hot rabbit suit during a performance in Edinburgh was one of the funniest things I've ever seen.

Dawn and Jen

French and Saunders were also very much up there in terms of 'potential'. They had met while doing drama-teacher training at the Central School of Speech and Drama and had discovered a mutual taste for the ridiculous. They spent many hours improvising for their own amusement and soon were brave enough to get up on-stage. They were immediately impressive, which, given the male-dominated climate at the time, is saying something. Later on they would audition for and eventually join the Comic Strip, where they performed for a while without payment. They had no idea that everyone else was being paid and, quite rightly, there was a righteous beef and polite but intense negotiations until it was all sorted out.

D and J supported each other and laughed a lot at the material they came up with, and thankfully the audiences agreed with them. They used physical comedy, characters, dance, singing, and played with dialect and rhythms. Also, because they'd both been teachers, they could handle stroppy, drunken audiences with no trouble at all.

In those days Dawn was the outrageous clown, and Jennifer would often play the straight person. But, unlike Morecambe and Wise or Abbott and Costello, they would later interchange those roles, which would be the making of them. They were both brilliant in whichever role they took on. Dawn would eventually play an important role in my life.

Getting back to Alexei, though: he was the embodiment of

39

everything that was sharp and new and fresh about the alternative comedy scene at that time. He was literate and moved with grace on-stage – he wasn't built like Nureyev but, boy, could he dance like him. He was surreal in his choice of subject matter and could be blisteringly sweary and sweaty when called upon to be so. He swore – A LOT!

On *Tiswas* we respected the old-school comedy – from *The Two Ronnies*, *Python*, *The Frost Report* and club comics like Frank Carson to Dave Allen and some of those dudes from *The Comedians* who cracked gags about mother-in-laws, big-boobed babes and foreigners that looked like me. Bearing in mind all that traditional history that Tarrant loved, I think he was a bit in awe of Alexei – so new and alien and rude. The alternative comics were basically foreign to him, which is probably why his enquiries had led him to hire just Alexei for *OTT*.

I remember one routine where the live audience got so hyped, Alexei yelled at them, 'All right, all right! You can wipe the sperm off yer seats now, thank you.' That was one of the many times the complaints phone actually melted at Central TV. The other time might have been when an 'entertainer' called 'the Rat Catcher' – dressed as Robin Hood and with the accompaniment of genteel medieval lute music – proceeded to stuff live rats down the front of his tights.

OTT was also famous for half-naked girls in bikinis running around, a live breast exposure during a snooker match, foul language, more custard pies, buckets of water and – my personal favourite – England winning the World Cup without once having to play a match.

It was like being in a submarine several fathoms under the water and being torpedoed from all sides. Somehow, we all managed to keep our heads, face front and remember our lines.

The great thing about the whole experience was that I got to meet and befriend Alexei, who, during rehearsals on show day, would stay in his dressing room with his wife Linda, only walking onto the studio floor when he was needed. He scowled in a dissatisfied manner a lot of the time.

We bonded properly during a terrible tennis sketch on location. In between takes, I was brave enough to begin a conversation, the opening gambit of which might have been, 'This sketch is rubbish, isn't it?' and we've been mates ever since. He told me that his main problem with *OTT* was that it wasn't his show, so he had to just endure it.

In the world of the Comic Strip, performers were used to much more autonomy, wrote all their own material and got to road test it in their own venue. They had become notorious in a short space of time: some nights at the Comic Strip venue in Soho, London (known as the Boulevard Theatre to aficionados), folks like Jack Nicholson and Robin Williams would hang out in the front row. In its time it was the epitome of hip, and Alexi was at the pointy end. To go from that to the former home of the Crossroads motel in Birmingham could have been seen by him as a backward step. No matter – however Lexi felt about his role in the show, Tarrant was grateful for his presence and let him do whatever he wanted.

But I'm getting ahead of myself. Trust me – the first show was a doozy.

I remember the feeling of exhaustion as the opening episode came to an end. We'd done it! Then it was a shower, a change of clothes, and within half an hour the entire cast was driven to the famed Greek restaurant, the Limassol, in the city centre, where we were treated to the kind of monumental bollocking from Chris that beggared belief. He'd bought us all a big meal and supplied free alcohol, then, after we'd eaten and were on our second alcoholic beverage of the evening, flipped his lid and proceeded to tell us just how *useless* he thought we'd been that night. It was unbearable.

But the worst part was . . . he was mostly right. For some reason, we'd all thought that the residual glow and goodwill from *Tiswas* would transfer automatically to this show. It kind of did. But only a bit. And expectations were way too high. There was no way we'd ever be able to top what we'd already achieved. This was a different show altogether from our Saturday-morning effort. Our previous achievements did not matter at this point. Plus, this new thing felt too big, too new, too shiny, too rude, too bold, too sexy and too out of control – more so than any other show we'd seen before. The whole experience was knackering, and there I was in the middle of it all. Damn . . . *OTT* was hard work.

Here Comes Manning . . .

And then, just as the show began to improve (about week seven), Alexei had to leave for an Australian tour with the Comic Strip. He'd signed a contract; he couldn't get out of it. He was gone. Disaster. I thought, 'Well, whoever they bring in to replace Lexi will have to rock hard to compete.'

So, what did our wise producer and lead presenter, Tarrant, do? He booked Bernard Manning to appear in Alexei's spot!

Bernard Manning was a blue club comic through and through. His *raison d'être* seemed to be to annoy as many of the audience as possible. He wasn't the only comedian doing material that would upset you if you were a black or brown person in the club. There were a few London comics who majored in blue jokes and did dodgy impressions of foreigners. Liverpool's George Roper was always telling jokes about Irish people; Mike Reid had a reputation for being very blue and sending up pretty much anyone who didn't come from the East End. At the time it felt like 'bigoted/racist/sexist jokes by white comedians in ill-fitting clothing' had become a genre in its own right, and was very popular in the late seventies and early eighties. Manning had his own club, called the Embassy, in Manchester, where he could get up and say whatever he wanted. And if people didn't like what he was saying, they could get the f*ck out. Bernard's technical skills as a comic were in no doubt. But his subject matter – in his words: 'paddies', 'nig-nogs', 'pakis', 'chinks', 'krauts' (the list was endless) – was relentlessly offensive. But he was King Manning and so didn't care.

43

I remember there was a key wide shot during *OTT*: Manning was centre stage, machine-gunning the audience with inappropriate jokes, while the rest of us were sat at the desk behind him, with stunned looks on our faces. We hadn't realised it was going to be that version of Manning. Tarrant's forced grin looked like it might split his face in two. He always maintained that the Manning booking was to 'shake things up'. Well, it certainly did that for me. I didn't want to be involved with anything where 'Bernard Manning' was the answer to 'What happens when Alexei's gone?'

Sharon and Paul's Reaction to *OTT*, Episode One

The reaction to the show from everyone in my family – from people I cared about – genuinely shocked me. Until then my family had usually been pleased for me, proud of my appearance on stage and TV. *OTT* was the first time a chink in my reputational armour appeared, though it wouldn't be the last.

I drove to Mum's house the day after episode one to have a rest, a bath, Sunday roast, rice and peas and hard food (dumpling, yam, green banana, cho cho, etc.) – and generally just hang out with the family.

When I drove into Mum's street, it was empty. There was no one around. Uh-oh . . . It was like a John Ford western: tumbleweed rolled across lawns, recently abandoned children's scooters lay on the pavement – it was a ghost town. When I got in the house, it didn't look like anyone was around there either. No matter. I unpacked my bags, ran a bath, got in and took a looooooong relaxing soak. As soon as my eyes closed, I heard them in their broad Dudley accents.

Paul spoke first: 'What we gonna say to him?'

Then Sharon: 'I dunno. It was terrible.'

'It was worse than terrible, it was . . . terri-horrible.'

'Yeah, it *was* bad.'

'He should be hung, drawn and quartered.'

'Come on, he's our brother.'

'All right, just quartered.'

'It wasn't funny enough.'

'The writers should be dropped from a high building into a large pile of dog doo-doo.'

They both laughed here.

'They was all over the place.'

'There were no good ideas ...'

'The joke shop musta bin shut.'

'Or knocked down.'

Sharon and Paul

This went on till the bath went cold. I got out, dried off, dressed, went downstairs and faced the music over the dinner table. They repeated what they'd just said, but this time to my face, with both barrels. Mum was defensive on my behalf. She knew that I'd been working hard: 'Leave him alone, he's worn out. You tink it's easy putting a show together like that? Chris Tarrant is a good man. He eats one of my h'alcoholic Christmas cake from me every year. This is just the beginning of the series; it won't be this bad next week, and then the week after that they'll find a way to make it *not as bad as the week before*, until by the time they reach the end, it will be quite good. Now eat your food and leave your brother alone.'

I went back to work the next day, reinvigorated. I had already taken a phone call from my agent Robert Luff, saying that he would do his best to buy me out of the contract, and did I want to be in the Black and White Minstrels again? Anything was better than what he'd seen a couple of nights ago.

I assured him that we could turn the whole thing round and was determined to help do that.

And so, in the space of a week, we came up with Joshua Yarlog, the Zimbabwean impressionist who could only do English impressions in his own voice. We appropriated the preacher Nat West from *Three of a Kind*, and I performed Delbert Wilkins (the Brixton milkman) live.

Joshua Yarlog

The second episode wasn't as bad as the first one; indeed, from that moment onwards, every show was an improvement on the last. Sometimes by an inch, other times by a country mile. We rehearsed, we worked hard, we ate an inordinate number of hotel breakfasts with thick-cut chips. In the end there was some good stuff here and there but, in all honesty, we suffered from a lack of planning. You can't hit something if you haven't got a target. To my mind, there was no sense of what the show was *for*. Just being a grown-up version of *Tiswas* wasn't enough. It might have been better to swing for the fences and attempt something bigger, bolder and fresher. In the end we wound up somewhere in the middle. Ugh.

We all took responsibility for it – there was no point in pointing fingers. We just didn't quite nail it.

2

BEGINNING TO RISE

Three of a Kind (and Having a Plan), 1981–1983

The beginnings of *Three of a Kind* were happening at around the same time as *OTT*. The differences in the two productions were very clear. The shows were like chalk and cheese in that there are many delightful examples of cheese, and you only get used to eating chalk if you're desperate and there's nothing else.

Three of a Kind's producer, Paul Jackson, had worked his way up the BBC ladder and was ready to exert all his passion and energy on a new kind of TV comedy. In 1980 he'd already produced and directed a show called *Boom Boom, Out Go the Lights*, which featured as many of the new breed of comics as you could stuff into a half-hour format for £8.50, a toffee apple and half a shandy. The show featured Alexei Sayle, Tony Allen, Rik Mayall and Adrian Edmondson, Keith Allen, the Blues Band with Paul Jones, and many more, showcasing as many of these alternative acts as Jackson could. He missed out French and Saunders, but he'd realise his mistake later.

Paul had vigour and vim and verve and was immensely persuasive: when he wanted to convince you of something, he would get real close to you, bury his nose in your cheek and then talk a mile a minute. You had to give in to his demands just to get him to reverse. He was exciting to work with; his boundless energy was contagious.

During our interview for this book, Paul recalled having been told there was an Ernest Maxin show lying around on tape at the BBC called *Six of a Kind*, and that he should watch it because

Lenny Henry and David Copperfield worked quite well together and might be worth sticking into the original format (called *Three of a Kind*). All it needed was a girl.

He watched the show and, though he loved Ernest's old-school light-entertainment stylings, he didn't really get what the programme was doing. But for some bizarre reason, he liked David and me. He even came to see me work at the String of Pearls in Wembley. This was a hotel cabaret/disco that was a chosen rendezvous for vagabonds, ragamuffins, pimps and thieves.

Paul came and watched me do a turn. Luckily, it was one of the good nights. The act seemed to flow, and the audience had stopped trying to get off with each other for long enough to enjoy all the stupid jokes and impressions. He came backstage afterwards, introduced himself and told me he was trying to put together a new sketch show and maybe I'd be interested in taking part. He was so close to me as he said all this that you couldn't have slid an American Express card between us. That close. I was in.

We both went to the Grosvenor House Hotel on Park Lane to watch David Copperfield do an uproarious corporate gig. After an hilarious hour and ten minutes of mayhem, the game was afoot – David was signed up too.

All we had to do was find a girl. We were dispatched to the Royal Court theatre on Sloane Square to watch a semi-improvised play called *Four in a Million*, directed by Les Blair, in which there was someone I'd never seen before: Tracey Ullman. The characters were club performers, guitar vocalists, comics and girl singers – all marooned in scruffy bed-and-breakfast lodgings, pounding the northern working-men's club circuit. Everyone was good the night we were in, but Tracey absolutely stood out. She not only danced and sang but also made us cry, then howl with laughter. Who does that? Tracey Ullman, that's who.

David and I were in complete agreement: Tracey should get the gig. She'd be an asset. And, oh my God, she was.

The series benefited from her intense approach to character work. She had this ability to disappear into characters or just simply blow you away with ideas during something as mundane as a wig fitting. She wasn't afraid to improvise during rehearsals, which would discombobulate the writers. She acted as if *she* were writing the show and often treated the sketches merely as a serving suggestion, and would change things on the fly if she thought she had a better idea. I was in awe of her. I'd never seen anyone behave like that before – when I'd performed on sketch shows prior to this, you received the material, looked at it, rehearsed the arse out of it and then performed it in front of a live audience. It either went well or it didn't.

Tracey interrogated the material: 'Why is this funny? What if we did this? Would that be better?' She played with the characters, chewed on them, turned them over and over repeatedly in her mind. She talked all the way through this process, unafraid – no idea was too stupid. She had ideas up the wazoo; she impersonated relatives, friends, celebrities, people she'd just met or overheard in the pub, people she'd never met. Every day at rehearsal, I'd sit there completely flabbergasted and think to myself, 'I want to do that.' Tracey was inspirational.

Working with Tracey changed me. Every time we came to the table in the rehearsal room and considered sketches for the show, we'd throw out the dumb and sexist and racist ones first, then we'd think about everything that was left and argue for our favourites to be in the show. They might need work, but we had made a pact among ourselves that we wouldn't do material that was lazy or stereotypical. Looking back, I'm sure mistakes were made, but at least there was a plan. We'd made a manifesto and stuck to it. That's why I believe *Three of a Kind* was the success it eventually became. It was basically a sketch show featuring parodies, quickies and musical numbers. The three of us enjoyed the process of making it from beginning to end; we had a target and a specific audience we wanted to reach.

Tracey filled in some of the gaps in my memory during a recent Zoom interview:

Tracey Ullman: I started off as a dancer in the Second Generation in all those cheesy summer shows, and I met people like Les Dawson and Little and Large – I did a panto with them. I remember Les Dawson used to say to me: 'Why are you doing this? You're a funny girl.' I said, 'Yeah, but what else can I do?' And Les Dawson said, 'Go and see Benny Hill.' I said, 'I'm not gonna do that, I'm not gonna dance around in a bikini – that's silly.' Then I tried to do legitimate theatre. I had a very good agent called Lou Coulson. She said, 'You've got to get sensible.' She made me do the Young Vic, and I was at the Royal Court working with Les Blair. We improvised a play in about eight weeks. It was clear to me early doors that I wasn't the typical actress. I couldn't do Received Pronunciation [posh voice], and I loved making things up.

Paul was very clever with us. He knew there was this new wave of comedy on the way, and that change was coming. *Three of a Kind* was so different, particularly the scenes we were doing like Simon and Julie – all that reality telly/mockumentary stuff.

Tony Sarchet used to write Simon and Julie – a gormless couple who would do TV interviews at the drop of the hat. They'd been abducted by aliens and may have been bitten by vampires too, but spoke about these events in a very low-key, BBC2 documentary manner. I asked Tracey what she remembered about our relationship with the writers' room, and the creative process, and she replied:

Tracey: We'd get to North Acton rehearsal rooms on a Monday morning and we were fearless. We used to go down to the basement make-up areas at the BBC, with make-up ladies Sally Sutton, Sula Loizu and Naomi Donne, and they'd experiment on us with wigs and prosthetics and colourings. The amount of chemicals they put on us, it's a wonder we didn't mutate! But we didn't care because we were young!

Tracey also reminded me that during tapings of *Three of a Kind*, I would get upset because the lighting department would fail to illuminate me properly during certain parts of the show. We'd do these three-handed jokes against a white background, and if the punchline was mine – and it didn't matter what it was – the audience would be squinting and saying, 'Who the bloody hell said that?'

In subsequent shows I started asking for 'THE NEGRO LIGHT!' Soon after that, they got their act together.

The Meeting in the Big Room

Paul Jackson had appropriated a big room at the BBC, to which he had invited as many writers as would fit. They'd scoured the BBC database for comedy sketch writers – anyone who'd ever had two-thirds of a joke broadcast on TV or radio was invited to attend. We arrived and were taken aback to find about 350 writers packed into this room. None of them were black or brown. There were about three women in the room. The rest were all blokes with varying degrees of acceptable hair (several comb-overs, a smattering of toupees), supermarket carrier bags, briefcases and Marks and Spencer's jumpers, a plethora of old-school/Footlights/Oxbridge types, some Russell Group university people, along with one or two dandruff-shouldered TV veteran hacks thrown in for good measure.

Paul spoke briefly about the intention of the show. He wanted it to reflect what was happening during that period of the eighties: alternative comedy, a Thatcherite government, rebellion with regard to racism and sexism, etc . . . new rules for the road. He was exciting to listen to.

Then he asked us to speak individually. David got up first and just said he wanted the show to be as funny as possible. Once he'd said that it was 'job done'. Then he sat down.

I got up and said I didn't want my race to be the butt of the jokes. I wanted the attitude to black performers to change. It was time that we were the makers of the joke, not simply the taker. Enough was enough. I sat down.

Tracey got up and spoke eloquently about the tropes of young women in sketches on British TV – usually the mini-skirted secretary, filing her nails in reception; the gobby traffic warden; the hen-pecking wife; the object of desire – all stereotypical depictions that she wanted no part in. She said, 'Thank you.' And sat down.

I don't think anyone in that room had ever heard performers speak like this before. There were political shadings to everything we said. We didn't just want to be mouthpieces for anyone who wanted to stick it to every girl who'd ever refused to snog them at the school disco. We wanted to play real characters.

That was the theory anyway. It's good to have a plan because, even if you deviate from it occasionally, you can always shunt yourself back onto the tracks: 'Hey! We said we weren't gonna do this type of sketch!' The difference between *OTT* and *Three of a Kind* was that the Beeb had more resources for material and more time because it was pre-recorded. A live show like *OTT*, every week for twelve weeks with no breaks, was a huge commitment – it involved so much advance preparation that, by the time it came to making the bloody thing, everybody was exhausted before they'd begun.

So *Three of a Kind* went ahead on BBC2. We pre-recorded four shows in front of a live audience for series one and were met with a favourable response. I enjoyed the jigsaw-puzzle, piece-by-piece aspect of building the show, the rehearsal process at BBC North Acton, the line learning. I loved the staff canteen there. We'd finish rehearsals and then go and have lunch; you'd walk in and there would be Ronnie Barker and David Jason, two Daleks, a Dr Who and Wendy Craig – it was magical. I'd sat in awe in Dudley watching all these people on telly, and now here I was queuing up with them for sticky toffee pudding and a brew.

I asked Tracey about the vibe of the rehearsal/writing/performing processes of the show. She mentioned several times that some of the material we had to do was a bit 'corny' or 'cheesy':

Tracey: Sometimes you felt it too. And all we'd do is, I'd say, 'Lenny, this is corny,' and we would get through these bits. Paul would be great and go, 'Look, just do that, it's just a little gag in the middle.' He was so cool and modern and young – he really did a good job back then. We were lucky to get him. He knew that we were frustrated sometimes and that we were just these young kids going a bit mad – I mean, I was twenty-one! You were twenty-three, David was a bit older than us. Yeah, sometimes it was corny, but it got better every year. I remember that first year and I was really nervous. I was doing silly things like Moira McBitch and I knew I had to be bold, and I think that's what we've both been doing for our whole careers. You don't know if anything's gonna be any good unless you try. Kim Fuller was great; the rest of the writers' room was important – Bob Sinfield, Tony Sarchet, Andrea Solomons, Rob Grant and Doug Naylor, James Hendrie and Ian Brown, Hale and Pace. They all worked so hard. There was also this opportunity for them to write for a girl that could act. You didn't see a lot of that type of thing back in the day, it was mostly boys in that Cambridge pantheon. I had a go at Mike Palin when I worked with him on my show and said, 'How come you never had any girls on *Monty Python*?' And he said something like, 'We were frightened of girls.' He was very apologetic.

Three of a Kind was a different time – sometimes it *was* corny, but we got over that stuff.

You had a ton of energy, Len! You were really enthusiastic, worked hard. David [Copperfield] worked his nuts off. He was sort of a big brother to you, and you and he had this lovely old-fashioned rapport.

Me: I do remember roaring with laughter for most of the day. David's northern bluntness and rudery always got me.

Tracey: You knew how to laugh with *him* and you knew how to work with *me* – we were so different, and you bridged the gap, Len.

Me: I'd only been going eight years by then. David was much more experienced, almost indestructible. He has this attitude of [Doncaster voice]: 'I can sing, play the piano, crack gags *and* do voices. And I can do a vent act at a push. I can do well over an hour!'

Tracey: There was a noticeable change between season one and season two. It was really weird, 'cos suddenly we were this trio of young stars. Everyone seemed to love it. The only thing was, there were some *terrible* jokes in it. We'd do these quickies, like David saying, 'I'm just gonna run the bath', and then you'd see him run across the screen with a bath on a lead . . . terrible! And then they'd cut to us doing Simon and Julie, and that would be different, good and interesting.

Me: So the good stuff outweighed the dodgy moments?

Tracey: I've never been in a mainstream show since. I've always been in culty things. I think it was an achievement to be on Saturday-night BBC1 getting the ratings that we did. There was a bit of a dispute at times over who had written what, because we used to improvise and riff in the rehearsal room, and then the writers would take that material and try to incorporate it into something they were already doing. Kim used to listen to me rambling on about documentaries that I'd seen – I wanted to do a woman living in a flat with living fungus – and he'd go away and structure that into a mini single-camera documentary, and it was great, y'know? You were more of a writer than me, Len.

Me: I never felt that. What I did have was energy. I used to go into writers' meetings and have loads of ideas, because I thought that was what was required of me. I still feel that being in a room with your fellow writers should be fun and full of laughter – it shouldn't just be coming in and handing in two dozen sketches in a Tesco carrier bag. It's being funny in the room – that's writing too.

Kim Fuller Changed Everything

Once the first series went out, my star was on the rise. People weren't looking at me and going, 'There's that black kid off *New Faces* that does impressions.' Now I was that kid who'd won *New Faces*, been on *Tiswas*, faltered on *OTT* and was now on *Three of a Kind*, which had somehow pushed me up nearer the surface.

Mainly because I had discovered a writing soulmate.

His name was Kim Fuller. For the longest time, he was my bro from another mo. From the moment I met him, I just thought, 'This guy's hilarious.' Not only that – he was cine literate, had watched loads of telly, was a bit of a surrealist and was also well up on the history of British comedy. AND he loved Richard Pryor. Get in!

Kim Fuller

All About Kim

I asked Kim, how come he was so funny? Also – where had that particular stream of weirdness come from? Here's an edited version of what he said:

Kim Fuller: When I was at school I read *Lord of the Rings* when I was sixteen – we all read it. I was mad keen on the Goons: I loved Spike Milligan growing up, and all the radio stuff. I used to listen to *Round the Horne* on a Sunday with my granddad. He'd be boiling up a Fray Bentos pie in a tin for me.

With all these influences in mind, I'd fool around at school, and used to think people like Kenneth Williams were hilarious. When we were in Cyprus, my mum took me to see *Carry on Nurse*. I didn't understand it, really – Mum had to explain some of the double entendres to me.

I remember getting a copy of *Ulysses* by James Joyce when I was about sixteen, and we were in Ghana and I didn't really understand it, but I loved the words and his facility with language. I think that's why I like Spike Milligan's *Puckoon* – I remember reading that bit where Puckoon looks up at the church clock and it's stopped, and he thinks to himself, 'Ah well, at least it's right twice a day . . .' That surreal logic just appealed to me, made me laugh. Obviously, when I got to Reading University in 1969–70, it was the Pythons.

At the time I met him Kim was an ex-teacher and jobbing comedy writer who'd had submissions accepted on *Not the Nine O'Clock News*. When I interviewed him for this book, he revealed to me that he was late for that first big meeting for *Three of a Kind*, but he'd heard enough to know that he wanted in. He found his way into the BBC bar and told Paul Jackson that he'd like to be considered for the show. So Paul asked him to send in some material. Back then, he was writing with Vicky Pile (*Green Wing, Smack the Pony*) and was churning out material for various sketch shows at a rate of knots. He was young, wore skinny black jeans and pointy red shoes and was kicking ass – taking names and not killing nobody.

He had a surreal way of looking at things, breaking them down, funnying them up and spitting them out. He wrote loads of good things for *Three of a Kind* and eventually took over from Ian Davidson as script editor and head writer. Every song parody I did on the show – from Eddie Grant and Break Wind and Fire to Theophilus P. Wildebeeste – Kim wrote. I loved working with him; he made anything possible.

We wanted to take the piss out of *Brideshead Revisited*, so we did. We wanted to do *Fame!* ('I'm gonna live forever!'), and we did that too.

The other writers – James Hendrie and Ian Brown, Tony Sarchet, Bob Sinfield, Ian Hislop and Nick Newman, Murray, Rix & Wilton, Gareth Hale and Norman Pace, Andrea Solomons – were also funny and productive. But when Kim was eventually given the role of overall script editor he took the reins with great panache.

During seasons one and two we accepted unsolicited material: people from all over the UK were allowed to send in sketches and jokes. So the end credits would be longer than the show most weeks. But reading and assessing that mountain of material in the run-up to production was a slog, to say the least. David, Tracey and I would take boxes of sketches away on holiday with us and read everything, when we should have been kayaking.

But as season one proceeded into season two and beyond, the number of contributors slowly reduced, until we had exactly who we wanted in the room. We put in the work and enjoyed ourselves and didn't have much to moan about – though the three-hander sketches at the beginning of each show were a *bit* repetitive and eventually annoying. They all went something like this:

Lenny Henry: I'm a struggling actor. I only get walk-on parts.

Tracey Ullman: I'm a struggling actress. I only get walk-on parts too.

David Copperfield: I'm a struggling stunt man. Mine are the parts they walk on!

Or:

David Copperfield: I'm going out with a married woman. If I ring her and a man answers, I put the phone down.

Tracey Ullman: I'm going out with a married man. If I ring him and a woman answers, I put the phone down.

Lenny Henry: I'm a shareholder in British Telecom. Thanks to these two I'm making a fortune . . .

Although we got to perform a mini rogues gallery of characters, complete with a variety of voices, it did feel a bit vaudevillian standing there, doing these hoary old gags. (The show openings were different in season three – we played three numpties who talked at cross purposes in an entertaining and silly way.)

I wasn't mad keen on drag, but somehow I kept finding myself in women's clothing. The more outrageous the better. The laugh that exploded from the audience when I emerged fully made up as Ruth Madoc in *Hi-de-Hi!* was possibly the loudest I'd ever heard for anything. After that, I'd do drag in one or two episodes. (Even in the early noughties I found myself dragged-up as Beyoncé and Kelis – enough with the high heels already.)

Three of a Kind won all kinds of awards: Variety Club of Great Britain; a BAFTA for best entertainment programme in 1983; Tracey won a BAFTA for best performance in a light entertainment programme, also in 1983. That year we won the Silver Rose of Montreux and the international press prize at the Rose d'Or, the Montreux television festival. The Silver Rose was a big deal for our show – but none of us were asked to attend the ceremony. I don't know why. This was obviously something that the important BBC executives attended. Us kids were not invited. But we knew about it once we'd won, and we got to hold the trophies (Paul arranged that we'd get one each!) and have our pictures taken. I really felt that I had broken the surface of this fathoms-deep show-business ocean where only the strongest swimmers survived. At last, along with Tracey and David, I felt confident in what I was doing; we'd made an award-winning, funny, characterful, Saturday night, mainstream sketch show that viewers watched and enjoyed in their millions – we were chuffed.

Awards are the way the industry measures its progress – certainly for us this meant a rise in wages, programme budgets and self-esteem. We were up there and going all the way.

And then we broke up the band.

Winning the Silver Rose
Clockwise from left: John Howard Davies, Me, Tracey,
a BBC exec., David, Paul Jackson

3

GOING SOLO

DOING SOLO

After season three of *Three of a Kind* it was decided that we'd gone far enough.

Tracey was off to pursue a solo career. She'd made a record (a remake of Irma Thomas's 'Breakaway') which had charted, and she'd begun a musical partnership with the brilliant Kirsty MacColl.

I'd been promised my own show – *The Lenny Henry Show* – for the BBC and was happy to go ahead as long as Paul Jackson remained as producer/director. Paul was the comedy man of the moment and we got on, so this seemed like the right decision. However, he wanted to expand and work on other TV shows as well mine. This idea of creating and presiding over a portfolio of programmes is commonplace now, but it was seen as an over-reach by his superiors, and as a result he left for more favourable shores. Unfortunately for me, by taking his talents elsewhere, *The Lenny Henry Show* (for the moment anyway) was rudderless.

I got a call from Jim Moir, later the head of BBC Light Entertainment. His office upstairs at the BBC smelled of old-school entertainment – a heady mixture of cigars, cigarettes, dodgy whisky, golf and success. I was probably the first black comic to sit in that chair on the other side of Jim's desk. He talked me through the Paul Jackson scenario and advised me to let it go – Paul was out like bell bottoms. Forget him. I was reassured that Jim himself was right behind the new *Lenny Henry Show*; it was what he wanted me to do next for the corporation, and I would play a big part behind the scenes. He suggested just one producer/director for the project – a man called Geoff Posner.

Geoff used to be a floor assistant on shows like *Doctor Who*, *Top of the Pops* and *Dad's Army*. At the BBC in those days, a floor assistant worked their way up from making the tea and running basic errands to eventually directing and producing their own shows. This could take many years. However, this complete immersion in the programme-making process, from soup to nuts, meant that anyone who'd been through it would know exactly how to make a television programme – of whatever kind – to a high standard.

When I heard the name Geoff Posner, I didn't recognise it, but once we'd met, I remembered that I'd worked with him on *Crackerjack*, *The Ronnie Corbett Variety Show* and *Seaside Special*. Geoff was the cool bloke with the big hair and moustache who told you where to stand, when to walk on, which camera to look at and when to get off. He was kind and warm, and he laughed at the jokes. The minute I met him, I was excited. He had great ideas and wanted to help me make the best show possible. He had directed *Not the Nine O'Clock News* and *The Young Ones*, then subsequently my show, and went on to produce and direct French and Saunders, Victoria Wood and many more.

The greatest thing about working with Geoff was his sense of calm at big events. In later years, I'd guest-host at big live TV events such as Amnesty International or Comic Relief or the Queen's Golden Jubilee at Buckingham Palace, and at those things they generally don't tell you who's directing. But Geoff would always come down from the production truck and say hello – 'It's me today, Lenworth – have a good time' – and talk me through which camera to look at and everything else. I'd always calm down then. If Geoff was running tings, then tings was gonna be run right.

I interviewed the delightful Mr Posner via Zoom to get his take on the whole origin of *The Lenny Henry Show*:

Geoff Posner: I remember a particular Ronnie Corbett show and thinking you were so full of energy. You were nervous, of course, also very conscious of being in close proximity to Ronnie Corbett – I observed you being very respectful. He was an important person in your career. I didn't say to myself, 'I'm gonna be working with that man in four years' time!' however.

Geoff says there are two main instances in his career when the audience went completely mad. The first one was our silly parody of Michael Jackson's 'Thriller', and the second was our version of a TV documentary series called *The Rock 'n' Roll Years*, in which I impersonated the Temptations, Pelé, the Jackson Five and both Ike and Tina Turner, and performed a parody of Michael Jackson's 'Bad' video. All on a budget of six crisp pound notes and a two-day-old crème brûlée.

Geoff: We assembled a group of writers that we thought you might like to work with. They had lots of meetings with you. As a result, there wasn't a big gap between what you wanted and what they wrote. Occasionally I'd read stuff and go, 'Meh,' but most times I'd read things and jump up and down and go, 'We've got to do this!' To me, that was the best reward of all because I'd obviously go through the sketches with you in mind and say, 'Well, I hope he likes this, hope he likes that.' But I would never dream of taking an executive position over material. One of the things Ernest Maxin used to do was choose the material and then show the act how to perform it! He was a real Hollywood-style producer in the old sense.

I never thought of myself like that. To me, my job was making it happen and pushing it through so that secretly I'd get what I wanted. But also so that you were happy. Hopefully, whoever I worked with would feel the same thing. It was their show, their name on the front of it – they've got to be confident enough in the material to perform it in front of that audience. As script editor in chief, Kim was partly in charge of making things happen and, for the most part, he would come through.

First Rock 'n' Roll-Style Solo Tour, 1983

This is my first tour poster. No old-fashioned suit from Wall Heath here: I'm wearing a leather jacket and a white shirt. I look deliriously happy. I'd had the experience of going on the road with the *Tiswas* posse and seeing how rabid and crazy their audience was. I wanted some of that for myself. Phil McIntyre and Paul Roberts – tour promoters extraordinaire – had come to visit my manager Robert Luff to ask for permission to represent me out there on the road. Phil McIntyre was a bearded bear of a man with a no-nonsense attitude and considerable wit. Paul 'Robbo' Roberts wore a striped school blazer, impossibly tight black jeans and Converse trainers. Mr Luff liked them straight away, even though they were young whippersnappers from the north. They spoke eloquently about how they'd introduce me to a new audience, different from the type I'd been used to.

I jumped at the chance to not be in a suit and bow tie, with the usual depressing three-piece cabaret band – 'Ted on t' piano, Bert on t' bass and our Daniel on t' drums.' I wanted no more of that; surely this was the moment to change everything?

Mr Luff gave them permission to put me on tour for twenty dates, all at colleges and universities. I was over the moon – this was going to be great. I'd never done this type of gig before.

What it looked like:

Hooray! This is rock 'n' roll!

What it was actually like:

I ate a lot of curries, sometimes after the show, sometimes before, a couple of times during. I remember getting changed in the toilets a lot. This happens at college shows, because you're usually performing in the canteen, standing atop trestle tables that have been hastily shoved together with no thought for health and safety. I kept saying to Paul, 'But in summer season you're given your own private dressing room, with access to your own bathroom. There's usually somewhere to hang your clothes, take a shower.' And he'd reply, 'Aye, lad, but yer not in summer season any more, are ya?'

Unis didn't have any *facilities* unless you chose to get changed in the locker room. Sometimes I'd manage to scam changing in someone's office. That was always good; they'd clear out a load of books and files and furniture and coats and spare umbrellas, and then, once the space was clear, they'd spray air freshener everywhere. However, whatever they did, there'd still be the residual aroma of stale meat pie, manky feet and three-day-old beer farts.

The shows, though, were something else. I'd be on for an hour, supported by acts like Ronnie Golden ('stand-up chameleon', ex-rock 'n' roller), the Panic Brothers (Everly Brothers from up north), the Mint Juleps (a diverse all-girl doo-wop band from south London) and more. I loved touring like this. Actually, this did feel a bit like rock 'n' roll.

The Mint Juleps – Monica, Lizzie, Debbie

By this time, I was performing what would eventually become the *Live and Unleashed* set in embryonic form. Kim Fuller had come on board as my chief writer, at Paul Jackson's behest. After Paul came to see me at the String of Pearls, apparently he'd said to Kim, 'Go and see Len in cabaret as soon as you can – it's an emergency!'

Kim and I hung out together a lot and talked comedy. Now, I'd done a bit of that with David McKellar, but he was a lot older than me and had other aspirations, whereas Kim was closer in age to me and liked stuff that I liked – Woody Allen, Linton Kwesi Johnson, Earth, Wind & Fire, Richard Pryor. In fact, when Geoff Posner suggested that I do 'a bit of chat' (i.e. some stand-up) at the beginning of *The Lenny Henry Show*, Kim saw me flinch and didn't miss a beat: 'Yep, we can do that, no problem!'

Stand-Up Aspirations/Working with Kim

The reason I flinched was because I'd never done stand-up proper before, and if I was going to do it on TV, I wanted it to be in a similar vein to what I'd heard and seen my favourite American comics do. Kim understood. He got it. We talked a great deal about Richard Pryor and Bill Cosby. George Carlin was strangely formal with his stuff – his was the sketch style where a premise is presented and the comic plays all the characters. The Steve Martin model was too weird, but it was great for attitude – we don't care, we're just doing comedy/jokes. Cosby was impossible: a) he had a prodigious memory, and everything in his childhood was funny; b) he was just too good – the voices, the sound effects, the subject matter – plus, he was spotlessly clean! He'd done it all. We were going to have to find things that were unique to me and excavate material from that.

For the first time, I was collaborating with a proper comedy maven, someone who really knew his onions and was prepared to help me. Kim understood that I hankered after fame in the US. I wanted to perform on stages where Pryor, Cosby, Steve Martin, Robin Williams and George Carlin had been. I knew it was going to take me a while, so these British stages were like baby steps. I was in for the long haul and, now that I'd set my aim at a target, things were beginning to work.

Every time I did an American character on *Three of a Kind* or *The Lenny Henry Show*, what I was actually doing (in my head anyway) was collecting bits for my showreel. We did a hundred

77

variations on the NYC cop crime scene, as well as the hot shot lawyer, the soul music star, the glamorous gossip columnist – just to show people my range. It worked. Or at least I thought so. How was I going to gather such a variety of clips any other way? I hadn't worked on TV in the States so it had to be like this – me playing all those different kinds of black person.

Recently, a black journalist asked if I'd understood at the time what my role was to the vast amount of diverse viewers watching: 'You were representing every black person in Britain. That's what you were doing, Len. So if you got an accent wrong or upset people because you said something that misspoke their culture, you were dissing an entire group of people. You were the only one, Len. You understand?'

For a while in the eighties and nineties I was just like Christopher Lambert in that film *Highlander* – 'There can be only one.' For an extended period of time I was the only black comedian on British television with his own show. Gina Yashere and Stephen K. Amos joked that, basically, the only way they, as young black comics, were going to get ahead in the UK was for Lenny Henry to drop dead. One in, one out.

Despite the brutality of that joke, I was absolutely grateful for this privilege and worked very hard to sustain the levels of humour and invention with each successive series. I tried not to stay in one place but to always keep moving, going from sketches to *Lenny Henry Tonite*, a six-episode portmanteau series where the subject matter changed every week. In contrast, in 1987 and '88 *The Lenny Henry Show* consisted of twelve sitcom episodes about the life and times of Delbert Wilkins. I loved each and every one of them, but the pressure to keep coming up with new material was relentless. American comedy writers call this endless grind 'feeding the monster'.

The lack of competition was also telling, and made me angry at times. In the nineties I formed a production company called Crucial Films, and our main remit (it seemed to me at the time) was to 'create some vehicles for other black comedians'. We instigated a writers' programme called 'A Step Forward' (early nineties) and found several writers for a new show called *The Real McCoy* (mid-nineties). I also did another sketch show with comedy writer/producer Geoff Atkinson, Kim Fuller and a few others, where we included performers such as Felix Dexter and Ninia Benjamin, Tameka Empson and Jocelyn Jee Esien from the *3 Non-Blondes* show, and Llewella Gideon from *The Real McCoy*, which provided a platform for this burgeoning black talent. I also tried to create sketch show vehicles for Curtis Walker and, later on, Gina Yashere. The pushback at the time was hurtful – it felt like commissioners were saying, 'We've got you, Len. Why do we need all these other people?' It was very frustrating.

Things are changing a little bit these days, but not quickly enough. There doesn't seem to be much investment beyond two series for anyone to really make a mark. *Famalam* had 'potential' but has stopped after three series; *Little Miss Jocelyn* ran for two series, as did Stephen K. Amos's show. Javone Prince just had the one series, which was a shame because there were some good ideas there. What I *do* know is that all of them deserved to run for longer than they did. A sketch show needs time to bed down so that the audiences can get more and more familiar with the lead comic's style and sensibilities. In the sixties and seventies Mike Yarwood, Dave Allen and Morecambe and Wise had endless goes at making their shows come correct. The same luxury has not been afforded to comedians of colour, and that's a damn shame.

Nowadays in the UK we have Mo Gilligan and Big Narstie winning BAFTA awards and heading into multiple series commissions, while Judi Love seems to be winning over the general public via her stints on *Strictly Come Dancing*, *Loose Women* and *Celebrity MasterChef* – I can see her hosting her own show in the near future. There are a whole bunch of new (or at least newish) black comics doing the rounds of panel shows, podcasts and sizzle reels even as I write – big up Darren Harriott, Athena Kugblenu, Sophie Duker, Dane Baptiste, Kane Brown, Slim, Quincy. Keep rising.

1981–1983

Meanwhile, back during the making of *Three of a Kind*, I would sometimes come into work with the weight of the world on my shoulders. Paul Jackson would ask me what was up, and I'd tell him about some function I'd been to where a black person had chastised me for failing to uplift the black nation via the content on *Three of a Kind*. It seems crazy to think that a mere comedy show could shoulder that burden but, today, American programmes like *Dear White People*, *Insecure*, *Atlanta* and *Black-ish* demonstrate what the chastiser meant. There is this idea that black folk on TV have a responsibility to represent their people in a political, positive and creative way, without showing any of the faults or failures of that particular community. Which is all fine as far as it goes, but what a shame that we're now not allowed the joy of playing bad guys, robbers, thieves, pimps, embezzlers, ghostbusters, white-collar thieves, murderers and the rest. I guess it's because we've been so stereotyped repeatedly as lowlifes, but without the brilliant insight, writing and creativity that other roles seem to embody. Whenever a black guy is in a sports film, how come he's never the coach? He's always the janitor who somehow, almost magically, helps the failing athlete find his mojo and go on to win the championship. Will Smith does this in *The Legend of Bagger Vance*; Carl Weathers as Apollo Creed does it in *Rocky II*; Morgan Freeman as Red helps Andy to find a Zen way to do his time in *The Shawshank Redemption*. Unless black people are given the resources to produce their own TV shows and movies, the situation will not change.

So, here's me in the eighties with all that on my shoulders, the only black person with his own TV show – well, apart from Trevor McDonald, and Floella Benjamin and Derek Griffiths presenting *Play School*. This would eventually change, but not for a long time.

We once performed a Kim Fuller nativity sketch on *Three of a Kind* where we played all the kids as well as the parents. The sketch had gone down really well and there were lots of positive comments. Then Paul got a letter from someone who said that 'as a card-carrying Christian and church member of many years', he didn't need 'a n*gg*r on television taking the piss out of the Lord Jesus Christ'. Paul chose not to tell me about that letter until later. His modus operandi, while producing *Three of a Kind*, was that when complaints or letters like that came in, he had to 'keep that shit away from Len or he might explode' – a good rule of thumb, I think.

So, yes, black people all over Britain were watching everything I was doing and wanting whatever that was to be a more truthful representation of their existence. But how was I supposed to do that? I was barely into my twenties, and nobody had provided me with the manual on how to survive in show business.

Sometimes I'd nail it straight out of the box. For instance, Fred Dread: I always thought he was a good and powerful character, based on the poet Linton Kwesi Johnson's political outpourings in a reggae ryddim at the time. It was fun to do. Peter Brewis, *Three of a Kind*'s musical director, listened to the LKJ albums and wrote out his version of a track for his group of all white musicians to play. The brilliant and surprising thing was that when they locked in, they sounded like they were from Trenchtown, innit. Kim wrote the lyrics, and we were off. It's still one of the best things I ever did on the telly. I appeared wearing a bowler hat and sunglasses, before a drumbeat and the rhythm kicked in. Then, at the end, the bowler hat was removed – to reveal eight-foot dreadlocks! Fabulous. I don't know why it gave me such pleasure, but I do know that people, particularly black people, stopped me in the street and wanted to big me up in the days that followed. A nice feeling.

The Act – Basic Structure

I was still doing a very basically structured stage act at this time:

Opening song/rap

Stand-up

Character, maybe the Blues Singer

Song

Stand-up

Character, maybe Nathaniel Westminster, the preacher

Song

Character, maybe Delbert Wilkins

Stand-up

Character, maybe Deakus

Song

Character, perhaps Theophilus P. Wildebeeste

Song

End

This was how my act looked for ages. Once Kim and I had set the template for 'how to do Lenny Henry successfully on-stage', I stuck to it religiously.

But in the pre-*Lenny Henry Show* period, the stand-up wasn't really the important part of the show. People wanted to see the characters, like Josh Yarlog, Delbert Wilkins from Brixton, David Bellamy, Trevor McDoughnut, old man Deakus and Theophilus.

At the time, the stand-up routines were basic connective tissue to get me from one character to the next. I didn't put much stock in them because I didn't really see myself as a 'Folks-great-to-be-here-take-my-wife-please-tip-your-waitresses-thank-you-good night!' type of act. I'd seen a lot of those guys doing the working men's clubs and summer seasons and they were always great, but a bit one-dimensional. Even though they had good jokes, they weren't as much fun as the characterful comics – the impressionists, the people who did several things, rather than just one.

Tommy Cooper, Dave Allen and Tony Hancock were huge stars in British stand-up comedy, but the Americans had gone light years beyond simply by digging deeper. Their comedy didn't seem to be about wearing a silly hat or using silly props. American comedians created funny scenarios, which is probably why so many of them went on to write situation comedies. In their own self-created world, every line, every nuance or catchphrase led to them building a hilarious environment, with them at its centre. This was a world where everything was their kind of funny, and it was their job to tell us all about it during appearances on *The Ed Sullivan Show*, *The Tonight Show*, *The Late Show with David Letterman*, *The Dick Cavett Show* or *Saturday Night Live*. Comics could develop their personalities beyond the odd quirks and quips about the wife or mother-in-law; there was much more to excavate from one's personal life, if you were prepared to go that far. This idea frightened the living bejaysus out of me.

Up until 1984 I hadn't really seen myself as a dyed-in-the-wool stand-up comic. If true stand-up meant excavating the truth about Lenny Henry and making it funny for the punters, my first question was: 'OK, but who the hell is Lenny Henry?'

Truth is, I'm only just discovering that now – that's why my first memoir was called *Who Am I, Again?* Most of my career has been spent hiding behind hats, wigs, beards and silly costumes . . . what do you mean, 'the *real* me'? But this sudden demand for 'the real Lenny Henry' didn't frighten Kim. He just dived in and dragged me with him.

Kim wanted to create a Socratic environment where we could talk about and explore anything we wanted. He had never done this with an artist before, but he'd guessed (rightly) that the way to get the best out of me for this new show would be to dig deep into my personality, mannerisms, childhood, teens, schooling and so on through a sustained series of analytical conversations. This method terrified me due to the fact that, at that point, I had told no one about my birth father, Bertie. I didn't want anyone to know about my unusual childhood circumstances – that my mother's husband was not my biological father – although they weren't *that* unusual. When we were working on my semi-biopic, *Danny and the Human Zoo*, the director, Destiny Ekaragha, asked the assembled cast if anyone had multiple parents or siblings, and almost three-quarters of the room raised their hands.

So, Kim and I did discuss everything – but not quite *everything* – about my childhood and my teens, growing up, parties, drinking, early attempts at sex, dating. I talked and talked and talked and talked and talked until I was blue in the face – and, eventually . . . we got somewhere. Miraculously, material began to emerge from this process and, because I was allowed to be in the writers' room from the beginning, I was able to make more informed choices; I wasn't just being presented with a *fait accompli*. I could choose, rewrite, riff or improvise with this content in any way I saw fit – because it was mine.

And then, one week in Luton, Kim and I set out to discover whether this material was ready or not. The difference was shocking. I was much more confident; I knew the material backwards because I'd lived and breathed it for several weeks. And the audience (the missing link in this process so far) laughed loud and long. Thank the gods. The Potential had finally come to fruition.

Work in Progress
(Prep for *The Lenny Henry Show* in 1984)

So, while in terms of shaping the television show Kim built in plenty of talking time for us as a team, I had transitioned from just being an impressionist/joke-teller to talking about myself and my life as a way of navigating between established characters from the TV shows. We were up and running.

However . . . it's tricky doing stand-up on the telly. I didn't want to give away my best material – we'd just established its efficacy. So, we had to generate new material that was appropriate to a TV pre-watershed time slot. Kim was a step ahead: he knew that for this kind of heavy lifting it was better to have a group-think-style approach, opening out the gathering of material to the rest of the writers. Bob, Tony, James and the rest, along with myself and Kim, sat in a room at Television Centre and brainstormed ideas for stand-up. We laughed a great deal – mainly whenever someone said something rude, and everyone would burst out laughing and say, 'Well, we could never do that!'

Not everything worked, but that 'choose a subject, now go' style of riffing was excellent as a starting point. We'd do that for several hours, and then the writer would go away and write a few pages. Thus, I was able to glean over an hour of new material from which to pick nine or so minutes for each show.

Feeling empowered, I asked the production team to find places where I could perform this material, in a work-in-progress fashion. I'd show up at the Croydon Warehouse or the Donmar Warehouse. There were a lot of warehouses. Sometimes in a tiny theatre where, say, there'd be a radical, agitprop play on about racism in a factory in apartheid South Africa . . . at the end, the director would get up and say, 'Anybody wanna hear some Lenny Henry jokes? He's here, and he wants to try out some new stuff!' And almost everyone would say, 'YES, PLEASE!' This became my M.O. I'd find venues where the most depressing plays were taking place. The audiences were so much more receptive to the material: 'Thank God, some jokes!' By now, of course, I'd visited comedy clubs in New York, Los Angeles and Chicago, where I'd seen comics trying out material for the Johnny Carson or David Letterman shows because they wanted to be 'ring ready'.

I was blown away by the positive reaction to the majority of the material. I shouldn't have worried about my transition into a confident stand-up persona; all I'd needed from the beginning was a brilliant script editor and at least six college-educated comedy writers at my disposal.

I guess it's different if you're a character comedian – you're creating a world with your character at its centre (like Emo Philips or Pee-wee Herman), so there's no need for it to be personal. You're making up stuff to suit that character.

I wonder why we didn't just create a Lenny Henry character? I suppose we did in many ways – only a small portion of the material in those shows was actually true. Things would usually begin with a truism and then quickly double back to make some kind of joke. I wanted things that sounded true, even if they weren't. Later on, I began wanting to be more truthful whenever I spoke on-stage. Which, of course, came with its own problems.

The Lead-Up to *The Lenny Henry Show*, Season One (Continued)

So, I've done my college tour. I've done *The Lenny Henry Sunday Hoot* on Radio 1 (DJ Noel Edmonds and his Crinkley Bottom went on vacation, so I filled in for him for thirteen weeks) and I'm about to make the series.

While at Radio 1 I was given a private viewing of Michael Jackson's 'Thriller' video. I lost my mind. I loved it – I wanted to be Michael Jackson. I practically ran to Geoff Posner's office at the BBC and asked him if he'd seen the video. He said no, so we got hold of a copy and watched it together. We agreed that we should attempt a 'Thriller' parody for episode one of the series.

Lenny as MJ

Geoff calculated that it was worth making a big splash, involving twelve dancers, two choreographers and a rather generous spend on make-up, costumes and prosthetics. It was a gamble, but our 'Thriller' parody defied all expectations. We knew it would be funny, but there was more to its success than that. There hadn't been a black comic with his own show before – and the fact that the first show out of the box was BAFTA-nominated and watched by millions of people was cause for all of us to be very thankful.

Kim wrote the lyrics (I helped), and Peter Brewis wrote the music (his was the hardest task: it had to sound enough like the original for the audience to get it, but it couldn't just be a copy, otherwise we might get sued). Geoff scouted locations and figured out how we'd budget the rest of the series once we'd captured this thing on film.

I don't know whether it was nerves, but I'd put on weight just before filming began – something that would turn into a lifelong issue for me. I remember putting on the signature MJ trousers for which I'd been fitted, and they split just before shooting. We had to put gaffer tape up the butt-seam to make everything copacetic. Fortunately, you couldn't tell when you watched it back.

We worked hard that night. I remember being knackered at the end of it. The original was shot over a twelve-day period; ours was all done and dusted in one night. But what a night! We shot some of it round the corner from Broadcasting House and the rest of it in woodland nearby, plus a bit in a graveyard in Harlesden. Just what your recently departed relatives needed: Lenny Henry, the size of a heffalump, moonwalking over their final resting place. I can only apologise; it was for the sake of television comedy!

The first time we played it to the audience, I was called up to the sound booth, where the technician was wringing his hands and complaining, 'They're laughing too loud – this is going to be virtually impossible to audio dub. What am I going to do?' He showed me the controls and meters that registered the sound of the audience – for every beat of the parody that mirrored and subverted the original, there was a huge laugh that bent the needles all the way into the red. I was over the moon! I think I said, 'Nice problem to have, we'll figure it out,' and then split to get changed into Trevor McDoughnut.

Once Geoff had edited the whole programme together, I could barely contain myself. I couldn't wait for the studio audience to see it. The reaction was nuts! They laughed non-stop from beginning to end. We were all very happy. But I was going to have to wait to see what the TV viewers thought – we'd made the series in the spring (as was the practice back then), but it wouldn't actually be broadcast until the early autumn. Nowadays, you'd go: 'Bugger waiting, we've got that "Thriller" parody. Let's put it out before anyone else.' But back then there was no YouTube, no streaming, no illegal bootleg downloads, nothing like that. We had to wait all through the summer, hoping that no one did a 'Thriller' parody before us.

The rest of the running order involved studio-bound material, such as 'The Harold Pinter Weather Forecast' and 'The Trevor McDonald Gospel News', three sections of stand-up and a couple of other, quicker things. In all it was a pretty solid first show.

I had no idea what it cost to make a BBC1 mainstream sketch show. I don't think Geoff knew either. I got the idea, though, that we would be allowed to start with a bang with our first show, and then later on we'd have to compensate by cutting our cloth to suit our coats, as it were.

I loved that show. Even though it was stressful coming up with the material, and my weight kept yo-yoing up and down throughout, it was somehow worth it.

The weight wasn't something I was that bothered about at the time. I think when I came back for season two the gain was noticeable: I wasn't the same Lenny as in season one. But I had been through a whole process of trying to control my body shape via every diet imaginable: the F diet, the Y diet, the whole food diet, the 'only-eat-what-you-can-fit-into-your-hand' diet, the cabbage soup diet (Oy! The flatulence – this was a reason for social distancing way before COVID-19), and many others. I hadn't been diagnosed with diabetes at this time, but clearly there were things happening with my blood sugar that should have been caught much earlier. This was going to be a lifelong battle for me – and other members of my family. I wasn't alone. We were all big eaters, and that was reflected in our body shapes.

At Christmas time we'd eat so much that we'd all fall asleep after lunch and then wake up hours later to find Mum cooking again – 'Jus' a lickle some ting to perk us up before H'eric and H'ernie!' Ye gods . . . it was Mum's fault – she was the Thanos of feeders. But we all bought into it; this was a big family with big appetites. When we were at home our mission (should we choose to accept it, and we always did) was to eat everything that was put in front of us. Is it any wonder, then, that when I embarked on a career and found myself in the Big City, with many more food choices than I'd ever had before, my waistline was affected so drastically? There were so many different types of cuisine – all within wheelbarrow distance of the BBC: Greek, Chinese, Indian, Thai, Indonesian, French, Italian – not to mention fast food and street food. I tried them all. And you can see the effect it had on me throughout the eighties and nineties: I'm like a second-string Marvel superhero: Forever Expanding Boy.

While all this was going on, Mr Luff convinced me that a return to summer season (not just any summer season, but a Blackpool

North Pier summer season) was exactly what I needed right then. I'd do it from May till October. Dawn and I were set to marry in October of 1984, and we wanted a full-on bells 'n' whistles wedding, with all our friends and family in attendance. This would need funding, so it was decided that I would go up north and do the right thing and get that cash for the wedding, even though I'd said to my nearest and dearest, 'Hey! If you ever hear me say, "Yo, guess what? I'm thinking about doing another summer season!" just haul me off and punch me good and hard in the face with everything you've got!'

Mr Luff told me it was excellent money and would easily pay for the big wedding we wanted: 'M'boy, if you're getting married and having the reception at the Savoy, you need to get the coal in, what?'

Dawn took on the role of wedding organiser throughout the summer, while I was in Blackpool. As always, she was brilliant at organising and threw herself into the melee of it all with alacrity.

4

DAWN

I first encountered French and Saunders at the Comic Strip, where I saw them marmalise audiences with their comedy stylings. I remember watching them portray Muriel and Diana, two upscale New York *ladies who lunch* discussing, among other things, 'clitoral frigidity'; enjoying myself immensely, I was totally convinced they were an American double act. Once I'd discovered they weren't I tried to recruit them onto *OTT*'s writing team. We were in rehearsals, and the absence of female voices on our writing staff was telling. So Tarrant gave me permission to ask French and Saunders if they would write for the show. I approached Dawn to gauge their interest. She refused, explaining that it took them months to work through their material, and that it would not be of benefit to us, seeing as we were going to be on telly in a minute. I was disappointed, but intrigued by their work ethic.

During this period, I'd been serial dating a variety of dancers from summer shows, funkateers and fellow clubbers. None of these relationships was based on companionship, fellow feeling or a 'meeting of minds'. Most of them were fuelled purely by physical attraction. Besides, I lacked attention span when it came to actually being with someone.

So, I found myself growing lonelier by the minute. I was yearning for something more substantial, but I just didn't know what that was.

The next time I met Dawn I realised that you could have a reciprocal conversation with someone and not have to perform or amuse them all the time. They could make you laugh too. A massive light bulb went off over my head. BONG!

In 1982, prepping for *OTT*, Alexei had invited me to come to London Weekend Television to watch a recording of David Renwick and Andrew Marshall's *Whoops Apocalypse* (a six-part sitcom about the lead-up to the end of the world). I was a fan and so couldn't wait to see it. When we arrived at the studios, I saw Dawn in the queue. She called my road manager and me over and asked if we wanted to sit with her and her friend Angie. 'Good idea!' we thought. The evening was great, but throughout I found myself mainly talking to Dawn about the show, the difference between the studio bits (loud) and the John Cleese bits on film (considered/planned), and studio sitcoms in general. It was a good conversation.

Afterwards, we left Alexei in the LWT bar and went off to a club in Soho called Le Beat Route for more conversation and many drinks. It was good, finally, to be able to talk to a fellow traveller in the comedy trenches. I was compelled by her. She was funny, clever, and I found her very attractive. I was in my early twenties, and at this point it seemed only natural for us to begin dating. We talked about everything – all aspects of performance, politics (my family voted Labour, but I hadn't really connected with the whys of it until I met Dawn), growing up, family, relationships, food, the future. When we spoke, we bounced around the subject matter and used jokes as a kind of structural glue. Even at the worst of times we used humour as both sword and shield. My mind was at last tuned in, focused and functioning as an equal in a relationship. In other words, I was in love.

Watching Dawn and Jennifer work together was always a joy – the grace deployed during their sketches; how one allowed the other to get laughs and then dropped out like a jazz musician so that their partner could solo always struck me as something wonderful to witness. I felt privileged to watch them do many gigs at places like the White Horse on Brixton Hill, the Assembly Rooms at the Edinburgh Festival, or on tour. They were brave and had a respect for each other; even if they didn't agree about a routine or a particular line, they were always ready to try things out for each other, in the moment. Watching them at the Comic Strip, the big element of the act that always cracked me up was Dawn's gung-ho approach to fronting things out via facial expressions or wordplay. She would dance and throw herself around with gay abandon and always get a huge reaction from the punters. There was an episode of *Girls on Top* where she had to take a running jump and drop-kick a door. What's not to love about that?

Jump Cut to 1984

Dawn and I aimed to have as big a wedding as we could to show our friends and family that we meant business. This might have been because of all the semi-glamorous Jamaican weddings at which I'd performed pageboy duty back in Dudley. To my mind, if we weren't going to get married in the right way – big church, reception, dress suits, food, friends and family jammed into a fancy-schmancy chi-chi hall with a big band and Big Al the DJ winding up the day's events with a big disco – then we might as well not do it at all. But this needed paying for. Dawn felt the same way: this needed paying for. Blackpool North Pier for twenty-two weeks with David Copperfield. Decision made.

But the big issue here was: what kind of addle-pated, imbecilic dimwit disappears to the seaside ON HIS OWN, over a hundred miles away, for over twenty weeks before he gets married – hardly seeing *anyone*, like family, friends, casual acquaintances, never mind your intended? Not a good call, Len. Not a good call at all.

A Sidebar on Hyperactivity

I've often been accused of being a workaholic. Certainly, wandering off to north-west England for six months to graft by the seaside sounds exactly like something I would do. No proper thought went into it, aside from the basic 'need money for gala wedding = find revenue stream'.

It wasn't that I was hyperactive. It's just that I had energy to burn. I loved to work. It's different if you're a plumber or a welder or a tree surgeon or did labouring like my dad. The fact is: show business didn't feel like work to me. There were elements of it that were difficult, and there were times when I struggled, but at no point did I ever want to give up and become a welder again. I never wanted to deviate from my chosen path: it was comedy or nothing!

And I had *so much to learn.* So, while I was in a position where I could work and earn and learn, I thought, 'Why not?' Why not go to Workington and do cabaret at the Skylight Rooms? Or appear on *Celebrity Sweepstakes* with Bernard Braden? Or go on *Blankety Blank* several times with that ridiculous expression on my face because I had no idea what I was doing there? I bounced and bounced and bounced around like Tigger on a pogo stick, and although there were many, many lows, there were quite a few highs too. The hyperactivity was just me enjoying all the opportunities that were thrown my way.

But there were several moments where I became overwhelmed and thought, 'This is too much.' Hyperactivity and overwork are displacement activities. They happen for a reason, and I wasn't sufficiently emotionally intelligent to figure out what that was. The pursuit of success meant that even when I came very close to breaking the surface – a BAFTA nomination or a positive review in the newspaper; or even Bob Monkhouse approaching me at a BBC Light Entertainment party and reciting a PC Ganja routine back at me – all of those things were nice, but they weren't the ultimate validation. I didn't really appreciate them as they were happening to me.

Even awards like the Silver Rose of Montreux that we received for *Three of a Kind* made me feel like I'd reached for the brass ring . . . but only brushed it with my fingertips. I'm like, 'What? No *Golden* Rose?' There was an unsatisfied need in me that perhaps pushed me to work harder in showbiz, at the cost of neglecting real life.

I'd go and see my family, who were all incredibly happy for me. As I look at my desk covered in photographs of me with Seymour and Mum and my driver Davy Luton, and my baby bro Paul, I see that familial relationships *were* being maintained – as far as my little fevered mind was concerned. But I was only just about staying afloat. There was no time to wave at the people standing on the shore waiting for me to come in. I was too busy kicking my legs, avoiding sharks. In my head, the way to do that was to present a moving target, to keep grafting, to keep learning, and everything else would be OK.

But for the majority of the time, even with all those rewarding moments that arrived with being more well known – having my own TV series; being nominated for awards – it felt like I was always but never quite breaking the surface.

Summer Season, 1984

I think I'd forgotten what it was like at the North Pier: walking in the freezing-cold rain to get to the stage door; coming out on-stage and seeing a steaming mass of people with damp tights and hair, all hoping you were going to cheer them up and being slightly disappointed when you only reach their expectations halfway.

It might have been my paranoia at the time, but I used to feel that there was a certain vibe from the audience that, although they knew who I was from the telly, they didn't want all that hip, semi-alternative, pro-black stuff I'd been doing in London. Where's all the impressions? Where's Algernon off *Tiswas*? OOOOOOOOOOKAAAAAAY!

I had changed. I didn't just want to do joke, joke, joke, joke, joke, joke, joke. I wanted to do characters and surreal and surprising material – and a lot of it didn't fit into that twice-nightly, hang-on-here's-a-ventriloquist-there's-David-Copperfield-in-the-audience-yanking-someone's-tie-off-their-neck kind of scenario. I guess when you're out in Blackpool with your family and you've just come in from a torrential downpour, you want cheering up; you don't wanna hear some tosspot banging on about the Brixton riots. I can see that now, but at the time it was like pushing water uphill. I adjusted as best I could. David Copperfield, of course, stormed it most nights. He gave 'em what they wanted: the ventriloquist act with the crocodile, the pratfalls, the silly voices, the killer song at the end. I don't think I saw him fail, not even once. I was top of the bill, finishing the show most nights reasonably well, and yet David (first-half closer) was ripping them to shreds almost every performance. I was humbled by the experience – and he made me work harder. The nights when the audience gave it up for me were truly exhilarating. But they'd made me graft for it. (*That's as it should be, Len. Stop moaning about it.*)

One night, Bernard Manning came to the show. I hadn't seen him since *OTT*. He sat six rows from the front, on an aisle seat. The perfect position for being seen – if that's what you wanted. He sat there like an oversized comedy sphinx amidst the muggles and roared his approval at every gag that *didn't* work. He did it all through the show; it was off-putting, to say the least. He came to the stage door afterwards to say hello and crack gags about how crap we'd been. David and I just stood there and took it all. Bernard worked us as though we were the audience at a two-person roast: 'All right, son? Tough night tonight? You were as funny as a burning orphanage . . . Call that an act? I'd rather stick me knob in a wood chipper . . . You died on your arse tonight, son . . . Funny as woodworm in a cripple's crutch.'

And then he'd switch attitude: suddenly he'd be all fake bonhomie and cigars: 'No, you're all right, lads. Nice work – I quite enjoyed it.'

Then he shook everyone's hand, relit his cigar and left us with: 'By the way, if ever you're going by my club [killer pause] . . . keep going . . .'

I had to remind myself that I had chosen this path and, in many respects, I was digging it: six nights a week, two shows a night, plus Sunday concerts in Scarborough, Yarmouth, Bournemouth and Torquay, which involved driving or training or flying there and back. Whatever you did, you had to make it back by the half-hour call for the first house on a Monday night. I wasn't twenty-six yet, was fresh-faced and bouncy, and though the whole summer felt like it was dragging along in the moment, in reality those six months slid by like a duck on roller skates. And, when they were finally over, I was relieved . . . but also completely knackered.

I came home and plugged back into real life, beginning with the events organiser – a lovely man called Andrew – showing Dawn and me around the River Room in the Savoy and explaining how many people it could hold. We were looking at the proposed menu, and I was thinking, 'Is there gonna be any Caribbean food?' I said that aloud, and he said, 'Ah, no, this is the Savoy, Mr Henry, we don't do that kind of thing here . . .' Mum had vowed that she was going to make the cakes for the wedding and, if we wanted, she'd provide Saturday soup and cook-down chicken as well. She eventually accepted that we'd already chosen a menu for the big day, but was pleased as punch that we wanted her to make all the cakes. She was actually brilliant about it all.

And when it came to making cakes, Mum's methodology was the same as it always had been: she baked them way ahead of time, burnt the buggery out of them, and then cut the burnt bits off (usually an inch), leaving the perfect cake in the middle, before icing them. Once satisfied with her handiwork, she loaded them into the car and drove to London, found her way (via Wembley, Brighton and Suffolk – no sat nav in those days, remember) to the Savoy and handed them over to the rather shocked chef, who was surprised that all the cakes were iced and ready to go, and only a teensy bit banged up from the journey.

While we were all at the church, the chef assembled the tower of cakes, but unfortunately in the wrong order. Mum went in to check on everything just before they were due to make their big entrance and went through the roof. She roundly upbraided the chef for 'not using his blouse and skirt eyes properly' and made him rearrange everything in the right size order! Which he duly did, with a multitude of apologies.

Choosing the Best Man

My quandary was: who would I choose as my best man? I opted for Tom, which was strange, because the initial part of Mum's h'integration plan involved my making friends with Greg. Then, through Greg, I met Mac. Tom came along later. He and I used to roughhouse a lot; we got on OK, but we were not best mates. Then he left Dudley and joined the navy. When Tom came home on leave for the first time, he was no longer a man to be trifled with. He had completely changed. The navy had toughened him up: he smoked now; he'd been around the world a bit.

Post 1975, Tom's peripatetic lifestyle echoed mine. He'd be on leave, coming to find me and hanging out in Blackpool or Bournemouth or Great Yarmouth, and then going back to sea. We were both AWOL from life in Dudley, having similar experiences (travelling, meeting new people all the time), reshaping our identities on a daily basis. I still wanted to hang out with Greg and Mac, but I wasn't seeing them as much – Greg was at uni, and Mac was learning how to navigate his way through the ranks of middle management.

Tom was best man, but for various reasons he didn't want to get up and make a speech. So Alexei Sayle, who was now a fast friend, said he'd do the honours. I reckoned that would be cool, as long as he didn't suddenly improvise and start machine-gunning the audience with F- and C-words. I asked him not to do that, what with Mum being a born-again Christian. He agreed, and we were set.

Erskine Thompson (or Erskine T – his DJ name) was my music

manager at the time. Here's why: in the eighties I was a funkateer and a clubber. I was always out and about throwing shapes on the dancefloor and pretending to play a star-shaped bass like my hero, Bootsy Collins. I was all about the music back in the day – therefore, all my mates (some of whom were in chart bands) naturally assumed that I'd want to make a record.

I'd spent quite a lot of the eighties under Erskine's watchful eye, making quite shouty funk demos in studios all over west

Me and Tom

London. I was signed at least four times, getting to know music industry people like Chris Blackwell at Island, Simon Cowell at BMG and Roger Ames at London Records. None of it came to anything, but it was good to have something other than comedy to occupy my mind. I figured, 'Hey, you never know, I might get a hit record!' I was hella deluded. Erskine was one of my many connections in the music business, and when I was looking for a DJ I went to him. He knew a dude called Big Al and procured him to be our host and MC for the evening dance. All good. The funk would blow people's minds. I was happy.

The reception was fun. It was amazing to see all my siblings – Bev, Seymour, Hilton (who brought four uninvited guests with him; lucky for him there was space [eyes raised· emoji]), Kay, Sharon, Paul. All my relatives. Colleagues from the business: the Comic Strip; make-up artists like Sally Sutton and Naomi Donne; Chris Tarrant and Robbie Coltrane and Ben Elton. And most of the Lockshen Gang (my Jewish friends from north London). Everyone was there.

Then the speeches were announced. They were scary because audiences of your peers – i.e. colleagues, workmates and other performers – can be a bit tricky. As I got up to give my speech – and this is indicative of how I was mentally placed at the time – I looked out and all I saw were pros. Yes, all my family and most of our friends were there in support, but there were a lot of people from the industry as well. Agggh . . . why did I invite all these people off of the telly? Why is the woman from *Hi-de-Hi!* at my wedding? Why's Roy Wood here? It's not Christmas! Saying all that, I did manage to get through my speech, and the guests responded in a generous way, which was great seeing as I was making it all up on the spot. From the expression on my face, it looks like I'm having fun, so I guess it must have been.

Thank God Alexei got up, did his speech and made us all laugh. He talked about how Dawn and I met and somehow managed to interlace it with jokes about Marxist–Leninist agricultural systems. Needless to say, my mum was confused by this material.

Once toasts had been quaffed, Dawn (at the behest of everyone yelling 'Dawn, Dawn, Dawn, Dawn!' at the top of their voices) got up and made a speech. It was great. She was really funny, did it off the cuff and stormed it with her usual skill, confidence and panache – no problem at all.

Then, just when we thought that particular portion of our day was over, Mum got up to say her piece. I looked at her, then at Dawn. *What's this now? This was not in the plan. Listen, if I was scared of being in front of these people, then why wouldn't Mum be quaking in her boots too?* But as she stood there soaking up the loving applause from all of us, she just waited, taking it all in. I just about restrained myself from tugging on her sleeve to make her sit back down, before she gave me a glance that said, 'Move from me, I have tings fe say.' And she did. I'm paraphrasing, but you'll get the idea:

Mum: I'm very proud to be here. I hope you all enjoyed the cakes. I made them. There's rum – be careful! I'm very proud of Len. Ever since he went on television, he's made us proud. He's been a testament to hard work and loyalty to this family. We'll always be grateful to him. And we're very happy to welcome my new daughter into the family. Y'know, I'm a big lady, I'm tall, and I've always been very rooted, with my feet on the ground. But today I'm floating six feet in the air because I'm so happy.

Thank you for listening to me.

My nieces Babette and Donna

Mac, Greg and Chris Difford

Geoff Posner (in the middle)

Then she sat down, and I looked out at all our lovely guests. Everyone was visibly moved. People were crying, wiping tears from their faces, or at least moist-eyed. I looked at Dawn, she smiled. I looked at Mum, she nodded. She'd smashed it. Why was I ever worried? She's the toughest of all of us. Why would she be scared of a bunch of showbiz turns? She could play Glasgow Empire on a Saturday night and have no problem.

Mothers-in-law assemble

First Time in Africa

We honeymooned in Kenya, at a place called Nyali Beach, and it was a massive epiphany for me. I'd never been to Africa before and continually felt that I was discovering my roots. It was an emotionally confusing time.

I loved Kenya (which was a good job: from 1988 onwards, due to Comic Relief, I'd be spending a lot of time there). I felt as if I'd come home. We went to a hotel called Treetops, which was an animal preserve where we watched elephants, deer and hyenas chilling at watering holes. I met Kikuyu warriors and observed as they performed enthusiastic dances for our group. I tasted indigenous food and quite enjoyed some of it. We visited an island called Lamu and fell in love with the place: it was tiny, with white beaches, no cars and great food. There were hippies everywhere, wearing floaty shirts and with dreadlocks in their hair, hanging out, maaaaaaan.

I've been told there's a possibility that I am descended from West Coast African folks. I'm sure I'll explore my heritage one day. However, my honeymoon was the first time I felt that being plugged into the birthplace of my ancestors was akin to being hooked up to the National Grid: a hugely powerful feeling of being directly interlaced with your roots and original purpose. Mind blowing.

Finally, *The Lenny Henry Show*, First Transmission . . . (Autumn 1984)

Just before all this wedding activity *The Lenny Henry Show*, season one, was transmitted. *Spitting Image* had also done a parody of 'Thriller', but I was glad to see that there was no repetition of the jokes we'd done in ours.

We watched our show go out and, at the end, Geoff rang to tell me how pleased he was. I told him I was proud of him. The show moved like a train and it had a great opening sequence. Watching it now, I'm struck by the imagery. It starts with me, wearing a bright pink suit, crossing London Bridge very early in the morning, shouldering a three-ton boom box and dropping rhymes like LL Cool J's dad:

I bin hanging around for eternity
Waitin' for you to turn onto me
But now you're here there's no turning back
Prepare yourself for a laugh attack
Lenny Lenny Len
Lenny Lenny Len
Lenny Henry Shooow
Break out of depression
Break into smile
Break into sweat
Break the four-minute mile
Give yourself a break
And break new ground

Break up, break even
Break down
Break! (echo) Break! Break! Break!
FONK-AY!

Delbert was there, providing back-up vocals. PC Ganja, the Rastafarian policeman, was also present, chilling in a shop doorway, accompanied by his dreadlocked dog, Selassie. There's a shot of me walking past a huge hoarding that turns into a giant screen featuring a giant Len watching tiny Len walk past. It ends with a funky synth-led horn riff, to which I bust some seriously supermegadope moves (in my mind anyway).

Geoff and Kim, the writers, costume and make-up had literally worked magic. The show was nominated for a BAFTA, and the ratings were decent for a first series.

My life was changing, my ambition was growing. I was almost at the surface. Would I make it?

Almost at the surface

5

SUCCEEDING UPWARDS

From 1985 to 1990

When doing a sketch show, the question that comes up constantly is: 'When do you start thinking about what's in the next series?' The honest answer is: 'All the time.' Because my name was in the title of the show, I wanted it to be good. At last, I had the opportunity to do all the things I wanted to do, with a team of people helping me do just that. But there were outside influences.

I had friends, family and now a partner who were all interested in the choices I was making. Quite a few commented on the fact that there were no people that looked like me behind the scenes on my show. There hadn't been on *Three of a Kind*. And although we had the legendary assistant producer Emma Thomas on *Tiswas*, no black people were involved in the creation of *OTT*, none on *Six of a Kind*, none on *The Cheapest Show on the Telly*. It was a common thing.

Because it was my 'normal', I didn't really pay it any mind. But, when in the course of my day I did meet people of colour, from Africa or the Caribbean – whether they were scene shifters or worked in the canteen or on security – there was always a conversation or some banter to be had about us being the only ones in the building. Eventually, it began to gnaw at me. How could the biggest public broadcaster in the world not have *any* black people in a production or editorial capacity? There didn't seem to be any black people in gatekeeper positions: the producers, editors, commissioners, and so on. One expected all the important meetings to be with white people – that's just how it was.

My friends would point out that, even though I was having a good time on the show and making the odd point with regard to black people's lives in the UK via characters like Deakus and Delbert, there was no significant sea change as a result of what I was doing. I was making a sketch show that was perfectly fine for what it was – a bit of stand-up, some characters, sketches, parodies, a song here or there – but it wasn't quite Richard Pryor, was it? It was tough because I loved my work: solving performance, script and joke problems – this was what we all loved to do, deciding on content and then endeavouring to make it better.

But I didn't write. I hadn't had any training in that regard, I'd attended no creative writing workshops. I was just me. I had a lot of energy and always brought that to the table; I would 'go off on one' in character a lot, improvising and fizzing and being rude (very much in the same way I used to for my school pals Greg, Mac and Tom), trying to get to the nub of what was funny.

Kim would ramble on for hours about 'funny': he loved to talk about the nature of comedy, the why of a comedic situation, and then, given a large glass of red and a couple of hours, he would turn that conversation into material. I'd always been there with him during these conversations, adding my thruppence worth and making him laugh.

Joe Charles used to say, 'Lenny, it's extraordinary: you go in there and explode – then they get the writing credit!' At the time I thought Joe was just being a snark. But he had a point.

As I've said, my favourite comedian in the world was Richard Pryor. When he passed away from multiple sclerosis, he was eulogised by some of the greatest comedians in the world as writer, producer, actor, philanthropist and, most importantly, one of the greatest comic minds that ever lived. Pryor would enter the writers' room, explode, riff and satirise black folks, white folks, politics and movies. Because of this he was credited as a comic *and* a writer. In movies like *Blazing Saddles*, *Which Way Is Up?*, *Car Wash* and *Blue Collar* Pryor brought his own sensibilities to everything he said and did. Although it has been alleged repeatedly that a great deal of his output was dictated by whatever intoxicants he was inputting, the vast amount of recorded material available via albums, TV appearances and movies is testament to just how gifted he was. He was of immeasurable value, and was seen as a wayward, yet problematic crazy-ass comedy powerhouse.

What I didn't realise at the time was that if you were in the room asking, 'Why is this funny? Why is that funny? What if we said it like this? What if a geezer from Dudley said that?' you were helping to shape whatever was trying to be achieved.

On *Three of a Kind*, at the beginning of each series, Kim Fuller and the other writers would get Tracey, David and I to talk about what we'd been watching on TV or at the movies, in the theatre or clubs. Tracey was really good at this: she'd always just seen some documentary or some bizarre woman who'd done some weird thing and who spoke in an odd, affected way – 'LIKE THIS, LEN!' She'd get up, there and then, and capture the essence of the silly/serious subject matter and the tragedy of that person's life via voice, character and attitude. AND THEN someone would go, 'Well, that's funny, but who's gonna write it?' Things would sometimes get lost in translation.

Because Kim spent more time with us, he actually understood what we were talking about most of the time. As our relationships developed (particularly near the end of the show's run) we had other people within the various writing teams who we could talk to. I got on well with Bob Sinfield and James Hendrie, and

Tony Sarchet and Andrea Solomons – later with Annie Caulfield too – all of whom liked to hang out and have beers and watch me act the fool. Or so it seemed at the time.

This helped a great deal.

The most important thing for comedians is a first audience or bounce: someone who'll say, 'That's really funny, but what if you did this?' And then they'll (hopefully) say something that makes you crease up. That's what you pray for in the room. Often when writers are gathered together, it takes ages for everyone to warm up because there's the worry that being funny together is rather embarrassing. What about the shy person who's funny on paper but has communication issues in the room? Sometimes the loudest people dominate; they're not necessarily the funniest, but often they carry the swing, through personality and weight of ideas. Comedy is tough.

Writers' rooms in the US are different from those in the UK, simply because the idea of being in a room full of sandwiches, cigar smoke, sweat and naked ambition – where your jokes better be as funny or three times funnier than the next guy's – reflects the hustle and grind of life on the street for them. If you wanna make a buck, you gotta make 'em laugh; if you don't make 'em laugh, you don't eat . . . 'So come on, make with the funnies, you guys. I'm payin' by the hour here . . .' Comedy is seen as a business in the States, a factory or a sausage machine – you keep churning it out week after week.

Yes, we have generated hours of funny content in the UK – of course we have – but we do have a tendency to stop after two or three seasons. Usually because of shy-writer syndrome. We send someone away to a quiet room, lock them up, then transfer money to their bank account and hope the next series comes out funny, intact and as good as it was last time.

Because of financial concerns, the writing-room model doesn't really get much traction in Britain – although you can generate volume. When it comes to who actually owns the intellectual property, it can turn into a bun fight. There are rules of engagement: I suppose whoever generated the idea and set the tone, the thrust and the comedic world, and wrote the first couple of scripts will probably be the person who runs the room and hires like-minded people to write in his or her style. That show runner will always be able to turn whatever the room generates into an episode because they were there from the beginning, understanding the central core premise and keeping that flame lit throughout the six or so seasons of that show – eighty to a hundred episodes.

It's still shocking to think that there were only twelve episodes of *Fawlty Towers*.

Twelve episodes of *The Young Ones*.

Twelve episodes of *Girls on Top*.

Maybe twenty-four episodes of *Blackadder* . . .

Hollywood prefers the 'lock a bunch of funny people in a room and wait' model over the single auteur model that we tend to use here in the UK. Although I benefited from this system, looking back I always wanted more involvement in the process than I was allowed. Maybe the producers thought that if they let the performer join in with the writing process, it would take too long or might upset the apple cart. Ronnie Barker wrote as Gerald Wiley for the *Two Ronnies* and got a lot of his stuff on the air. But he had to adopt a pseudonym to do that.

I got my first ever writing credit on *Three of a Kind* and, from then on, I assumed that my name would appear as part of the writing team – even if all I did was go in the room and explode, that's something, right? It might not be sitting down and burning the midnight oil, but exploding, riffing, improv, voices . . .

how could all that not be part of the process? I'm still asking the question because I have a high regard for writers. I had a real attitude towards bad jokes or sketches. I was a bit dismissive, if I'm honest, and didn't take in how long things had taken to write. Nowadays, I'm a little more careful when assessing a script. Having been through the development process myself, I get now how horrible a careless evaluation can be.

Producing material is a tough row to hoe. The good people are good for a reason and, if you're privileged enough to be anywhere near them when they're on form, beg, borrow or steal whatever resources you need and hold onto them. They don't come along very often and, when you lose them, you'll find them hard to replace.

We all want to be the kind of comedian who writes all their own material, but those people are few and far between. Victoria Wood, Ben Elton, Richard Pryor, Steve Martin, George Carlin, French and Saunders: they all knew or know funny people who can write, but they all chose or choose to generate their own material because . . . they trust(ed) it. They'd rather make their own mistakes than someone else's. That's probably right for them, but I always needed someone to bounce off before I felt that the material was working. Although Kim was my main man for many years, there were other people I liked working with too, so I side-hustled. I'm not sure if that went down well with Kim, but I'd get impatient sometimes, especially when he went off and worked for other comics like Jasper Carrott, who I was in awe of at the time.

Carrott did a devastatingly clever routine about the voting process that brought the house down – it was so on point, so smart, so clever, every joke topping the last one, and it was all delivered in Carrott's user-friendly, curmudgeonly yet charming manner. The whole voting process was compared to losing one's virginity. I think it ended with the phrase 'premature election'. Woo hoo! Kim wrote that.

It was always alarming to me that the writers, at the end of the series, would be released into the wild and go and write for some other show. I was very jealous and didn't like that at all. But what could I do? I wasn't seen as a writer.

I'd visit Geoff Posner's office at the BBC, and there would be a shelf with box files for all the shows he'd worked on during the year: *The Lenny Henry Show*, the *Victoria Wood* show, *The Young Ones*, *Carrott's Lib*. I always envied those other shows. I wanted to be the only show Geoff and his team did, but that was ridiculous – my show took a month and a half to generate three weeks of filming, six weeks of audience shows and then perhaps a couple of months to edit and prep for broadcast. What would the team do for the rest of the year?

What I was yearning for was a model where we were always in production and I was at the core of that production, whether I was starring in it or not. Unless some kind of miracle occurred, this was *never* going to happen.

Early Hankerings for a
Production Company

My point is, we were generating a great many ideas. Not all of them fell within the remit of a sketch show, but some of them could have been sitcoms, or game shows, or quiz shows, or straight-up parody shows. But we didn't have the financial model for that kind of setup. Programmes like *Saturday Night Live* can do that because they have the resources and they've been around since God was at infant school; they're seen as the gold standard for producing characters and ideas that might have legs beyond a sketch show (some that really work: *The Blues Brothers*, *Wayne's World*; others that don't: *The Ladies Man*, *MacGruber* . . .). The frustration of not being able to go to the next level with some of our ideas pained me. But we swim on and sometimes lie back and kick our legs for a while . . . at least we're staying afloat.

Season Two of *The Lenny Henry Show* (Spring 1985, for Autumn Transmission)

What I remember of this season was the parody that ended episode one. I was, and am, a huge Prince fan. So, of course, as with the 'Thriller' video, I wanted to pay homage. Peter Brewis wrote the music, and Kim and I would attempt to recreate 'When Doves Cry' and 'Let's Go Crazy' and fit in some jokes (visual and verbal) around the whole thing. At this point, I was somehow . . . much bigger (weight-wise) for this show than I had been the year before, so all my clothes had to be resized. I wasn't that worried. My weight had fluctuated from the minute I entered show business. It was almost like paying the toll master: 'Oh, you want to sail across the River of Success, do you? For that you must gain thirty pounds for the privilege.'

When I arrive for my fittings to play the tiniest funk god in rock, I'm about seventeen stone. No matter, I sort out all the costumes, make-up and . . . I'm fine. I'll be exactly like Prince – just the Incredible Hulk version. I do the filming, and it's great, the jokes work, everybody's happy, but, as I watch the show and enjoy it, there's this undermining niggle about my weight: I'm the size of a house. When did that happen? *You don't look like Prince, you look like a hippo trapped in a purple circus tent.* As noted earlier, this would be a recurring motif throughout this period of my life: weight control. I'd do whatever I could: diet, SlimFast, shakes, mostly veg, mostly protein. I even went to that doctor, the one you're not supposed to go to – the guy who prescribes a green pill and a pink pill and a white pill, and then, the next thing you know, you look like a stick insect with an afro and you can't sleep at night because your Adam's apple is bigger than your head. Yeah, I went to him and lost a load of weight. I looked great, but my brain was mush a lot of the time.

I had all my rationalisations: 'Yeah, it's cool, my family are Caribbean; we're all big. We eat big food, we wear big clothes and we're proud of our appetites.' It was kind of true. Food was important to me, especially if it was home food. I'd drive the hundred or so miles to be at my mum's house the minute the mutton soup with dumplings and yam was cooked, simmered and ready to serve.

'Oh, Len, I didn't know you were coming here today.'

'Oh, don't mind me, it's just Bev may have mentioned you doing the red pea soup today. Is there any left?'

'How many people you have with you?'

'Oh, about thirty-seven.'

'Bring them all, mi cook enough food fe all a yu.'

Mum always cooked too much, and we were always expected to clean our plates. Even if we weren't that hungry. But it wasn't Mum's fault I was looking so big – it's just the way things were. I didn't know it at the time but most of my family have an issue with diabetes. My weight was yo-yoing up and down not just because I was a greedy pig. I had been hard-wired by the gods to have this sugar intolerance. As I loved sweet things, this was not going to end well.

There's also that guilty feeling when you arrive for fittings and your measurements have changed. Costume designers and producers don't mean to, but they can be a bit judgemental – 'Ooh, put a bit of weight on, have we? We'll have to take that all the way out.' Or, 'Bloody hell – size of that arse.' Or, 'You won't get into that without a shoe horn and an entire tube of lube, darling.'

I was very self-critical, and this was embarrassing, although I pretended it didn't matter.

I remember a TV critic making jokes about how big my thighs were, and being destroyed by the comment. I was dressed as Tina Turner, and she said my thighs were like tree trunks in suspenders. It really upset me – and pushed me to embark upon yet another ridiculous eating plan that involved carrot shavings, cucumber balls and clear chicken soup. Ugh.

The second season of *The Lenny Henry Show* was nominated for a BAFTA that year. A key way of marking your progress in most industries nowadays is via award ceremonies. If you win an award, it's an indication that you're doing something right. Unless it's one of those where you pay for the award. BAFTA seems to be a venerable organisation where peer-reviewed work is key to the decision-making. It's also a fantastic night out for the industry. Everyone gets dressed up, there's snacks before you go in, and they get out the good glassware and china. They ply you with champagne and other alcoholic drinks. It's almost like they want a huge fight to break out mid-show: 'She's mine, Barry!' 'Mind yer own business, Piers!' 'Kaneesha, hold my Malibu and coke, man. I'm gonna box my man's ears!' 'Tarquin, y'bastard, stitch that!'

But that never happens. People politely move to their seats when the time comes and sit there for ages as they are skilfully navigated by their gracious host (Graham Norton – very funny; Stephen Fry – unflappable; Billy Connolly and Angus Deayton – both hilarious and brilliant) through the highs and lows of their year in television and film. I think it's good that they've split TV from film – that used to be such a long night.

When I hosted the BAFTAs in the early nineties, it took place at the Albert Hall; they'd taken out all the floor seats and transformed downstairs into a massive cabaret venue. During the show all you could hear was the multitude of folks chinking away at their crockery far off in the distance. I read half-baked jokes from the autocue in a vain attempt to extract laughter from this disinterested and distant crowd. I had some moments – a Diana Ross medley at high speed before she came on; some Coen brothers gags – but generally had a pretty rough night. Mel Smith approached me at the after-party and said, 'You had such hope in your heart when you walked out there.' And I did. I thought wearing an Ozwald Boateng suit and having the band play 'Boogie Wonderland' by Earth, Wind & Fire as I made my entrance would provide the armour that I needed to get through nearly five hours of reading links off autocue while chug-a-lugging coffee backstage in order to stay frosty as the evening rolled on and on and on. Unfortunately, that was not the case and I was not invited back. Ah well, I've been since and I've won since – lifetime achievement awards and such. It's much nicer to be there and actually win something than to be hosting and continually wondering if they're enjoying themselves or not: 'Did they like that joke? Hey! They liked that joke! Oh my God, they hated that joke. Move on, move on, move on.' I think perhaps the future might be Ant and Dec as presenters. If there are two hosts ploughing through the night, it seems to be much more enjoyable. Plus, they've got each other. I think there is something magical about working with someone you respect and adore, where only *their* approval matters. If you're in a gang on-stage, like the Pythons or the Goodies or *Famalam* or the cast of *Spaced*, it doesn't matter whether the audience laughs or not – it's vastly satisfying chaos up there.

One of the most enjoyable things I've ever done was *Tiswas* at *The Children's Royal Variety Performance*. We just did what we wanted, and we thought it was hilarious. Besides, it only mattered that Chris was laughing – nothing else bothered us. I also remember being on-stage at the Improv in Los Angeles. I did ten minutes and found it incredibly difficult – I got some laughs, but it was . . . *agghghghgh*! Next up was almost the entire Wayans family. Keenen wasn't there, but Damon and Marlon and at least six or seven comedy relatives were up on-stage, and they took it in turns to crack gags and do characters and portray attitudes. It was extraordinary and braggadocious. I loved it. Made me want to get a gang and be on-stage. You're judged by the company you keep – being a solo comic, no matter how good you are, means you're always alone up there, all the time.

July 1985

Westcliff-on-Sea, and it's the same day as Live Aid. I'd been invited to participate by the BBC, but I couldn't because of the tour. As I watched it in my dressing room, I knew instantly that this was a defining moment – but because of being on the stupid road, doing my stupid tour, I was missing the whole bloody thing. A moment of global empathy for all of us, and I wasn't there. I was really miffed.

We had a collection in the theatre and raised about two grand. At the end of the gig, I drove to Wembley to hand over the money to someone, but they'd all gone home or to the after-party somewhere. I'd missed it all. I paid the money into the local bank the following Monday. I was determined not to be on the back foot with something so important ever again. I had no idea . . .

1986

I'm a bit despondent. I was still doing sketches, for God's sake. I'd done *Tiswas*, *The Cheapest Show on the Telly*, *Six of a Kind*, *Three of a Kind*, *The Lenny Henry Show* but I needed a break from sketch comedy or my head would explode. That's what I told Jim Moir anyway . . .

Geoff Posner was great about us departing from the sketch model. Although it was only our second sketch show together, it was my eighth. I wanted to do something else. And the model I most admired was the Comic Strip. Their Enid Blyton parody, *Five Go Mad in Dorset*, had been a major part of the successful launch of Channel 4 in 1982; they became the channel's go-to single-camera comedy team from that moment forward. They all brought something bountiful and clever to the table: Peter Richardson and Pete Richens's genre-specific eye for detail; Rik and Ade's explosive energy and 'Johnny goes too far' attitude; Dawn and Jen's quick-witted parodic writing and clowning; Nigel's pin-point characterisations; Robbie Coltrane's spot-on impersonations and gravitas, which he could summon at will the minute he heard 'And . . . ACTION!'

Being married to Dawn, I would hear everything that was going on: the creative shenanigans, the on-set gags, the striving for a kind of synergy that other shows (including mine) weren't quite achieving. I was well jell and didn't mind who knew it. They were a team to be reckoned with. Although their shows were up and down, they had a consistency in effort, verisimilitude and craft that I craved. Hearing all the stories when Dawn came home from filming or an exciting meeting made me want to be part of a team. I envied the idea of a democratic group debating their next move, the inner power struggles, the accepted responsibility of writing for themselves – all of those things seemed better to me than continuing to do what I was doing on my own. I absolutely saw the limitations of being a solo act now. Although some might find having an important board meeting on one's own amusing, I hankered for company. The Comic Strip had a mission statement and an attitude that it was difficult to summon up solo.

I wanted to film for more than two weeks. I wanted a *sustained narrative*. That was exactly it: I had 'narrative arc envy'. I didn't just want to do little blobs of comedy; I fancied myself as an actor and wanted to show the world what I was capable of.

Late 1985 into 1986

So, the next series I pitched to Geoff was an anthology show, featuring me playing a different character each week. They'd be funny shows but unrelated, as in no story throughline; they'd be one-offs. I could sense a rapid cooling of enthusiasm as I continued the pitch: 'How does that work, Len? You're not going to do Delbert and Theo and Deakus any more? How MUCH will this cost? Do you have to do them *all* on film or could you just do *one* of them and then the rest on video? Did I ask how much this was going to *cost*?' The questions were endless. But because I wasn't the producer (that was Geoff), thankfully, it wasn't my problem. I just had to come up with the ideas.

My big idea was that we should hire different people to write each episode. I wanted Kim Fuller to remain my main man and to write a couple but, as for the rest of our team of writers, they didn't really fit what I wanted to do. I was looking for something that could stand alone or might even be a pilot for a sitcom in its own right.

Kim had been writing on my radio show, *The Lenny Henry Sunday Hoot* (music and silly characters on Wonderful Radio 1). We'd come up with a *Blade Runner*-style character called Gronk Zillman, Private Eye of the 31st Century. We thought that could be one of the episodes. Kim was also slated for another episode, so that was two shows down, four to go. I'd met Ben Elton many times. He was affiliated with the Comic Strip via the Comedy Store gang, and had sometimes sat in for Alexei when the big man was detained elsewhere. I asked Ben if he'd write a half-hour show. He said 'yeah' almost immediately. It would be about a motorbike courier's worst day and would be called 'Pratt Outta Hell'.

Me doing the *Sunday Hoot* – 'Last night a DJ saved my life'

I'd seen Tunde Ikoli's plays upstairs at the Royal Court Theatre, *Scrape Off the Black* being the most notable. I was not only moved by the characters and their predicament, but also loved just how funny the play was. I wanted Tundi to write a sitcom/playlet about a Caribbean barber shop in London. We called the piece 'Popsi', and it was based (a bit) on my barber off the Edgware Road, who would amble to the betting shop halfway through trimming your hair! There'd be arguments about music, politics, food. He'd stand there and declaim: '*You see, the H'inglish man don't know food! You know who know food good? Jamaican people! Before we come to this country them did never understand how to season them food. Them did never eat rice and stew chicken and curry goat. Before we come here, all dem people like Churchill an' Henry the Eighth – all them would eat is fish an' chips an' mushy peas an' steak an' kidney pie and mash potato – not even a salt! Not even lickle peppah!'* etc. He'd carry on like this while simultaneously massacring the top of your head.

Geoff got hold of Ian La Frenais and Dick Clement – the geniuses behind *The Likely Lads*, *Porridge* and *Auf Wiedersehen, Pet*. They were keen on writing about an inter-racial middle-class couple (played by me and Dawn) with a baby on the way who get involved in a police stake-out, led by Jimmy Nail. It was called 'Neighbourhood Watch'.

I'm not sure how we got hold of Stan Hey and Andrew Nickolds – they were solid writers who'd worked on the TV series *Agony* and *Hold the Back Page*. They had the sitcom gene and knew their onions when it came to conjuring up comedy scenarios. I wanted to do a version of my mum's story, set in the Midlands, maybe shot in black and white. Stan and Andrew knocked it out of the park. Both being journalists, they understood that they'd have to do some research. So they went to Dudley and interviewed my mum! I had to go with them, just in case she'd cooked salt fish fritters for twenty-eight. I had to prepare Mum for the whole process:

'Mom?'

'Yes.'

'I want two blokes – two white blokes – to come to the house and–'

'Why? They goin' fumigate the place?'

'No.'

'They doin' the plumbin'? That toilet upstairs hasn't worked properly since you brother–'

'Mum, they're not coming here to do the plumbing.'

'Well, what two white men doing coming to my house when I haven't even run a hoover over the front room – or had the windows clean since Whoppi kill Philip?'*

'They're called Stan Hey and Andrew Nickolds and they're writing the new series. They want to write about what it was like coming to England in the 1950s.'

'Oh, well, they gonna want food when they come. That's going to take some tellin'. They eat food?'

Stan and Andrew interviewed my mum, talked to me a bit and then went away and wrote 'What a Country!', about a young accountant coming to H'inglan and having to work in a factory because nobody believed he was an accountant. He had adventures, endured racism and bullying, but eventually overcame all of that by using his brain. I thought it was one of the best shows of the series.

And, finally, Kim's second offering was a musical that involved Greek gods and a guy who works in a supermarket who can't find love and is considering suicide. Simon Brint wrote the songs, and Debby Bishop was in it. It was enjoyable to make, but a bit of a mess in the end. Certainly, Geoff and I didn't think it was our best work.

The work that went into 'What a Country!' schooled me on structure and performance. I wanted more work like that and less of the sketch-show-style, back-of-a-fag-packet, 'that'd be funny', 'hang on, let me change that' type of methodology. Things were changing, and there was a new target to aim at now: the half-hour sitcom model.

* By the way, I have no idea who these people are.

So that was the *Lenny Henry Tonite* experience – 1986 – boom! Gone, just like that. Hard work but, interestingly, not as hard as coming up with six half-hour sketch shows – mainly because you were only dealing with a writer or one set of writers per show. It seemed more manageable.

It didn't quite have the same heft as the Comic Strip, but at least it was ours and, at the time, a cherishable attempt by me to tell a *Windrush*-style story. It really meant something to me, which is why I followed it up with . . .

1987 – The Year of Delbert Wilkins, Season One

The decision to use Stan and Andrew as head writers on the Delbert Wilkins show was strictly determined by my experience on *Lenny Henry Tonite*. Working with situation comedy writers was a completely different experience to that of grafting with sketch writers – particularly in that when you put together a sketch show, it's very much a piecemeal affair. My days on *Three of a Kind* and *The Lenny Henry Show* meant that I had grown accustomed to the very ramshackle, undisciplined, anything for a laugh, 'just chuck out the rubbish bits' attitude towards the assembly of material. There would always be ideas, but we tended to make it up as we went along. Kim's best quality is his ability to almost spin comedy gold from thin air, bouncing off whoever is in the room and crafting comedy moments of wit and invention. All of that is great for sketches – they're only two or three minutes long. However, mapping out a series of six thirty-minute mini-comedy dramas is something else. A whole other discipline of thought, intention and execution was needed. What was interesting about *Lenny Henry Tonite* was that Kim and I found it quite a difficult form. I was dependent on him to make the thing work, and although we had cool ideas, they were a bit sketchy and all over the place. But the other writers, the ones who'd been used to the sitcom form, managed to come up with conceptual, long-form, half-hour narratives that had the sitcom pace and the rhythm and humour that fulfilled the brief perfectly. They were all different, but they seemed to have a thematic structure that worked within the parameters of what we were trying to achieve, i.e. 'Tell us a funny story in thirty minutes, Len.'

I was frustrated that Kim and I didn't nail our episodes – clearly, we needed more experience in the thirty-minute format. But the others had all written half-hour comedy shows before, and it showed. In terms of what they handed in on the page – structure, characterisation, jokes per page – it was all there.

So that really affected what I did next, which was twelve episodes of *The Delbert Wilkins Crucial TV Show* (it wasn't actually called that, but that's what it was: a sitcom about Delbert). I was determined that the character should evolve during the show, and I wanted it written by people who understood the sitcom form. Geoff Posner and I really enjoyed making Stan and Andrew's single-camera black-and-white film for *Lenny Henry Tonite*. We shot it in Dudley in various locations, and I loved the actability of the whole piece. I didn't have to try too hard to be a black guy who'd just arrived in the UK and found himself in a hostile environment. Choosing Stan and Andrew to write Delbert was a no-brainer. Kim was vexed with me at first – he had been the original Delbert writer and had really helped to shape Delbert's kick-ass attitude. Delbert's gags were always on point and hilarious. But the sitcom needed something else. The character needed to be fleshed out, and his friends, girlfriend and family also needed to be shaped and made realistic. There were always mini-monologues in the show (called 'The Delbert Wilkins Guide to Cruciality'), where Delbert would haul off and take the mickey out of the police or the government or the Brixton lifestyle, and Kim and I would sit down and do those. We'd also do a punch-up on Delbert's dialogue. But Stan and Andrew dictated the shape and the other characters that peopled the show.

Although I felt bad that I had upset Kim, my brother in comedy, with this choice, it was the right thing to do. I'd grown impatient with the sketch-show mentality, and this was a perfect opportunity to swim to the next island, scrabble ashore and evolve into something else.

More on Delbert Wilkins in 1987 an' 1988

Delbert was my good luck charm for a long time. He was hip, funny, sharp and had street cred. I'd never had that, but Delbert Wilkins, with his slicked-back or pointy hair, sharp moustache, wicked suit and cheeky Charlie chatter, was definitely one of the cool guys. British comedy tends to favour the underdog who gets everything wrong and, in his own way, triumphs in the end. The British comic tends to not get the girl, or the million pounds, or the big promotion. Winning isn't seen as a particularly classy goal; participation, playing the game, that's the ticket.

But my favourite comedians – Richard Pryor, Steve Martin – and my favourite films – *Ferris Bueller's Day Off*, *48 Hrs*, *E.T.*, even *Jaws* – all involved protagonists who overcame ridiculous odds to triumph. They were cool when the time came to be cool; they didn't lean over and fall through an open bar like Del Boy or get dragged away while on roller skates like Frank Spencer. Comedy protagonists were more like Bugs Bunny or Anansi, the trickster spider from African mythology: they were heroes who invented a clever way to outwit their opponents. In *Silver Streak* Richard Pryor flips the whole situation when he enters a railway car with the bad guy and pulls a gun on him: 'You ain't sayin' shit now, Mister.' Eddie Murphy in *Beverly Hills Cop* disses the bad guy to his face and blags a hotel room by throwing a massive wobbly, pretending to be a gay journalist from *Rolling Stone*. I somehow can't see Norman Wisdom doing those things . . .

Creating a cool comedy character was dangerous – there was a high probability that he wouldn't be liked by the general public. If he got the girl, the house, the car, the money, the promotion . . . what were we rooting for?

So the idea of making Delbert into a situation comedy was fraught with worry. I asked for Kim to perform punch-up duties on Stan and Andrew's scripts, because he wrote the best jokes for Delbert and got me into a position where I could go on-stage and do that character anywhere with confidence, knowing I could throw down with anyone.

The character of Delbert came out of the Brixton riots in the early eighties. The whole place was aflame, with furious residents protesting about mistreatment from the police; everybody was mad as hell and they weren't going to take it any more. There were lots of issues – deaths in police custody, stop and search, overt racism – and it was all kicking off. I saw a black Labour politician on TV one night, so angry he was practically foaming at the mouth. He was rendered almost inarticulate. I really felt for him and also wondered what it might be like if there was a young dude from the street up there on *Newsnight* or *Question Time* dealing with all the interviewer's prying questions with skill, panache and flair.

I'd met a wonderful choreographer and dancer called Kelvin, who had an amazing speaking voice. He was south London to his core, black and beautiful. He had this laid-back, funky, almost sing-songy Brixton tone – every sentence ended with 'Ya knaa mean?' Or 'Y' get me?' He also had this ridiculous Woody Woodpecker-style laugh. I loved everything about this guy. Maybe *he* could be the model for this new dude I was thinking about?

There were several attempts at Delbert. The first one was during *OTT*. He was a young dude who came on TV to tell it like it was about what was going on in the streets of Brixton and why – only I didn't know what he looked like. My brother Paul and his mates were always hanging out at my mum's house. I'd been to the street market in Birmingham, up the road from the TV studios, and had bought some clothes – berets, one-piece overalls, dungarees, Doc Martens – all bright colours and as camp and street as could be. The guys put me straight on my garms – in broad Dudley accents:

'Len, are you insane?'
'You can't represent like that, dread, you haffe come correct.'
'You look like that old lady that collects the bottles with the
    shopping trolley up Dixon Green.'
'That looks all right but it's the wrong colour, man.'
'He shouldn't wear glasses.'

In the end, when I did Delbert on *OTT* he was the Brixton milkman selling dodgy gear off the back of a milk float. It kinda worked.

Alexei's the one who said he should be 'half-a-teef'. I wasn't sure. What he actually said was, 'Shouldn't he be the kind of geezer who'd nick the gold teeth out his gran's gob?' It certainly gave him an edge, to not just be fast talking and a hustler, but also giving the cops a good reason to stop him on the street – he *had* done something wrong; his car boot probably did have black-market drink, clothes, fags, drugs and puppies in there . . .

We played with that for a while. But, in the end, I wasn't feeling it. The whole idea of a cockney loudmouth lowlife was nothing new – there was David Jason as Del Boy in *Fools and Horses*, George Cole as Arthur Daley in *Minder* and Flash Harry in the *St Trinian's* films, James Beck as Private Walker in *Dad's Army*. We were used to this trope, brilliantly executed by these wonderfully dextrous, articulate, hip, slick actors. But making Delbert just a straight-up roadman, a teefin' clart, was not the way to go. One of the problems with the police activity in Brixton was profiling: stopping and searching black people when they were out and about minding their own business, just because they looked like someone from a dodgy photograph they'd half looked at on their way out of the station. Much better to have Delbert be the mouthpiece of the innocents, the guy who, while being arrested, does a running commentary as the police make mistake after mistake:

> **Delbert**: So I'm cruising in my Ford Wicked. I got my seat so far back I'm driving looking out the skylight, ya knaa mean? Anyway, I got my radio turned up so loud a Great Dane explodes three streets away . . . thass how loud my stereo is, man! So Babylon's behind me in a minute, get me? He waves at me, I wave back. He tells me to slow down, and I do, 'cos I done all my errands for the day, ya knaa mean? So he comes up to the car, yeah? He puts his head through the window, which worried me 'cos I hadn't wound it down yet. He says, 'Can you identify yourself?' I looked in the mirror and said, 'That's me!'

I loved it; any variation like that made me laugh. The po-po were trying to pull over a geezer who had more rabbit, chutzpah and game than they could possibly imagine. Delbert had an answer for everything; he knew the law and wasn't going to let you get away with anything. Plus, he was a dude in his twenties. He was interested in girls, raving, music. He was a DJ; this was at the time of Jazzie B at the Africa Centre and Norman Jay and all them DJs and MCs running illegal raves all over London. The whole pirate radio lifestyle was wicked but fraught with danger. You'd play a fifteen-minute twelve-inch tune by Brass

Construction, and halfway through you'd have to climb out the window because someone had grassed up your location.

Delbert: You have been listening to Crucial FM. I am Delbert Wilkins and that was only one and a half minutes of Brass Construction 'cos we got to get gone out this window before the boys in blue bruk down the door, man! We'll be back a week Friday. Boom! Winston! The window, man. Babylon come!

By the time we were talking about Delbert as a sitcom character, he'd done several little sets, or monologues, on *Three of a Kind*, *OTT* and *The Lenny Henry Show*. Looking back, I don't know why we didn't just do all our favourite characters in every episode. Like *The Fast Show*, where they rinsed out all

Delbert and his Ford Wicked

their catchphrase characters every week until we were looking forward to them saying their special thing: 'Suits you, sir.' 'Me? Here?' 'You ent seen me, right?' 'Does my bum look big in this?' 'You know, a tin of Farrow and Ball paint is . . . very much like a woman.' Brilliant! The characters returned week after week, having their adventures and making the same mistakes over and over again. Back in the day, we thought doing Delbert and Deakus and Theo every week was somehow cheating. If we did the same characters week after week, wouldn't the viewers get bored?

The upshot of all this was that I felt there was more mileage in Delbert. In the monologues we set up he had a friend called Big Winston, a girlfriend called Claudette and mates called Freaky Deaky and Double Bump. They all lived the lifestyle of the midnight groover, the funkateer, the raver – driving around the streets late at night playing pirate radio very loud and yelling, 'TUNE!!'

I remember talking to the TV producer John Lloyd about it. He was an expert on getting sitcoms off the ground, having been in on the creation of *The Hitchhiker's Guide to the Galaxy* and *Blackadder*. We were walking around Shepherd's Bush one night having had a drink together, and I was explaining the whole thing:

Me (very enthused): Delbert's gonna have this wicked car and him and Winston are gonna be cruising and then suddenly they'll see the police and there'll be this car chase!

John Lloyd: Yeees . . .

Me: And then Delbert and Winston take evasive action, and there'll be great music – like Cameo, 'Knights by Nights' – and they'll just miss crashing into a milk float and two geezers carrying a huge sheet of plate glass across the street.

John: Yeees, and–

Me: Hang on, and then Delbert'll do this ninety-mile-an-hour dash across London Bridge with all the lights lit up. It'll look like a movie!

John: Lenny, do you have any idea how much money it costs to make a sitcom?

Based on our previous budgets, with the best will in the world the Delbert sitcom was not going to look like a cross between *Soul Train* and *Beverly Hills Cop*. It was going to be a British studio-based sitcom about a young Brixtonian man-child with delusions of grandeur and aspirations to be the best-dressed DJ on the radio. He and Winston'd be running their broadcasting tings from the back of a Greek café, with the police popping in for cups of tea and tzatziki and flatbread, never realising that Del and Win were pumping out big tunes mere feet away from them. We'd record most of it in front of a studio audience and play in pre-recorded scenes intermittently.

Stan and Andrew really got the voice of the show, capturing what it was essentially about. They found out what Delbert was scared of – losing his voice, looking stupid, his mum – and they made those things paramount. In series two Delbert got beat up by some bad guys and couldn't talk properly for two episodes. In another episode he took Claudette out for their first date and ordered a fancy sea bream *en papillote* (fish baked in paper); when it arrived on the table, he picked up the paper and wiped his face with it because he was so nervous.

The other thing we discovered was that no matter how good your sitcom lead, he needs a world around him, people to relate to, otherwise he's just talking to himself. So we had Pip Torrens as a lovelorn police constable and Gina McKee as the object of his desire. Nimmy March played Claudette, Delbert's new girlfriend and, eventually, mother of his child (who was named Crucial, for goodness' sake).

The revelation for me, though, was Vas Blackwood, who played Winston. I'd seen him in a play by Mustapha Matura called *Welcome Home Jacko*. It was set in a youth club, and Vas played one of the lickle youts hanging around for the titular protagonist. I couldn't take my eyes off him. He handled every line with aplomb, and shone physically. He did lots of great stuff when you weren't supposed to be looking at him.

We'd spent a great deal of time working on the written jokes, making sure they popped and were concise when they needed to be and overly verbose when it suited us. Delbert was a word-smith and a gag merchant. He hoovered up good lines, so it was essential that the setups were correct. But Vas decided that he would do his lines exactly how he wanted. He would ignore all direction and advice and just roll the dice on every single line. I used to get angry with him:

Me: Vas, what's going on, man?

Vas: How'd you mean, Len?

Me: It's just . . . you've got to say this, here, how it's meant to be said, so that I can say my bit the way it's written.

Vas: The fing is, Len – I'm an actor, yeah? And, not bein' funny, dread, but there's a fahsand ways to deliver a line. I'm just trying to make it so that we're both funny, y'know. Otherwise you might get lonely up there.

He used to drive me potty. In my selfish way, I wanted him to pick a mode of delivery and stick to it. But, in the end, Vas was right. He couldn't deliver a straight line if he tried, and it was frustrating. But when we got into the studio and I saw the audience's reaction to him, I got it. Vas's Winston was in a world of his own. He was ungovernable, so we let him do what he wanted because a win for him was a win for the show. So I relaxed – just about. He continued to drive me to distraction, however. We'd complete the morning's filming and break for lunch, and then, after everyone had eaten, you'd be going to make-up and costume for last-minute checks, and you'd see the runners looking for Vas:

Runner: You seen Vas?
Me: No. Is he not in the trailer?
Runner: No. I don't know where he is.
Me: Oh God. Didn't we tell him off about this yesterday?
Runner: I did.
Me: Oh God – we start in five minutes and he's not here.

And then Vas would come down the road on a skateboard, with his shirt off and tucked in his pants, looking impossibly ripped, drinking half a Guinness and with a dodgy cigarette dangling from his lower lip. He was incorrigible.

I loved the show. Loved it, loved it, loved it. I got to play records. Lou Mahoney played my Uncle Jake (a tailor, which is why Delbert's suits were so funky fresh); Rudolph Walker was my absentee dad (art imitating real life, unbeknownst to anyone but me). The first season did well ratings-wise; the second was just as good. People were saying 'well hard' and 'totally sponditious' and 'well crucial, y'knaa mean?' at me in the street. Vas and I even got asked to play Delbert and Winston for a building society commercial!

It was important to us to film in Brixton, on the front line, so that we represented it properly. We'd film in a church or marketplace where you could see that this was an area where black, brown and white folks lived together. Delbert was a breakthrough character for me. Doing just one character was better, more manageable. When I got home at night, I wouldn't be worrying about how I was going to play a doctor, the captain from *Hill Street Blues*, the lead singer of Break Wind and Fire, Prince or Gary Coleman from *Diff'rent Strokes*. I was going to be playing Delbert for two months, there was a story throughline, and I would speak and move like Delbert for the entire duration. Bliss.

I was asked to write record reviews as Delbert for *Smash Hits*; Delbert got his own show on Radio 1; I was given clothes to wear on the TV show by Jasper Conran and Betty Jackson. We weren't rising to the surface any more; we were on the top more often than not, in a custom-built speedboat with go-faster stripes down the side and a mammoth Bang & Olufsen sound system that could dissolve a seagull from six miles away. Life was cool.

I decided that the second series (1988) of Delbert would be the last. Stan and Andrew's eyes were looking elsewhere. We loved the show but we were all eager for the next thing – and then the next thing after that. I wanted to stay on or near the top. Obviously, Delbert would play a big role in my future – but I was interested in making other things too.

There was a sidebar event here. I was asked by a young filmmaker called James Bruce if I was interested in a book called *The Suicide Club* by Robert Louis Stevenson. I'd never read it and didn't really know James, but he was vouched for and turned out to be a really nice bloke. We got on, basically, so I read the book and saw that it was a trilogy of stories about a secret gentlemen's club in olden days London, white aristocratic types who'd meet up to discuss how they all wanted to die but hadn't got the courage to do the dirty deed themselves. Turns out that the main rule of the club was that, after a tense card game, the loser was given the mission to whack whoever it was that wanted to die soonest.

I thought it was a bit of a slim premise but SO wanted to film in New York City and Sag Harbor for six weeks – and stay in an apartment on Central Park West for a while – that I just said yes.

I got to work with Mariel Hemingway, Michael O'Donoghue (one of the originators of *Saturday Night Live*) and Robert Joy, who featured in Woody Allen's *Radio Days* and a whole bunch more. I met a very charming southern costume designer called Mckinley Kirby (we called him Kinlo). He'd done some voice work (ADR) on a film called *The Silence of the Lambs*; he had no idea what the film was like but said it had been great fun and he couldn't wait to see it.

Making *The Suicide Club* was odd, to say the least. The cast and crew traipsed up to Sag Harbor, which is an old whaling community, described in the book as: 'An incorporated village in Suffolk County, New York – in the towns of South Hampton and East Hampton on Eastern Long Island. For many years, its main means of supporting itself as a community was through the hunting of whales.' It's quite an interesting place, but we didn't see any of it because we were all jammed into a tiny hotel (the cast, crew, catering and producers – everybody) trying to make head or tail of the script. Which, it suddenly became apparent, we were expected to improvise daily so that a very nice man called Matthew could write up whatever it was we'd pulled out of our butts to film the next day. Strangely, this seemed to be a system that kinda-sorta worked. God knows how, but there was always something to shoot.

I think it might have been a vanity project for Mariel Hemingway. Her husband was very much all over it in terms of production and costs and how much for each pizza, so I'm pretty sure he paid for it all. I remember getting into a car to drive back to Manhattan from Sag Harbor and being chased for many miles by some teamsters (heavy union-type dudes) who were pissed at us all for making a non-union picture. I don't know what they would have done to us had they caught us. I also have an abiding memory of when the film was first shown at the London Film Festival. I was with James at the screening – as the only Brit in the movie, they thought it would be a good idea to have me along to promote it. Mariel did *not* make the trip – maybe she knew something I didn't? I didn't watch the screening because I had an idea that the film might not be the next *Godfather*. I listened through the door and heard no applause as the credits rolled.

Then, suddenly, I was whisked to the seating in front of the screen and made to face a large room full of journalists, one of whom opened the questioning with: 'Lenny, why did you bother to make this film?'

I looked at James but he just smiled and shrugged.

The panel continued in this way until I was able to spin myself very fast like The Flash, drill my way to the centre of the Earth and escape. Thank you for letting me spend time in New York, but please punch me in the face repeatedly if I agree to do something without reading the script properly ever again. I should have remembered this entire experience in the early nineties . . . but more of that later.

Comic Relief:
First Red Nose Day Proper, 1988

I'd been around Richard Curtis a fair bit in the early eighties. He'd written material for *Three of a Kind* and had also (with ace musician Phil Pope) written the very funny 'I've Given Up Drinking Today' for *The Lenny Henry Show*. Back then, I knew of Richard because he wrote and performed with Rowan Atkinson. Their sketches and characters were featured on *Not the Nine O'Clock News*. They had made several albums and put out videos of their show. They were the AC/DC to *Three of a Kind*'s Brotherhood of Man (that's what it felt like to us at times). *Not the Nine O'Clock News* was a TV show that was all about topicality and naughtiness, whereas *Three of a Kind* was a lifestyle comedy of more traditionally intended sketches and characters. By the time I got to *The Lenny Henry Show*, I'd been around Richard a fair bit and liked him a lot. He was a funny guy who supplied many of the great ideas for the corking sketches with Rowan. Most importantly, though, Richard and I were colleagues, and from that sprang our relationship proper.

Post-Live Aid, Richard had gone to Ethiopia to see for himself what the situation was like there. Michael Buerk's harrowing reports on the BBC news had caused all of us to contribute money to the emergency over there. Live Aid had come and gone and made us all feel good about giving, but there was a sense that the comedy community could do something too. Something funny for money, something that might not just be a once-in-a-lifetime thing. While in Ethiopia, Richard was shown around a medical facility. In one room everyone was dead; in the next they were half alive, with a small chance they might survive; and then, finally, he got to a tent where people were more likely to live than not. The hustle and bustle of triage treatment, the under-staffed nursing facility, the weary doctors all moved Richard to want to do something bold to help out. He came back to the UK and asked Rowan if he could figure out how we could all do a benefit show for Comic Relief, which had already been set up under the umbrella of an organisation called Charity Projects, with Jane Tewson (who'd founded Charity Projects in London back in the day as a response to homelessness in Soho).

Rowan was cool about us doing the benefit after he finished his show at the Shaftesbury Theatre, and the whole Comic Relief vibe was born. It was filmed by BBC2 and went out as an *Arena* documentary film. We raised a lot of money with that first programme.

Afterwards there was a party at our house to celebrate and, possibly drunk and high on the success of what we'd just achieved, I said, 'Maybe we should do a night of telly where we do our thing and raise money for the same charities – make it a regular thing?' Richard, not so drunk and with his fundraising hat on, needed no further prompting. He took this half-shaped thing and moulded and worked at it until it slowly evolved and became Red Nose Day and Comic Relief. He generated a team featuring producer Paul Jackson as chairman; a board of trustees, including myself and various others; a deal with the BBC; an arrangement to make red noses; and fun packs for schools and colleges, who were instructed to 'do something funny for money'.

During the run-up for this show, Richard and I wrote letters to various stars and celebrities to ask if they'd take part. Quite a few of them equated appearing in a charity appeal show for Africa as a political statement, and so refused to be involved. Luckily for us, the majority of younger performers were more than happy to get involved.

The first Red Nose Day show, hosted by me, Griff Rhys Jones and a very young and smartly dressed Jonathan Ross, was a huge success. It was also very messy – and live. We discovered that we had to be light on our feet throughout – Richard tended to rewrite the autocue as you were speaking. There were so many links that the whole thing blended together into a morass of puns and silliness. Perhaps a more diligent producer might have said, 'Enough with the *Dances with Wolves* jokes.' But no one did.

The first Red Nose Day – Griff, Me and Jonathan

Griff used to get very cross when we were writing the links for the show. He wanted more comedy and better writing. The answer to which was: 'You've got Richard Curtis, Griff – you'll have to manage.' He almost jammed a fork in his thigh while yelling, 'We Must Make This Funny!' He was a scream in the room, and I loved his passion for making things better. I learnt a lot from Griff. Jonathan was totally laid-back from the very beginning. He and I would bring our favourite comics into rehearsals and read them behind the desk in between takes and while they were playing the films in.

Ethiopia

I'd been sent out to Ethiopia with Helen Fielding as my producer and the film-maker Butch Studdart to make a series of mini-documentaries for the night of the broadcast. Even though I'd been to Africa on my honeymoon, I wasn't really prepared for what I saw. In the wake of the recent famine, and with thousands of people upping sticks and moving across borders to camps where the emergency services were already pushed to the maximum, I found filming my bits to camera stressful. We had people on the ground from the local charities (most of them white), who took us around and spoke Eritrean and were able to give us the bullet points of why we were there. It was harrowing for me at the time, I felt so out of place, but as usual the purpose

– the why of being there, and what we could do to help – over-ruled such feelings. There were so many emotionally involving characters and stories – like the old Ethiopian man who'd lost his daughter and grandchildren during the famine and who, at the end of filming, approached us and said, 'If ever you people in Britain have a problem like this, just let us know and we'll come and help you out.' Or the children who laughed and laughed and laughed at us after we had found a small hill on which to sit and eat our lunch of squeezy cheese and crusty bread from the local garage. As we ate, before setting up the afternoon's shoot, we couldn't help noticing that many of the other villagers had come to laugh at us too. I asked our translator why they were laughing. He went off and came back with a big smile on his face and said, 'They are laughing because you are eating your dinner on the dung heap.' We laughed at that too.

Once the films were all cut together, they were really heartfelt, emotional, moving and sometimes very funny.

I was ritually immersed in poverty and hardship from the minute I arrived in Ethiopia. I met people who'd lost everything and had nothing, kids with no family to speak of, totally dependent on the aid agencies that Comic Relief was helping to fund with the help of UK money. Later on, Richard was able to be there for some of the trips and he was always very encouraging, writing the texts of the appeal films and setting the tone. All the producers, like Helen Fielding, had been briefed comprehensively about the intentions of each mini-documentary. This was hard to get right. The overall narrative of the Comic Relief mission was to give 'a leg-up and not just a handout'. It was always meant to be about indigenous people having the wherewithal to tell their own stories, with added narration and comment from me, Victoria Wood, Billy Connolly or Griff Rhys Jones, or whoever. The intention was to sidestep the traditional 'white saviour' trope of the posh-voiced, white-shirted broadcaster holding a microphone while standing in front of the suffering masses with distended bellies and flies on their eyes, and saying, 'These poor people here need your help. Please help them or they will die.'

Among the most memorable moments from that first year of filming was when I had to walk with a young woman to a well to get water. She did this every day. The point of the film was that she shouldn't have to walk for an hour, daily, with a heavy pot of water on her head. There should be a water source in the village. I tried to carry the full pot of water, and it was so heavy it nearly broke my shoulder. She, however, carried it with ease and didn't know what all the fuss was about. So we abandoned that part of the filming. We did an appeal to the people back home and, at the end, we wanted her to say 'thank you' to everyone who'd donated money. There were several takes, and they were all good, but the more times we did it, the more nervous she got. I noticed that she was struggling with the words and, as I tried to help, the two of us realised how silly the whole situation was. We both got the giggles. Fortunately, the whole thing was caught on film and was broadcast throughout that night. We became the charity that not only got involved with these projects, but also, given the opportunity, could find humour in certain situations, which coloured the films with warmth, personality and joy, not just doom, gloom and death.

We raised fifteen million pounds for charities all over Africa and in the UK. We had done good and there was a lot to be proud of – but it wasn't over, not by a long chalk.

Coast to Coast, 1987

In the midst of this extraordinary run of events came *Coast to Coast*. This was a script written by Stan Hey about a Liverpudlian DJ and a Motown-loving American drifter who team up, become friends and wind up driving an ice-cream van across the UK, with some gangster-owned counterfeit printing plates in the back. They are, of course, pursued by those gangsters (beautifully played by Peter Vaughan and George Baker), aided and abetted by a dodgy scouse British Rail employee called 'Kecks McGuinness' (Peter Postlethwaite). Sandy Johnson of *The Comic Strip Presents* fame was set to direct. I think Stan was persuaded to think about me for the Scouser because I'd been on the telly for a while now and had the kind of recognisability that might help get the film made.

Turns out, that's exactly how it went down. I met David Thompson, the head of single films at the BBC, and he became a champion of mine in terms of making the transition from just doing sketches and comedy to proper acting work. David gave the project the green light and, suddenly, off we went. I practised my Liverpool accent with a mate called David Knopov, who seemed to be in my hotel room 24/7 throughout the first five weeks, saying typical Scouse things and making me repeat them, like, 'Dey do doh, don't dee?' And, 'All right dere, lar?' Or, 'Barry White? I likccgh hm burrriwoodengohwidem.' (In other words: 'They do though, don't they?' 'All right there, lad?' And, 'Barry White? I like him – but I wouldn't go with him.')

We worked and partied hard, patronising the local clubs, bars and discos. We met a lot of people involved in the Liverpool music scene. Everybody seemed to be going to the same pubs and bars, checking out the same bands. I was still young and felt indestructible – on the scene, feelin' keen, lookin' mean. I was buying records like *Parade* by Prince, Anita Baker's *Rapture*, Janet Jackson's *Control*, produced by Jam and Lewis, anything by Trouble Funk, Teena Marie, Terence Trent D'Arby . . . and hanging out – though working hard made me feel less guilty. I was away from home for eight weeks on the trot. This was the norm back in the day.

We stayed at a remarkable hotel called the Adelphi, which, in its day, was incredibly impressive, its grand Edwardian architecture standing strong and steady in the midst of the city centre. According to their website, Charles Dickens named it as one of his favourite hotels.

WHEN WE STAYED THERE, WE DID INDEED HAVE GREAT EXPECTATIONS, BUT IT TURNED OUT TO BE A BIT OF A BLEAK HOUSE.

FIRE ALARMS GOING OFF AT ALL HOURS OF THE NIGHT.

WOOP! WOOP! WOOP!

THERE'D BE THESE EVACUATIONS.

AND I'D BE STANDING IN THE CAR PARK IN THE MIDDLE OF THE NIGHT, GUESTS STARING AT ME IN ME PYJAMAS GOING:

ARE YOU THE BLOKE OFF THAT ADVERT? DO YOUR EYES!*

*I'D DONE AN ADVERTISEMENT IN WHICH, WHENEVER I ATE A PARTICULAR SNACK ITEM, MY EYES WOULD ROLL AROUND MY HEAD CRAZILY.

I ALSO HAD:

OOOOKAAAAY!

THERE WAS THIS TO BE DEALING WITH:

HEY LENNY LAR, KATANGA MY FRIENDS!

AND THE ICING ON THE CAKE:

DO DELBERT, LENNY LAR!

IT WAS EXHAUSTING. IT'S A WONDER WE GOT ON THE SET AT ALL.

Most of the cast and crew were staying there, and we all had odd experiences involving items of value disappearing from our rooms and horrors that were beyond the pale (loud disco music till 2 a.m., sticky carpets, screaming hen parties, lads beating lumps out of each other for fun . . .). John Shea, the American star of *Coast to Coast*, took to having a glass of wine, taking a sleeping aid, stuffing in earplugs and sleeping through the chaos. He always seemed rested and calm when he arrived on set. I, on the other hand, had *Murder on the Orient Express*-style luggage under my eyes, a faulty memory through lack of sleep, and God knows what else.

It was a fun shoot. On the first day of rehearsals, Sandy decided to film a scene where my character, Richie, had a pile of old Motown records and was playing them in a purist/Northern Soul acolyte way. This was real music; never mind all your beats per minute, techno, shag-happy house and the like – Richie played the Temptations, the Four Tops, Stevie Wonder, Junior Walker and the All Stars, Smokey Robinson and the Miracles, the Velvelettes, Martha Reeves and the Vandellas. It was about Tamla Motown, and Richie was all over it like a rash. I could relate to someone obsessed with this kind of music. I'd been around Northern Soul DJs and understood their pernickety nature when it came to collecting white-labelled musical obscurities from the past. 'Hey, lar, dis was recorded in a broom cupboard in Detroit by the Motown house band. They got paid in readies and peanut-butter sandwiches, and the lead singer's David Ruffin doin' a Hungarian accent 'cos he don't want Berry Gordy to find out he's been bangin' out his pipe singin' for a rival record company, y'know whorra mean?'

So Sandy set up a shot of me, as Richie, playing records using DJ equipment (two turntables and a microphone) on the morning

John Shea arrived. Sandy radioed for him to be brought on set asap and asked him to just react to whatever was going on. John was greeted by me playing Motown's greatest hits. He grinned as soon as he heard the tunes, nodded his head, shook his shoulders and snapped his fingers. I liked him immediately. He was a consummate actor – not so much method, but theatre-trained and rather strict. Our first proper scene involved me waiting to meet him in a restaurant. Stan had Richie pretending to be a CB radio operator – 'Over, Red Devil, it's me, Scouse Git; yes, over, over, over' – all in a broad Liddypool accent, almost heckling myself with comments and voices and sound effects. As soon as Sandy shouted, 'Action!' I began, but, after a while John walked off the set, approached him and said something to the effect of: 'Uh, Sandy – is he gonna do it like that?'

I totally panicked: '*OH NO! He thinks I'm crap. What am I gonna do?*' I was full of shame. I didn't know how to act. I should just go back to the working men's clubs, that's where I really belonged. Horrific self-doubt came and feasted upon this banquet of insecurity – all in the space of two minutes as I continued to watch John and Sandy deep in conversation.

Here's what Sandy did.

He came over and spoke to me, very quietly, in his cool, Scottish burr: 'OK, Len, very nice. Now, let's do all of that again, but take your time this time, OK? And maybe take the volume down a notch?'

And that was it.

After two or three takes, he said, 'Great. Moving on. Nice one, Len. Lovely, John . . .'

And that was it.

I hadn't had any acting training whatsoever, apart from watching Tracey Ullman's excellence at close quarters and having

Norman Beaton yelling in my ear, 'Do it better, boy!' when I was seventeen. Acting on film was different. I'd made commercials and shot parodies on *Three of a Kind* and *The Lenny Henry Show*, but the idea of sustaining a performance over ninety minutes was daunting. What if you put on weight during filming (highly likely to happen)? What if you forgot the dialect (also very highly likely to happen once we left Liverpool and there was no more Knopov)? What if I just couldn't do it? Of course, the answer was to hurl myself off the cliff and dive into the deep waters of 'JUST DO IT, YOU PILLOCK' and hope for the best. In my brain, all of this negativity was countered by: *'Sandy knows you; Stan's worked with you and likes what you do – that must count for something. Just work hard and see what happens.'*

So that's what I did. And I learnt so much from John Shea. He was elegant and mysterious, and he loved to rehearse. We got into a routine of running the lines quietly and then, when the camera turned over, hardly raising our voices – whether we were being funny, scared, passionate, whatever. John didn't like big, over-the-top performances, so I had to learn to do the opposite of what I'd normally do and be real and natural for a change. When you watch *Coast to Coast*, you can see me, scene by scene, altering my performance to suit the style of the piece. Luckily, Sandy shot the film in sequence, so after a rough(ish) start you can see me physically and vocally settling into a performance groove that stays on point to the movie's climax. This was the first on-screen performance of which I was proud. It was rough around the edges but, due to the quality of the script and the players, it worked. My inexperience seemed to come across as chaotic, fun and passionate. Although Clive Barnes of the *New York Post* gave me a B+ for my dialect, he allowed that the film worked well and that the double act of John Shea and Lenny Henry was a treat.

I loved working on the project and wanted to do a sequel – we all did – but there was a problem with the music rights. Stan and Sandy had done a road trip across America from Sag Harbor to Los Angeles, zigzagging through the deep South. The research had been done for a follow-up story, in which Richie and John's character go on a wild goose chase to find a blues singer of renown. It sounded hare-brained and crazy, but that was what it was like at the time. You did something that worked, and immediately everyone was hustling to do the follow-up because, hey, that might work too. I think Stan wrote a long story outline for *Coast to Coast 2*, but it never got picked up – probably too expensive and a music rights nightmare. Ah well, on to the next thing . . .

I love this photo. It's the first shot that Trevor Leighton took of me.
Trevor was my photographer of choice from the early eighties
right up until 2000. Very nice chap.

Doing the cheesy *Three of a Kind*-slightly embarrassed grin.
Dunno why . . .

The Lenny Henry Show – doing stand-up on telly pretty
much for the first time. Thank God for Kim and the other
writers – it could all have gone a whole other way . . .

In the coat – the mighty Delbert Wilkins of Brixton.

In the cardigan – Deakus, who comes from ahhhmmm . . . Jamaica!

In the purple Dandy Highwayman look – it's Prince!

Gurning during a stand-up gig at
the Albany Empire. We used these
shots on the back of the *Stand Up
...Get Down* album cover.

An in-store signing for
Stand Up ... Get Down
(note the same T-shirt).

A Comic Relief promo shot: *left to right* – Jennifer Saunders, Gareth Hale and Norman Pace, Tony Robinson, Jonathan Ross and me in a ridiculous but gorgeous Red Nose Day suit.

Myself and the Champ – the Juliet to my Romeo for Comic Relief – Misterrrrr Frank Bruno! 'Y'know what I mean, Harry?'

During filming for *Live and Unleashed* – in heavy prosthetics created by the brilliant Norma Hill. Steve Martin left a message on my answer-phone when he saw it.

As Richard Pryor (PG 13) in *Live and Unleashed*.

My big movie debut role – Miles Pope in *True Identity*.

As Michael Jackson (*above*) and presenting (*right*) on Mandela Day.

A whole bunch of Chefs: *left to right* – Erkan Mustafa, Roger Griffiths, Gary Parker and Claire Skinner . . . All wonderful.

Theophilus P. Wildebeeste, the world's sexiest soul singer, decides to go into space. 'Ride My Rocket' was the hit single.

6

RISING . . . RISING . . .

Delbert, Second Season;
The South Bank Show, 1988

So, the second season of Delbert began with three episodes featuring a near silent Delbert. Note to self: 'Never upset the writers.'

Stan and Andrew had Delbert beaten up by tough guys who broke his jaw. Delbert couldn't talk and, when he tried, he sounded like he'd done ten rounds with Frank Bruno. It was a good story beat – Delbert looked cool with the swollen jaw. The series did pretty well and bowed out with a viewing audience of about nine million.

Also in 1988 I was the subject of an episode of *The South Bank Show*: Leonard Bernstein, Pier Paolo Pasolini, Tom Stoppard, Elizabeth Taylor . . . and now a black kid from Dudley who says 'Katanga, my friend' in a dodgy, unspecified African accent! Film-maker Andy Harries had got in touch. He'd shown an interest in my career and wanted to make a documentary about where I was at in 1988. It was a good question. I'd been in the business since I was sixteen; in 1988 I was in my thirtieth year. It was time for an appraisal, and *The South Bank Show* was the most prestigious place for that to happen. I was very honoured to be asked, as I'd always been an admirer of Melvin Bragg's luxurious hair, which seemed to flow Medusa-like on and around his head whenever he entered the room. Andy was a pistol, a hotshot, a go-getter. By the time he met me he'd directed the documentary series *Africa* (1984) and had worked on several editions of *The South Bank Show* and *Arena*. He'd also directed the pilot for Jonathan Ross's *Last Resort*, which went to series shortly afterwards. He had a production company with Paul Greengrass called Sleeping Partners. I liked him because he was unstoppable and knew how to get things done. I admire that in people.

When we were filming *The South Bank Show*, Andy talked about all the people he knew: artists, musicians, broadcasters, journalists. He seemed incredibly sophisticated to me. I'd seen the show and knew they rarely talked to people like me. I'd done working men's clubs, summer seasons in Great Yarmouth, the Minstrels show, and carried it all on my shoulders like a massive boulder of pain that kept getting heavier.

'Why me?' I asked.

'It's time,' Andy replied.

He wanted to show people just how much I'd achieved since leaving the Black and White Minstrels in 1979. When he put it like that, I said, 'Yes.' But I wanted to include everyone I'd worked with, so, Kim Fuller was involved, and so were Stan Hey and Andrew Nickolds, because Andy wanted to feature Deakus, Delbert and Winston, and the stand-up as well. He wanted to plonk me down in the middle of Manhattan and take me on a whirlwind tour of the comedy clubs, trying out stand-up material. The biggest and most famous club in New York at the time was Catch a Rising Star. Andy thought it'd be a good idea to close out the documentary with me doing a set, and American bookers talking about my prospects. This was going to be scary, but fun!

The trouble was, usually with a *South Bank Show* they might commission a little something from the subject – a new John Cage piece or a mini-Alan Bennett *Talking Head* by a guest performer – but, at times, mine felt like a special edition of *The Lenny Henry Show*, with odd bits of interview cropping up every so often. It wasn't just me talking to Melvin and clips from past performances; it was new material mixed in with Melvin asking me about my beginnings, and then my mum chatting away, and finally ending with me in New York City, performing at Catch a Rising Star. All the bits and pieces we shot in the UK seemed to go well, but the climax of the piece in New York . . . for that segment, the ideas were a bit sketchy. I'd never done stand-up in America, and it felt like a huge ask to just go there and start doing it, like now! I was in a panic. Fortunately, Kim Fuller came with us to supervise the New York set.

These days, a young comic with the opportunity to visit New York City and do a set in one of its most storied venues would first pinch themselves and then write pages and pages of jokes, which they would workshop, trim and focus until the material shone like a new pin. Then they'd go to the Big Apple knowing they were ready for anything that could be thrown at them: multiple bookings, requests for an appearance on the *Tonight* or *Letterman* shows, and so on. When I interviewed Andy for this book, I remembered how unprepared I was:

Me: When we got to New York, I had a massive dip in confidence because I just wasn't ready, and you said to Kim Fuller, 'You've got to sort this out.' You didn't tell him how or why, you just said, 'You've got to sort this out. I can't film any of this.' And we went to work – you somehow made him feel that he had to knuckle down and work with me. Because he could have easily gone, 'This isn't gonna work, his bottle's gone, f*ck it!' But that didn't happen because of your relentless badgering. And you knew that our relationship was . . . intense. You just said, 'You've got to pull your finger out.' Kim works really well with people that are strong with him and give him a good structure.

Andy: I remember you went on-stage on the Monday or Tuesday, and it was a bit grim, wasn't it? We had a good week besides that – we went to Nell's and met Prince and hung out, that side of things was great – but I was anxious about it because I knew that if I couldn't get the bit of footage that showed you triumphing on a New York stage, on the brink of US fame, the film was going to be a bit of a dud. I tried not to show you just how nervous I was – but inside I was having a bit of a panic that we might not make it.

Me: You didn't mask that very well. The way you put it to us was, 'You guys better get your f*cking shit together.'

Andy: But the thing was, what that week did for me – and I talk about this when I'm doing lectures or public speaking to interested parties – is that it made me really understand just how raw comedy is . . . and the exposure of being a stand-up comedian. I saw you pulling yourself together: you had to write a set with Kim that would really work, and it did. That started my comedy experience. If a rock band does a duff gig, they just have to play their way through the set and get on with it. But comedians have to go on and get through it and try to figure out what's working and what isn't working, and navigate their way through that. And it got better. You discovered that whole thing of being a black Briton in New York. You did that first – it's a trope now with modern-day British comedians – but you were the first one to do that stuff, and the New Yorkers really identified with what you were saying. In the late 1980s New York was quite heavy, edgier on the streets. There weren't many black Britons on the streets out there, and you expressed that in a humorous way. As I remember, the set went down pretty well, and I was proud of the show in the end.

I relaxed a little as we wrote and hung out. As long as Kim was there, I figured we'd be all right. We had strong building blocks in characters like the Blues Singer, the Preacher and Theophilus P. Wildebeeste, the sexiest soul singer in Christendom. But what I was desperate for – and what was lacking – was some top-quality stand-up. The first night I went on-stage at Catch a Rising Star the words turned to ashes in my mouth. I was exposed: everything I was doing was Pryoresque, and noticeably so. None of the material spoke to being black and British with a Jamaican heritage, which is what I should have been talking about.

We went to all the comedy clubs to give me a taste of how things went down in this new territory. We wrote material every day; I got up and tried it out most nights. We wrote about being black and British in America and being mistaken for hoodlums. 'People kept saying to me, "When you go to New York, watch out for the big black guys."' There was a good opening line: 'Good evening, my name is Lenny Henry – yes, there are black people in the UK. We're called "the accused".' They liked the whole 'the cops pulled me over and I opened my mouth and sounded like the Duke of Edinburgh and they let it slide'-type material. It was a genuine blast to be on-stage over there.

We got material from my lived experience. I found twenty dollars on the sidewalk that had been accidentally dropped in front of me by a guy and his girlfriend. As I approached them with the money, they looked back then began walking faster. So I walked faster until, eventually, we were all running. I was shouting, 'Excuse me, you dropped this.' The guy's shouting over his shoulder, 'No, no, buddy. You keep it!' (In real life they just sped up and eventually ran like hell.) One day I was profiled and followed around a shop by a security guy with a radio: 'Check out the black guy . . . I'm following the black guy.' That went in the show as well. Everything else was material I was already doing, and it began to gel. The section we cut together of us in NYC really worked. I felt it showed me off to a good advantage. A lot of people saw it, including my mum.

And all the way through that process, Andy kept saying, 'We should do something else. What do you wanna do? What ideas do you have?' He was like a runaway train. He wanted to make more content, generate more ideas. I was blown away by his enthusiasm; he was probably one of the first people I'd met with as much energy as me. I mentioned to him that very few British comedians had made a feature film of their show. I could be the first one. So we made *Live and Unleashed* and, for a moment there, I thought it had changed my life for ever.

Lenny Live and Unleashed, 1989 and Just Before . . .

It would be the first stand-up film by a British comic to be shot like a movie. I was very, very, very interested in this – thrumming with excitement, in fact. It seemed to be the perfect time to do something like this. I was on tour anyway, so making a film at the end of it wasn't going to be such a big deal. But Andy didn't want it to be just a stand-up movie; he wanted wrap-around material, characters, some kind of spoof before it segued into the comedy bits. So, once again, we asked Kim to supervise the new material. He put together a mini-power room of James Hendrie, Lennie Barker, Annie Caulfield, him, me and a couple of others. Everyone made it their job to think of funnier lines, things that could top already good punchlines – that's how we rolled. I honed the material till it squeaked and I felt confident about it. But Andy wanted more. He thought we should get a gospel choir for the Reverend Nat West. So we did a routine where the reverend kept going into sexy soul songs in the midst of his sermon, and the choir got carried away and joined in. It was fun to do, but it didn't make the cut. We shot a mini-introductory film, with Robbie Coltrane playing a bolshy cab driver. Robbie had it down cold, and we kept rehearsing. Then it turned out that Andy couldn't be in the cab directing us, so I had to monitor the performances. We did eleven takes, and then I said, 'Print it!' We wrote a fantasy sequence where various comics (played by me) were waiting and saying stuff to me on my way to the backstage area. Being Steve Martin meant that I had to get up at four in the morning to begin the prosthetics. Norma Hill was key make-up artist that day and she did a brilliant job of making me as Steve as could be.

We filmed at the Hackney Empire. When we got into the theatre, me, made up and dressed as Richard Pryor, harangued me from the balcony (in strangely PG13 language for him); and then, as I reached backstage, me, made up and dressed as Eddie Murphy, gave me a hard time. All shot for a whole guinea and a bag of pork scratchings.

I remember on night one of recording the show, I had a very sore throat (which always seems to happen on the first performance, I don't know why). I'd been looking after my voice all the way through the tour leading up to this moment. I couldn't believe that my voice just wouldn't play ball. I did exercises, steamed, and nothing worked. I just had to bite the bullet and get on with it. That show was fine, but I stayed in bed all the next day and told everyone not to phone. The tour had been quite gruelling and I needed to rest my voice. The next night was better – I knew where the cameras were and could play to them occasionally. Andy's directing at this point was mute because once the show started and the cameras were running, he couldn't talk to me during the performance. He trusted me to get on with it. He really pushed us as a team, making sure each department was doing what they were supposed to be doing. I couldn't wait to see the first assembly.

Gerry Hambling was helping Andy with the edit. He'd overseen the post-production on films like *Mississippi Burning*, *The Commitments* and *Midnight Express*. When I went in to watch the edited sequences, I didn't really understand who Gerry was. I kept asking for takes that didn't exist and trying to get him to go round the corner on some shots because 'it might look better from there'. He was very patient with me and eventually produced an excellent edit of the show. We'd done it. It's one of the shows of which I'm most proud. *Live and Unleashed* was made on quite a low budget for Steve Woolley and Nik Powell's Palace Pictures. The album came out on Island Records. The film ran for a good long while at the Haymarket in London and it made its money back! I'd drive past the cinema sometimes in the evening and point out to anyone that was listening: 'Hey, that's me! I'm grafting and I don't even have to be there.' This was the life. Oh yes.

Cannes Film Festival, Darling (1989)

When I went to Cannes Film Festival to promote the film, it was abundantly clear that there wasn't much money being thrown at it. Andy and I were taken to a nice restaurant, where I ate bouillabaisse for the first time, which was like eating a live aquarium. Fish kept bubbling around and breaking the surface, their eyeballs staring at me accusingly before disappearing beneath the liquid. But there was nothing about my film anywhere: no posters, flyers or handouts. I had to go and say 'hi' to everyone at a discotheque!

I was introduced in French and only just about recognised my name. I got up and said 'hello' and made some jokes, and the microphone fed back loudly all the way through my speech like an ear-sizzling Ted Nugent guitar solo. The more I tried to move the mic closer to my mouth, the louder the feedback got. After a few minutes I gave up and handed the DJ his microphone back. No one clapped. I was utterly dejected. It was like dying on my arse at Keighley Variety Club all over again. Cannes wasn't supposed to be like this. However, I *did* get to see Spike Lee's back as he walked away from me. An abiding memory is of having breakfast with Steven Soderbergh, who was about to win the main prize for *sex, lies, and videotape*. He was a cool guy, very natural and friendly, and obviously talented.

I came back a couple of weeks later for the Cannes TV Festival, where *Live and Unleashed* was up for auction. This was a more corporate affair. I had to do a short live presentation, and, clearly, the television posse knew their business. The audiovisual crew spoke English, and there was a producer who asked which clips he should show and then had them edited and cued up for the Q&A after my performance. It was a packed house, with lots of bids for the film. I sang 'Bad Jokes' and I may have done Theo for them. It went well, and the BBC bought the rights.

The reaction to *Live and Unleashed* had been good, and the film had attracted the attention of Harvey Weinstein and Miramax Films. In those days, once they bought the American rights, they would do something called 'audience testing' almost immediately. This involved inviting a group of people to a theatre, where they would watch a screening of your film. There would be a discussion afterwards about what they did and did not enjoy about the presentation. Then the audience would be asked to fill out cards that might possibly say:

I loved it.
I liked it.
It was ok.
Meh.
I didn't like it. I HATED IT!

Andy went to some of these test screenings and, apparently, the cards that came back were mostly positive, with very good scores. He figured the film would be a great calling card in New York and LA. All we had to do was get Harvey to agree on a limited screening in both those cities; the reviews and attendant publicity would do the rest.

But ...

I had been spotted by a movie executive, a lovely man who'd seen the TV festival performance on tape and then asked for a copy of the film. He watched it and then called his bosses at

Disney/Touchstone. He wanted to put my hat in the ring for a movie from which Eddie Murphy had just walked away. He thought I could step in and fill Eddie's shoes. I was so happy that all the questions I would normally have asked slipped from my mind. Questions like: 'You know I'm not Eddie Murphy, don't you?' Or, 'Who's gonna direct it? It's gonna need to be someone I know, right?' And, 'Why's Eddie walked away? Is the script rubbish?' There were endless questions, but I wasn't paying them any attention. I'd been approached by Disney/Touchstone about a major motion picture, with my name above the title. I was away with the big-time Hollywood dream fairies and, *lalalaaaalaleeee*, Disney wanted to sign me for a three-picture deal. This was it, everything I'd been working for since the beginning of the eighties! I was at first stunned, then gobsmacked, then thrilled, then genuinely frightened. There was no question of me turning it down: I'd wanted to be in a movie since I was four years old in Dudley, a little black kid pretending to be James Bond or Simon Templar off the telly, running up Rollason Road with my fingers shaped into a pretend gun and shooting at imaginary bad guys. I'd spent most of my childhood jumping in and out of bushes and catching invisible hoodlums with my improvised kung-fu kicks. Every time I drew a picture in art at primary school it was of Robert Vaughn in *The Man from U.N.C.L.E.* – the pointy quiff and a vague representation of a suit, with a skinny tie and a gun. Or Sean Connery, with his pointy quiff toupée and his shiny suit, standing next to a pretty girl in a bikini. This was all I'd ever wanted to be and do. I'd never seen a black person doing these things in a film or TV show, so I just drew them and imagined myself doing them. We had Greg Morris in *Mission Impossible*, which ran from 1966 to 1973, and he was cool. We also had Mark (Don Mitchell) in *Ironside*, but all he did was push Raymond

Burr around in his wheelchair. I hadn't seen much of Sidney Poitier in the movies, but I would have been majorly inspired by him if I'd been allowed to see *Lilies of the Field* or *In the Heat of the Night*. I remember seeing Woody Strode in *Spartacus*, maybe on TV, and for a brief moment wanting to be a Roman gladiator. That saying – 'If you can see it, you can be it' – is true. Whenever I saw a black person on TV, I immediately put myself in their shoes so that I could imagine what it would be like to be a teacher, a cop, a secret agent, a slave or a soldier.

My being asked to make a film – even one of Eddie Murphy's cast-offs – was the biggest event of my life so far, and I wasn't about to throw it away.

The first of what would be a three-picture deal – *True Identity* – was written by Andy Breckman, based on an original *Saturday Night Live* sketch. Performed by Eddie on the show, it was about him using make-up to transform himself into a white person and observing how white people behave when they think black people aren't around. I thought to myself, 'This is going to be extraordinary. This is going to be "the bomb"!'

Well, I was at least half right . . . use of the word 'bomb' is a big clue.

I read the script and showed it to a few people, including Dawn and Richard Curtis. Most, including myself, thought that it needed some tweaks, a bit of work. But I felt I could do something with it. Richard made several suggestions that were very funny. There were also some ideas that I had talked over with Dawn, like making the lead character English of Jamaican heritage and a huge fan of all things Americana; making him an impressionist and a mimic; and giving him a surreal and improvisational sense of humour. These were all things on my can-do list and, if they agreed to them, it was going to be OK.

After much discussion, I accepted their offer, and from that moment Dawn had my back completely. We discussed the deal and the schedule and made a pact that we would go through the entire experience together. From make-up tests and shooting on the streets of Manhattan to filming for several months in Los Angeles, Dawn made sure I was supported from beginning to end. We were flown over, business class, to LA to continue talks and do the preparatory make-up tests. The premise of the movie was simple: Miles Pope, a wannabe actor from NYC, flies down to Florida to make a commercial. On the return flight he sits next to a formidable-looking businessman (played by Frank Langella), who, unbeknownst to Miles, is a Mafia boss. The plane hits turbulence; everyone's screaming and thinking, 'This is the moment I die in a freakin' plane crash!!!!' The mobster grips Miles by the arm and confesses that he has killed people and done terrible things in pursuit of money and power. He wants to tell all this to somebody – anybody – before he dies. All the way through the turbulence he's confessing and confessing, and then, suddenly, the turbulence just . . . stops. Uh oh . . . Miles now knows this guy's name, the names of his victims and where the bodies are buried. He's in the deep and dreadful. From the moment the plane lands, he is in mortal danger. The mobster can't have him running around with his cry-baby confession uploaded to Miles's cerebral cortex. The kid's gotta be taken out. Miles knows he has to get the hell out of Dodge – so he goes to his friend, who happens to be a make-up artist (played by the director Charles Lane) and a dab hand at prosthetic makeovers. He tells his friend everything. His friend's solution is that Miles should become a white guy, therefore avoiding detection.

That's the movie: Miles on the run, putting on the make-up; the bad guys in pursuit, dealing with weird situations where

Miles has to do lots of different characters and voices to escape/
avoid/evade . . . yadda, yadda, yadda . . . the bad guy. Eventually,
he beats the bad guy and gets the girl.

The End.

'The nominees are—'

HOLD UP, WAIT A MINUTE!

There was a lot to do if I was going to resemble a credible
white guy. I recommended Norma Hill, who'd done such a good
job of turning me into Steve Martin for *Live and Unleashed* that
Steve himself rang my answerphone and left a long, rambling,
funny message, demanding money and gifts from me for bor-
rowing his entire visage – nay, his very soul – for profit and gain.

Norma was booked to do my make-up, but then, on arrival, it
turned out they'd also booked Michele Burke, who'd been nominated for an Oscar for her make-up and hair design on *Cyrano de
Bergerac* in 1990 (she'd worked on Gérard Depardieu's hooter).
Michele was to be the head make-up person, and Norma was
designated for the days when I was only required to wear normal
'Lenny Henry-style make-up'. I thought I could sort this out, it
was cool. I talked to my agent in LA, Susan Smith. She kicked up
a fuss and eventually got some assurances that Norma would be
part of the team that would preside over all make-up duties.

Susan was a force of nature. Her default position was, 'Get
the f*ck outta here, you f*cking, c**k-s*****g, motherf***er!'
Her mode of defence was to be on the attack at all times. She
swore like a docker who'd repeatedly stubbed his bare toe on a
girder. She fought like a tiger for me on more than one occasion.
Thankfully, she understood the problems of working for Dis-
ney/Touchstone – and they were many.

'Welcome to California –
Now Drop and Give Me Twenty!'

I'd already figured out that my size might cause some concern, so, before flying out in the spring of '89, I had been rigorous with personal training and nutrition – and managed to get down to fifteen and a half stone. Which is a good size for me – I can get suits off the peg and get down like James Brown. I felt good about my size and shape and was ready for anything. So imagine my face during our first 'meet and greet' when one of the executive producers carelessly said, 'You're quite a bit bigger than we all expected, so we'll have to fix that. We'll have the Disney nutritionist work on that with the company diet. You stick to that, you'll lose a ton of weight in no time.'

Oh God! To them I was a heffalump in a suit. When I got the Disney diet sheet, it was basically two lists of what I could and couldn't eat. Underneath 'WHAT YOU CAN EAT' it said:

Air
Rice cakes
Chicken
Tuna fish
Lean steaks
Boiled eggs
Bagels
A glass of wine once a week
Low-cal beer
Water

And underneath 'WHAT YOU CAN'T EAT' it just said:

Everything else

This plunged me into not only a maelstrom of low self-esteem, but also perhaps the toughest regimen of physical exercise that I've ever undertaken. I had to get up an hour before my call time to ride a stationary bike and then perform a series of Canadian Airforce exercises. I wasn't even going to be in the Canadian Airforce. There were two-hour bike rides every Saturday and Sunday – *and* gym sessions three times a week with Doug, my personal trainer at the Mondrian hotel, who resembled a 'condom full of walnuts' (© Clive James re. Arnold Schwarzenegger). Doug was ripped, shredded and muscular beyond belief. He could bench press a tower block and would often demonstrate this when there was no one else around. He could climb a rope in no time at all and, when we trained outside, would jump up on the consecutive rings and swing from one end to the other with no effort at all. I would usually get stuck on the second ring and then, with tears coursing down my cheeks, have to be helped down by Doug and the hotel maintenance guy.

This was my life now.

The bike rides were good. In LA it meant riding up and around the coastline for four hours. In New York it meant cycling from my hotel uptown all the way down to the Staten Island ferry and then turning round and doing the return journey. I would do this with a stunt man called Phil, whose job it was to keep me alive and set the pace as we bobbed and weaved through traffic. I managed to avoid being struck by insane limo and taxi drivers many times. I had to do these rides because there was a shot our director wanted of me riding a racing bike through the streets of

Manhattan as if I'd been doing it my whole life without a care in the world. I think during the majority of the shots my face, rather than not a care in the world, actually displayed an '*agggggh*, I'm going to die!' expression – either that or 'Learn to drive asshole! I'm riding a bike here!' The whole careless vibe evaporated as soon as I pushed out into drive-time traffic. What was I thinking?

So, between Doug and the Disney diet, I could actually see myself losing weight and gaining muscle – but the cost was high. I was allowed just the one glass of wine a week, along with a little bit of pasta or rice, chicken, salad, vegetables, salad . . . I was eating like a supermodel. For a while there, if you'd asked me my middle name, I'd have yelled: 'Misery!'

Although Disney were paying me decently and had sorted out luxurious hotels and per diems (a daily stipend in cash in a brown envelope), I felt that things were wrong with our relationship. There had been script meetings where I had been able to express my concerns (not that many, to be honest) to the writer Andy Breckman and the producers. For the first time, I felt like I had been heard. Then Andy was no longer there. I liked him; he seemed to be a funny guy who knew what he was talking about. He was gone.

Then they brought in Leslie Dixon, who'd written *Overboard* for Goldie Hawn and Kurt Russell. Dawn came with me to meet Leslie in a rehearsal room, and there were discussions about the existing screenplay and what could be done to make it better. Then came a new draft of the script. I don't remember what it was like because it wasn't around long enough to get comfortable with. Leslie was gone.

Suddenly, Charles Shyer and Nancy Meyers (later, they'd direct and co-write the *Father of the Bride* reboot with Steve Martin) were brought in for rewrite duties. By this time I was sick with worry. I'd never done anything that had been through this many rewrites. I thought there was something wrong. And there was.

The writing and rewriting of the script unravelled at speed and it soon became clear that, although there was a good idea in there somewhere, it wasn't quite coming together. Our director, Charles Lane, was part of a group of young black creative talents who had recently blossomed. Disney had appropriated him because they wanted a Spike Lee of their own. But Charles had a different sensibility to Spike. He was quieter; he was careful and considered in his speech. He'd won the Prix du Public at the Cannes Film Festival for his silent movie *Sidewalk Stories*. His humour was more Chaplinesque. So far, his movies had been made with a musical score and sound effects, but no dialogue. They were charming, black-and-white evocations of a late-twentieth-century African American Little Tramp – a bespectacled homeless dude beset by everything the Big City can throw at him. In *Sidewalk Stories* he gets lumbered with a badly behaved little girl and, at the beginning of the movie, tries to get rid of her, then by the end realises that he doesn't want to lose her. I loved it and thought that, despite his lack of experience at the grown-ups' table of movie-making, he was talented enough to weather the storm and come up trumps.

Charles was great: he took the whole script on board, listening to everyone's concerns about it. He simply communicated calm. All would be well because he, Charles Lane, would rewrite the whole thing, taking everyone's notes on board. He told me, 'Trust me, man. There ain't gonna be no problem.'

But there was. Charles's version of the script was 180 pages long. If you threw it across the room at a burglar, you could knock that sucker out. The dialogue was off; there was too much description. Everything that was good about the Andy Breckman draft was almost gone, and all the hazy, wobbly, dodgy stuff that had emerged from recent drafts had somehow stayed – accompanied by Charles's additions, tweaks and new plot twists. I was confused. Why was it so long? Where were the jokes? Charles seemed to have written himself into the movie (he got good reviews in the end). What was going on?

In addition to all this, there was dialect work with Ric Ericson, a genius of accents as well as an acting coach. He taught me Long Island lockjaw, how to talk like a New Jersey mobster, a native New Yorker, an African American southerner – all those things and more. Ric was a fantastically decent person and also a shoulder to freak out or cry on whenever the moment called for it.

By the time we began shooting, my head was in a bad place. Day after day, I was doing my best to represent myself in a decently funny way. But I was way out of my depth. Plus, because I was working in a dialect that was not my own, Ric would continually run in to correct my efforts *after every take*. He'd whisper in my ear, 'Say "boat".'

'Boat.'

'NO! Say "boaht" – like "vote".'

'Oh. OK. "Boahht".'

'Good. Now say "Pan Am".'

'Pan Am.'

'OK, good – you're good, you're doing good. You ready?'

'Yeah. I'm ready.'

'NO! Say "ready".'

'Man, I'm ready for Freddy.'

'You sound like Prince Charles. Say "boat . . ."'

I had the scene shifters, grips, sound crew, camera posse, hair and make-up all looking at me like, 'Eddie Murphy would be killin' this by now.' And they were right. I was sinking way, way, way low. The constant corrections were taking their toll.

And other things were happening.

The make-up situation was getting out of hand. It had been decided that I would wear a full mask of prosthetics covering my nose, chin – including my eyes – almost down to my chest. And my hands, up to my elbows. This was a big job. I was going to be a big walking mass of white-guy rubber. A prosthetics team who had just won an Oscar for their stellar work on *Dick Tracy* with Warren Beatty and Madonna were also brought in to join Michele and Norma. They were called Caglione and Drexler, and they were fantastic. They really knew their stuff. So now, with a make-up team consisting of Norma, Michele, John Caglione Jnr and Doug Drexler, everybody was an expert in movie and TV prosthetics, but no one could decide just how white and freckled I should be when I was the white guy. Make-up tests dragged on. I went from looking like Boris Karloff in *Frankenstein* to André the Giant in *The Princess Bride*; from Mel Brooks in *Blazing Saddles* to some guy one of the producers had met in a bar once. It was all very confusing, and no one was listening to how I felt, except for Norma, to whom I was able to grumble as the make-up was removed at the end of the tests. If she hadn't been on set every day, I probably would have gone nuts. She was very patient and encouraging and, along with Dawn, was able to get me to a place where I could go before the camera and do what was expected of me.

Caglione and Drexler were brilliant and gung-ho. Every time they put a panel of the prosthetic on my face, they'd do a high five or a fist bump with whoever was around and say, 'Good job!'

'Yeah, man, good job!'

'You're my hero.'

'No, man, you're *my* hero!'

They were good fun to be around, relentlessly upbeat, but all business when it came to establishing a calm make-up trailer, with everyone working hard. Somehow they all managed to reach a consensus. Disney even asked the renowned genius Dick Smith to come in and have a look at the final make-up. It was an honour to meet him. He had done *The Exorcist*, *Scanners* and *Altered States*. He walked around me, examining all the joins, looking at all the flesh-toned additions to the make-up. Caglione and Drexler gave each other low fives. Michele folded her arms and looked proud. Norma nodded her head, thinking, 'Yes, this is it.' Then, abruptly, Dick picked up a random make-up brush and a paint pot and started adding red dots to my cheeks, nose and forehead.

You could see all that 'rah, rah, rah' high-five stuff flying out the window, all that confidence dropping off the entire team's faces in large chunks. What was he doing?

His argument was that whatever we did, we still had a chunk of rubber on a living person's face. This wasn't a monster from another planet or a little girl possessed by the devil. I was going to be around other human beings, I had to fit in with other white people, so they should do whatever they could to make my complexion – especially under the lights – play nicely with the other un-made-up white folks around me. His pointillist-style expressionistic pattern did give a more realistic texture to my face. Everyone seemed happy.

Then one of the producers came in, looked over my shoulder, ruffled the surface of my carefully placed wig and said, carelessly, with a lemon-lipped expression on her face, 'Hmmm, he doesn't look like my son,' then left the make-up trailer with a concerned look on her face.

Weird.

New York was hella cold that year. We had to pick up a shot that we'd done in LA which hadn't quite worked. Tom Ackerman, our director of photography, came up with the weird notion of standing me up against a wall somewhere downtown, building a white tube around me from Styrofoam, with a white reflective surface on the inside, and shining a bunch of lights to resemble the LA close-up shot's daylight – and shooting my lines that way. It worked to an extent, but when you wear prosthetics, if the weather is a little chilly, the rubber begins to turn solid and you can't move your face.

It was at least twenty degrees below freezing that day.

There was one moment when people were able to tap my face like it was concrete: 'Y'all right in there, Lenny?' 'Damn – you could play racquetball with this guy's face. We got a heater anyplace? Lenny's eyeballs are freezing solid!'

During this whole period in Los Angeles and New York, I had no real contact with Mum or Seymour, Hylton, Paul or Kay. The only person from the Henry clan who came out to see me was my little sister Sharon, who came to New York in the dead of winter to show her support. Manhattan was hip-deep in snow and arctic frost. When she arrived at our location, I was in full Miles-as-a-white-guy mufti, and Sharon walked right past me, with no idea that the white dude with the wide(ish) nose was her brother. It wasn't until I said in broad Black Country, 'Sharon, I cor believe you'd blank me on a street in New York, man,' that she turned round and literally burst into tears. 'Oh my God, you'm a white bloke . . . what did they *do* to you?'

Hollywood Friends

Dawn and I got to know a small group of Brits out there – expat professionals who'd made the leap from the UK to the States, like Ian La Frenais and Dick Clement, who, after the success of the likes of *Porridge* and *Auf Wiedersehen, Pet*, were developing movie projects such as *The Commitments* and *Still Crazy*. They'd also had a hand in Tracey Ullman's success with her multi-award- winning show *Tracey Takes On . . .* for HBO. They introduced us to people like Jeff Lynne from ELO. Jeff was born in Erdington in Birmingham, so I got to chat to him about that and how Roy Wood (his ex-partner in the Electric Light Orchestra) came to my wedding. Dick and Ian also introduced me to George Harrison. I really liked George – he was very funny and loved talking about comedy (particularly anything to do with *Python*), Vedic meditation and how I should try more vegetarian food, because that might help my digestion. I swear to God! Later, I went to a party at Ian's house in London, and George made a beeline for me and asked me how my digestive tract was now I was back home. Yeesh.

John Cleese was a presence too – he and his wife would invite us out for supper, and sometimes the psychotherapist Robin Skinner would be there. Skinner had written a book with John called *Families and How to Survive Them*. We all got on quite well. I think I may have moaned a bit too much about my 'first Hollywood movie blues' to all of these people. Whether it was Eric Idle or writer/director Jonathan Lynn and his psychiatrist wife, Rita, I cried on any shoulder that was available. I

Christmas in LA

Top: with Robin Skinner

Above: Richard Ericson, his
husband Louis Raymond,
and Rick Seigel

had a Greek chorus of mostly Brits that I'd heard on the radio or seen on the telly, all of them saying 'take no shit', 'put your foot down', 'don't let them treat you like that', 'take the money and run' or 'don't take the money, stand your ground, don't give up'. They all meant well, but none of them could convince me that this movie was going to be a success – there were too many portents of disaster in the tea leaves. I just had this feeling that all this effort, all this money, all these people were frittering away all this time for something that wasn't as well formed as it should have been.

One of many very funny evenings with Jonathan Lynn was when we were invited to hang out at a pizza joint with Eric Idle and Robbie Coltrane, with lots of gags and banter and japes and wheezes and all sorts of nonsense spilling over – plus more than my regulation glass of wine per week. Jonathan was telling the table that he had cast Steve Martin as Ernie Bilko in a movie remake of the famous Phil Silvers TV series. Robbie (a huge Bilko fan) is a talented vocal impressionist, actor and comic force. The second he heard the words 'Sergeant' and 'Bilko', he took off on a series of riffs where he not only impersonated Phil Silvers, but also everyone else in the cast too, pretty much making up his own episodes:

Robbie as Bilko: Come on, come on, come on, men, let's move, move, move, we gotta poker game to get to. Doberman, steal a bottle of bourbon and a truck, run every red light they got . . . get me to the casino before I explode. *Awww*, look at these cards [eyes to heaven]. God, come on, gimme a break, will ya? I got six kids and three wives to support – somewhere.

And:

Robbie as Bilko: Why, sir, how could you think anything duplicitous was taking place here, on this army base?

Or:

Robbie: Meanwhile, there's six privates tip-toeing behind the corporal's back with two giant chocolate cakes, a stripper and a huge vat of cocaine.
Me: I don't remember that episode, Rob.
Robbie: Swear to God, it was genius . . .

And on and on . . . it was a masterclass, performed at rapid-fire speed, with a clarity and high-joke quotient designed to make you choke on your chicken risotto. At the end of it all, Robbie wiped the sweat from his forehead and took a drag on his fag. Eric looked at Jonathan, took a long pause and said, 'So, d'you think you've got the right guy for the lead role in that Bilko movie then, Jonathan?'

It was nice living in an apartment off the Pacific Coast High-way. We were just up from a place called the Colony, where all the Hollywood muckety-mucks lived. Dawn and I were invit-ed to a pre-Christmas party at the house of Peter Asher (as in Peter and Gordon; he later became an in-demand music producer for people like Linda Ronstadt, James Taylor, Cher and more). When we arrived Robin Williams was there – and he knew who I was! He said 'hello', then did a tight ten-minute set. Like, for a short burst he was letting everyone know why he was known as wonderfully funny. It was brilliant, and then he was gone. I won-dered how many parties he was going to that night, and if he'd repeat the same material at each. It was like watching a comet cut through the sky, bright and sparkly and all too short.

Hollywood Swinging Continues

As filming continued, I realised more and more that:

a. I wasn't happy;
b. because the script wasn't very good.

Charles Lane was handling himself well and shooting lots of close-ups and mid-shots – everything he was supposed to be doing. I just didn't feel confident enough in the whole enterprise. In my mind I felt myself careening downhill towards a large wall in a car with no brakes. Writer/comedian Rick Seigel came out to see us in Los Angeles. Rick had befriended me on the Montreal comedy festival leg of my *Live and Unleashed* victory lap. He had interviewed me for his comedy magazine. We had a good time and vowed to remain friends. Rick and I started talking about what I was going to do after *True Identity* had wrapped. It was a good question. We were three-quarters of the way through and, although everyone was working incredibly hard, it didn't feel like it was getting any funnier. I had to prepare for when I got home. I had to have a plan. It was going to be tough – this was my big shot. Better British performers than me had come to the States and sunk. I was going to have to suck it up and work out my next steps.

One of the things that Disney wanted to do, before the movie came out, was to make a series of shorts and create a pre-*True Identity* presence for Lenny Henry. The producers asked if I wanted anyone from the UK to figure out how to do this, so I asked for my good friend James Hendrie to be flown over. Just before I'd gone out to begin work on *True Identity*, I'd been asked to star in James's directorial debut, a short film called *Work Experience*. James and I had a relationship that went back to *Three of a Kind* and *The Lenny Henry Show*. We had worked on Joshua Yarlog sketches for my TV show, in which a Zimbabwean comedy impressionist insists on mimicking British TV celebrities without any clue how to impersonate them. Although you probably wouldn't do that sketch now, at the time I liked the innovation of the material and the silliness of it. We did parodies of *Blind Date* and *The Singing Detective*. Josh had a soundman called Tunde and a wobbly camera operator called Ziggy, and very cheap production values. The scripts made me howl with laughter every time.

James and I got on very well. We would write stand-up together too, and the methodology was not as strict as Kim's. Kim would often talk and talk. I would do the same, and then he would go away and write before bringing it back, and we'd look at it all, mark off the stuff we liked and strike out the stuff we didn't. By contrast, James and I would sit together in the room and just try to make each other laugh.

Later, we wrote a piece about my daughter's infant school and how they'd asked us as parents to help her make a little house that might have been in the city of London in 1666. This was seen to be a dad-and-daughter mission and so, when she got back from school, my daughter and I set about creating a seventeenth-century London dwelling. Well, it took a bit longer than we all expected. My daughter was in bed by eight; I think I finally finished glueing on the last rafter at about 12.45 at night. Next day, we took it into school, and the sight of all these hand-crafted houses lined up around the car park was a joy to behold. So many parents had worked hard to make these things for the children. Some of them might very well have been listed by Kirstie and Phil. There was a very competitive vibe from some of the alpha dads with their own computer-based businesses who had made 3D printouts and then hired a team of operatives to build the houses from scratch in miniature – some of them obviously contending for a middle-page spread in the *Architectural Digest*. Then the head teacher came out and addressed the children and their parents with a loud hailer: 'Welcome, everyone, to our infants' rendition of the Great Fire of London!'

And he set fire to the first house.

Within moments the whole car park of little houses was ablaze. There were alpha IT dads crying, mum solicitors threatening to litigate like a mofo, exhausted single parents charging towards the head teacher in a kung-fu drop-kick pose. But they all had to get past me, 'cos I was strangling him . . .

James and I spent a morning shaping the narrative of that until it sang. It was a very funny routine – and I loved working with him. So, back when he'd asked me to star in *Work Experience*, it was the easiest 'yes' I'd ever given. It was a short film (eleven minutes) and it would form part of a TV series on Channel 4 called *Short & Curlies*. They would get a cinema exhibition and be offered up for inclusion in various festivals around the world. It was a three- or four-day shoot, directed and written by James, produced by Mary Bell, and the cinematographer was this great bloke called Robin Vidgeon, who'd worked on *Never Say Never Again* and *Raiders of the Lost Ark*! He had a little screen on his main camera, and before every take he would show me the shot so that I knew if he was shooting me full length or up close. His attention to detail and inclusion of me in the process will never be forgotten. Between this and James and I laughing a lot through-out, I don't think I'd ever participated in such an easy shoot. James wanted a low-key performance, no gurning or yelling, and his instinct was absolutely correct. When I saw what he'd done, I was excited – this was the kind of acting I wanted to do for the rest of my life!

Then we were nominated for an Oscar! I was working, so I couldn't go – so James went to the ceremony. I remember watch-ing it back on repeat and being moved to tears. John Candy and Rick Moranis read out, 'And the nominees for best short film . . .' and I was already overjoyed. To have something you're in mentioned in Oscar dispatches was brilliant. I felt like I'd leapt out of the water and was flying unaided already. But then to hear James's name read out as the winner . . . I had to sit down. I was breathless. He got up, in his over-large tuxedo, and thanked everyone, including me, and then sat down.

When he got back home we went to dinner at L'ortolan, the restaurant in Shinfield, near Reading, owned by John Burton-Race. James placed the Oscar in the middle of the table and we ate and drank and laughed and celebrated like animated charac-ters from the *Beano*.

James had skills as a director, comedy writer and ideas mer-chant. So it was a natural thing to invite my friend who'd just won an Oscar to come to LA and work on a series of short films to introduce America to the comedy of Lenny Henry. You'd have thought the Disney execs would be all over that, wouldn't you?

Sigh.

James flew over and we spent some time working on ideas, and then presented them to our prospective benefactor. I think there was a *Godfather* parody, also a black-and-white *Double*

Indemnity-type affair where I played everyone in the film. The producer looked at James and said, 'You guys, a short film is like a haiku. Everything has to be just perfect. Y'know, it's like a sonnet – you gotta know that every beat works and that the climax is satisfactory and has been set up so that the only possible conclusion is the one that occurs.'

James was on the next plane home.

Then I was told that I should work with some other writers. But my problem was that everyone they asked me to work with had no idea who I was, what I did, what I'd done, what I was capable of doing. So, every meeting was a torturous first-date situation, with me having to perform and do characters, hoping they somehow got me.

They didn't.

Each idea was rejected by the Disney producers, who were determined to produce small, beautifully formed haikus. Unfortunately, the haiku store was closed. This was NOT going the way I thought it would.

Luckily, the Greek chorus of expats were there to advise and cajole and nurture me through the experience, and, as always, Dawn was loyally by my side. But we were both aware that her aspirations had been put on hold, making her feel unhappy at times.

By the end of my time on the film I felt as though I was bumping along the bottom of the sea bed, chilling out with a sea toad, playing backgammon with the anglerfish, cracking gags with the kraken. No surface in sight.

My Hollywood travails were teaching me every day that you're nothing if you don't have control. Things were going to have to change. I started thinking about what I *really* wanted from this experience, besides superstardom, a fur sink and a solid gold bidet.

Apart from such aforementioned essentials, what I actually wanted was more control over my work.

There were black people in Hollywood running production companies and making things happen. The Hudlin brothers were making their seminal *House Party*; Suzanne de Passe ran the movie division at Motown. There'd been a huge up-flowering of black and brown directors and producers coming out of New York. Spike Lee was one of the most successful ones; Charles Lane was part of this surge, as were John Singleton (then about to make *Boyz N the Hood*), Matty Rich, Julie Dash, Charles Burnett and Robert Townsend. A massive door was opening for black talent. I knew I mustn't, under any circumstances, blow my big break and allow the door to close before I'd at least taken a shot at extending my luck. My name was above the title in a Disney movie and, for a few nanoseconds, that was important; there was a general feeling that people should have at least one meeting with me. So I set up meetings with Reginald Hudlin, Suzanne de Passe and a few others.

I had two more films to make with Disney, so, although it felt like *True Identity* was not going to be the next *48 Hrs*, at least there would be two more tries at the brass ring. I read scripts: one was called *Mr Destiny*, which eventually starred Michael Caine; the other was a project that had been around for a while called *Filofax*, which eventually starred Jim Belushi. I couldn't tell from reading the scripts why I was being considered for them and, in the end, neither did well at the box office.

But I did have an idea: chefs – articulate, persnickety, genius-level, argumentative . . . Chefs. 'Oh yeah,' you're saying, 'Gordon Ramsay, *MasterChef*, *The Great British Bake Off* and more and more.' But in the early nineties none of these projects were around.

Once *True Identity* was completed, there were premieres to attend, some promotional duties, but my heart wasn't really in it. I was excited for everyone to see what we'd managed to achieve, but I knew that it wasn't the real marinara sauce.

7.

THE FALL

Jeffrey Katzenberg gives Lenny some advice

LOS ANGELES, CALIFORNIA...

ON ONE OF MY LAST FEW DAYS IN LOS ANGELES, JEFFREY KATZENBERG, THE DISNEY HEAD HONCHO AT THE TIME, CALLED ME INTO HIS OFFICE.

HE LOOKED LIKE THIS.

I DRESSED UP IN MY RAZOR-SHARP JOHN RICHMOND SUIT AND ARRIVED AT KATZENBERG'S FOOTBALL PITCH-SIZED OFFICE EARLY.

I READ A MOVIE MAGAZINE, AND THEN SUDDENLY THE BOSS ARRIVED, LOOKING MEAN AND LEAN AND READY FOR ACTION.

WE WENT AND SAT DOWN IN HIS OFFICE. HE LOOKED AT ME OVER THIS HUMONGOUS DESK AND SAID:

COULD WE GET TWO COFFEES IN HERE, JANICE? AND SOME COOKIES. THANK YOU.

WELL, YOUR MOVIE'S NOT GONNA MAKE ANY MONEY.

OH.

YEAH, WE DID SOME RESEARCH... IT'S GONNA TANK.

AH.

BUT HEY, AT LEAST YOU'LL KNOW WHAT TO ASK FOR NEXT TIME, RIGHT?

BY THE TIME HE WALKED ME OUT, I COULD'VE FIT THROUGH THE KEYHOLE.

Pushing Water Uphill

Katzenberg's advice – 'You'll know what to ask for next time' – has stuck with me over the years. I've chewed over his words many times in my head, trying to get at what he actually meant by that. He wasn't talking about a stretch limousine or a moose-skin suit. I think he was referring to 'doing whatever it takes to get the project across the line as excellently as you can'. In terms of films and television these days, getting anything across the line successfully is akin to doing the lottery. A million things can go wrong, and it's a miracle that many things get made at all.

I think, as I consider his words repeatedly, grinding my teeth while doing so, that he was talking about choices. Every decision we make in the act of creation is important. Collaborations are key here too: who do you partner up with? Are they smart? Do they get things done? Are they always on time? Are they good in the room? Do they know how to raise money? Can you trust them?

Funnily enough, it's possible to make the same mistakes over and over again, even if you have had the words of wisdom from a Hollywood executive tattooed onto your forehead. The main thing I've learnt from what Katzenberg said to me is: don't rush. Take your time. Breathe. Talk to those you trust. There will come a day when instead of diving straight into the deep end, think about it, consider the sharks, piranhas and stingrays. Learn to plan better: if I do this, what if that happens? If I don't get this person, could I get that person? Who's in charge of quality control? And so on. Of course, it's easy to say all this now and, truth be told, I'm still learning about this aspect of career wrangling. But what I do know is that whatever they dangle in front of you, none of it is worth leaving your family and friends back at home for months on end. That's the most straightforward thing I've learnt.

Dawn and I flew home from LA, and the VHS of *True Identity* was in the bargain video pile at the Indian shop up the road before we'd even touched down. I was way down at this point . . . bumping along the bottom. I was going to have to navigate my way up and out of this five-mile pool of despond.

In the gap between *True Identity* and the return to life in the UK there was a changing of the guard. Robert Luff and I had reached a plateau. We'd achieved everything we set out to do, and all was good. But Robert was a man of a certain age now – still spritely, still compos mentis . . . most of the time. In the midst of a meeting, Mr Luff would suddenly start waxing lyrical about being in the Gordon Highlanders, or what it was like to hang out with Arthur Askey, or how the Black and White Minstrels had broken box office records at the Victoria Palace in a bravura run from 1962 till 1972. These occasional drifts of focus and subject matter could happen with anyone, anywhere – in a posh restaurant with the controller of BBC1, during drinks with an ITV producer, or even ensconced in his Earl's Court office, sat around drinking tea and eating perfectly chosen biscuits. He thought more fondly of the past than what was happening today. His response to anything regarding race or discrimination was always to say how proud he was of me, how I'd managed to navigate my way from my immigrant working-class background to being almost an establishment figure, performing at Royal Variety shows, with my own regular slot on the BBC.

He used to sidestep all talk of race and discrimination because of the huge political football he'd had to cope with for many years: *The Black and White Minstrel Show*. We would have had to discuss what it meant that he'd produced and made money from a show that, despite the good people involved, made my skin crawl.

As Mr Luff's forgetfulness became more and more noticeable, I became aware that a difficult conversation had to take place. I'd talked to my tour promoter about the old-fashioned nature of the Luff organisation. At first I'd found it rather grand and quirky but, eventually, I realised there had to be a more modern model for my management needs. I had to do something.

PBJ in the House (Early 1990s)

After *Live and Unleashed* and *True Identity*, I'd had a meeting with Peter Bennett-Jones. PBJ, as he's known to all and sundry, helped to form Talkback Productions. He then went on to create the Tiger Aspect television company. He also represents Rowan Atkinson and Eddie Izzard through his company PBJ Management. He's a bullish, intelligent man with a great love of Shakespeare and an encyclopaedic knowledge of comedy, good wine and cufflinks.

When Peter received BAFTA's special award, John Willis, the chair of BAFTA's television committee, said, 'Without Peter, British television would have been much less fun. He has developed some of the finest talents in comedy, as well as masterminded one of our best-known production companies. Yet he has still found time to help create and now lead Comic Relief. His contribution has been immense.'

When we met for the first time, in 1991, he showed a keen awareness of where I was placed career-wise. I had been on the road a lot. The first thing he said to me was, 'Do you want to keep schlepping around the country? Or do you want to make things?' It was a good question. Comedians can often seem like door-to-door salesmen, going from town to town selling ourselves. It's an exhausting gig – well paid, but exhausting all the same. By the time I joined PBJ Management, I'd had enough of being a 'road comic'. I wanted something different. PBJ took on the job of helping to steer me through the post-Hollywood experience. I remain eternally grateful for his guidance.

Back Home . . .

As soon as I crossed the threshold of my home, I began eating like a normal person once again, so my Skinny Vinnie status, as dictated by Disney, would soon cease to be an issue. The very first thing we did when we arrived was to order a curry. It was always my job to over-order the curry on a Friday night. This is how it would go down:

1 butter chicken
1 lamb balti
1 keema peas balti
4 plain naan
1 chana masala
2 saag aloo
4 onion bhajis
36 poppadoms

If family were staying, there'd be three times as much. I have no idea why I ordered so much. I think it must have been the inherited genes of my mother coming out – 'If yu cooking for six, yu might as well mek allowance for forty-eight.' Christmas dinner at our house was like the day after Ragnarök: plump and stuffed bodies strewn all over the place, but no speck of food to be found anywhere.

Mum gasped when she saw how slim I was post-*True Identity*. She insisted I sit down and eat an enormous eight-gallon bowl full of Saturday soup (red pea and mutton and hard food) all on my own. She wanted to see an instant weight gain in front of her very eyes or I would not be allowed to leave. 'Fenki fenki, licky licky bad mind Americans making my boy starve to death. Why they don't give him the sustenance he need to survive? Look at him. He's so skinny him favour stick h'inseck!' So returning home was a reunion with all the familiar things, my appetite being one of them.

I think uppermost in my mind was that I must try to generate and participate in good work to negate the perceived whiff of failure that was *True Identity*. Therefore, at the beginning of the nineties, I initiated and got to make a TV film called *Alive and Kicking* by Al Hunter Ashton, starring Robbie Coltrane and myself; also *Bernard and the Genie* with Alan Cumming, written by Richard Curtis. I was scrabbling, in a way, to make sure no one forgot who I was, so was willing to have a go at almost anything to prove that I was still worthy of the British public's attention.

But the hard work paid off: I won a best performance award for *Bernard and the Genie*; and *Alive and Kicking* won an important European award. I was starting all over again – working my way up towards the surface.

But the *True Identity* experience had affected me. If I didn't get back out there and realign my career, there would be reputational damage. I consulted friends and colleagues about starting a production company. I'd met several black people who were running their own operations in LA and thought to myself, 'They're not sitting at home waiting for something to happen; they're going out, saddling up, heading north and *making* it happen.' I wanted to do the same.

The Beginnings of Crucial Films

I wanted to be in control of my career decisions. I wanted my own production company to handle all my TV and film work. And I needed a safe space where I could write, direct *and* produce. That was how I wanted things in theory, but the reality was a whole other story.

I spoke to an entertainment lawyer called Mark Devereux, who, with the help of my friend and colleague Sebastian Born (back then a literary agent at James Sharkey's company; later literary manager at the National Theatre), sought out the various avenues through which someone like me could start a production company. The funny thing was, I had no clue, no specific idea of

Crucial Films

what production companies were supposed to do. I knew only that they made films and TV.

In honour of Delbert Wilkins, I named my new company Crucial Films. I already had the answerphone message: I wanted people to ring up after hours and have Prince sing that bit from 'Adore' that goes, 'It's cruciallll, *cruciaaaaaaaaal*.' We hired a managing director called Polly McDonald. She was a producer who'd worked with a prolific creator called Peter Tabern at a company called Childsplay Productions. She knew about start-ups and creating a slate of programmes and, most importantly, how to get things done. She was smart and had good jokes, equating production to being akin to 'pushing water uphill' or 'plaiting fog'. I liked her.

We got ourselves a tiny work space in Soho, across from a dodgy shop that sold vibrating things and had mannequins in the window with hardly any clothes on *at all*. In the first few days of Crucial, Polly and I would sit opposite each other and bat ideas back and forth. We were soon to acquire an executive PA for both of us . . . there were loads of ideas on the wall. We were off.

Eventually, we had a corking team working there. Crucial Films was incredibly hard work, even though we were fully funded by the BBC. Coming up with enough viable ideas for broadcasters was something I hadn't really thought about. Polly would arrive for work, and I would bombard her with notions and half-formed embryonic ideas, and she would write them all down and stick them on the board. Some of these things worked: *Funky Black Shorts*, *Crucial Tales*, *Thing* with Neil Gaiman (turned out to be *Neverwhere*), *Thing* with Alan Moore (didn't work out, but fantastic idea though, and it was great meeting Alan) and *Chef!* But there were many other things that stayed on the cards and never came to fruition. I didn't have a plan for how to execute these ideas and I desperately needed one.

I knew I wanted to create and work in a more inclusive atmosphere. On *True Identity* there had been a black director, soundman, electricians, grips, make-up people; back in the UK, I wasn't surprised to find the status quo unchanged. I wondered if having your own production company meant you could get a more diverse group of people working behind the camera. It took a while to set up, but Crucial was able, absolutely, to dictate who did what in terms of production, editorial and script. I used to ask Polly, 'Is there anyone that looks like me working on this show?' And, God bless her, she'd do her utmost to make that happen.

Waiting on Billie, 1991

At the same time, Dawn and I were in the process of adopting a child. We'd experienced a number of unsuccessful rounds of IVF but were determined to expand our family. We'd been talking about adoption for some time and decided to go for it. We weren't going to let the misery of our time in LA dominate our future; we wanted our lives to be full of kids and fun and laughter. So the adoption process began, and then we just had to wait.

One year later, Billie arrived. Happiness burst out and times were good.

But that doesn't mean everything was easy once we'd navigated social workers and self-questioning and Nappy Changing 101. Having been raised by parents who worked every hour God gave to put food on the table and clothes on our backs, we were both very aware of our forthcoming responsibilities as parents. Parenting was so hard for my mum: she would beat me to remind me of how difficult things were *because* of me. In the end, I knew she loved us and would have probably wrestled a tiger just for looking at us funny. We knew that parenting was a serious affair.

Every single aspect of raising a baby from scratch was unlike any experience I'd ever had. I'd held babies before (I've got three brothers and three sisters; Hylton had seven kids, and so did Bev – believe me, I'd been around full nappies) and was comfortable around them. But there was plenty of fear, such as bath time – what if you turn around for two seconds and she's suddenly underwater? Or that exquisite moment when she starts walking:

what if I turn around for two seconds and she's heading straight for the fire?! What if you go to the chemist and she's toddling along and you're distracted for one and a half seconds and you turn around and find her wearing overalls and working behind the counter of the pharmacy – without even negotiating holidays, dental and health insurance?

My mum and Billie were firm friends from the very beginning. She had many grandchildren already, but Mum always made us feel as though Bill was her first grandchild. Billie was invited to eat curry goat and hard food as soon as she had teeth: 'It will mek her strong. I used to gnaw at the bone when I was her age. Mek her eat it!' She was incredibly patient with Billie and marvelled aloud at how much energy she had. Mom did that odd thing that grandparents do, where she'd look at her, and then look at us, and even though she knew very well that we weren't related by blood, she'd say, 'She look just like the two of you,' and shake her head.

The nineties was a pretty hyperkinetic period for me. I had something to prove and so, rather manically, I threw myself into the work, even though, with a young child around, I could have slowed down a little and helped out a bit more. I did what I could, but I genuinely thought I had damaged my career and had a lot of work to do to fix it. So, I spent as much time as possible building Crucial Films. I was in offices all over London, pitching and trying to re-establish things in an attempt to distance myself from that fun sponge of a movie.

Meanwhile, other things were happening. *Alive and Kicking* got green-lit in 1991 too. I'd found an article in the Sundays about Davey Brice, an ex-offender and addict who'd straightened himself out by running a Glaswegian rehab centre and football team for junkies, pillheads and weed smokers who wanted to quit. I thought the idea of a junkie football team trying their best to stay in the game was inspirational and had potential for humour. I spoke about it with the writer Al Hunter Ashton (who won a BAFTA in '93 for his film *Safe*). I went up to Glasgow and spoke to Davey and various people involved with the centre. Al wanted there to be two Davey Brices in our film: the ex-offender and the hard-nosed drug counsellor. I would play an addict/drug dealer/gang member called Smudger, and Robbie Coltrane would play the hard-case drug counsellor. We shot it on a tight budget, with Robert Young directing. Jane Horrocks and Cal MacAninch were in it too. It was well reviewed, and I was over the moon. It was telly, but at least someone was paying attention. The film won a Monaco Red Cross and also a Golden Nymph award.

Charity Thangs

Just before the *True Identity* shitstorm, I was very lucky to be asked to make a second appearance for Amnesty in 1989 in *The Secret Policeman's Biggest Ball*. Dawn and I were invited to John Cleese's house (yup!) with Jennifer and Adrian. Jennifer was going to co-direct this enormous show, and we were all going to be in it. John wanted me to do a *Python* sketch and maybe a couple of other things. I read loads of sketches from his book and liked one about shopping for shirts. He wisely advised me to do 'Crunchy Frog' with Robbie Coltrane and Jimmy Mulville as a copper with a dodgy tummy. If you liked alternative comedy at the time, then this was the Amnesty for you: there was Stephen Fry and Hugh Laurie, French and Saunders, Rory Bremner, Robbie Coltrane, the *Spitting Image* puppets . . . plus a legendary performance by Peter Cook and Dudley Moore, who were just brilliant. They did a sketch called 'Frog and Peach', and Dudley did his Beethoven sonata at the end, which raised the roof and made the audience stand up and cheer.

Once Again, Red Nose Day . . .

The next Comic Relief followed shortly after. I remember more filming in Africa – lots of little kids following me down the street, yelling, 'Hello, how are you? I'm fine!' And that odd feeling in my gut about filming in Africa and yet not having people of colour on the production team or on cameras, sound or editorial. I didn't know how to communicate this for a while, so it was a continual internal struggle. I loved everybody involved but, generally, always felt it was a bit like 'shooting oneself in the foot' when it came to diverse representation on these particular films.

Hale and Pace (writers/performers who'd written for *Three of a Kind*, among other shows) wrote a song for Comic Relief called 'The Stonk!' which involved a brand-new dance. Victoria Wood wrote something called 'The Smile Song', which was on the B-side. This was the show where Tom Jones and myself (as Theophilus P. Wildebeeste) had a BATTLE OF THE SEX GODS! We sang a version of Bad Company's 'Can't Get Enough'. People had to ring in and pledge money to vote for who they thought was the sexiest. Tom won by at least a foot. Curse him!

'The Stonker' was the title of the Red Nose Day shenanigans that year, and the whole thing raised twenty million pounds! God Bless the British Public.

Meanwhile . . .

Bernard and the Genie

I'd had an idea about a genie – I'd always liked genies and the legends of *The Arabian Nights*. I'd written down three-quarters of a storyline with some jokes and showed it to Richard Curtis. He looked at it and said, 'Lenworth, this feels really stupid, but it could be something . . . leave it with me.' He took it away; then, a few weeks later, he gave me a large brown envelope. He invited me to read the contents of said envelope as he underwent a robust back mangling by his Chinese osteopath. I agreed to go along and sit in reception while he received the forceful pummelling. I read fifty pages of *Bernard and the Genie* that night, accompanied by the sounds of Richard's back cracking like a dry branch in a forest during a fox hunt and his repeated cries:

'OW!'

'Christ!'

'F*ck!'

'OOOWWWW . . .'

and

'Bugger!'

I basically laughed like a drain (do drains laugh?) throughout this entire spinal violation. Tears ran down my face. There were things that were cut from the script that I liked, but he'd somehow managed to get all of *The Young Ones* into one epic scene of magic, disappearance and rudery, and it pretty much stayed as written.

Richard's one of those people who, when they say something's going to happen, it does – the living embodiment of Katzenberg's maxim 'know what you're asking for'. Look at the immense work he's done for Comic Relief over the last hundred years. A lot of it wouldn't have happened without Richard at the pointy end working, chatting, charming, persuading, writing and shaping.

So, *Bernard and the Genie* had its Bernard (Alan Cumming) and its genie (me); writer and associate producer (Richard); director (Paul Weiland, who'd helmed many successful commercials

The Genie

– Walkers crisps – also the successful Mr Bean franchise); and Peter Fincham from TalkBack as executive producer. We were off.

Making *Bernard and the Genie* was the complete opposite to the *True Identity* experience. Richard was on set every day, and a comic tone was set. Paul, myself and Richard discussed things throughout each day: was this funnier than that? What about if I did this stupid dance here? It was such a pleasure to be unfettered and working with really meticulous and, most importantly, funny people. The delightful Alan Cumming was Bernard, the hapless hero: no girlfriend, no money, no job, but he finds a golden lamp, rubs it and is immediately attacked by a gibberish-speaking genie who wants to cleave him in two with a scimitar. Bernard says something like, 'I wish you'd stop attacking me!' And the genie stops. Then he says, 'I wish you could speak English.' And the genie says, 'Bugger.' And so it continues, in a light, romantic, magical, pre-Christmas vibe till the end. I would have done it for nothing. I was blessed and I knew it.

Comic Strip Stylings

I was very honoured to be asked by Peter Richardson to a meeting at the Groucho Club (renowned Soho drinking hole for media types, ne'er-do-wells and almost-models). This was in the halcyon days when you could work in the club and use your computer downstairs. We sat at a table and I read the role of a depressed American comic who comes to Oxford to make a comedy movie, while his girlfriend embarks on a degree in poetry without telling him.

I loved playing this guy and had a kind of hip, sarcastic sneer plastered to my mush throughout. I was pretty big when I made this little film: there are scenes of me with my top off that are not aesthetically pleasing. But, strangely, I didn't care. I was just happy to be working with people I knew and having no one come up to me, wrinkle their eyebrows and mutter, 'Can we change you for a skinnier model, please?' I wasn't sure about the ending of *The Comic Strip Presents . . . Oxford* (a group of dons in mortar boards and capes stomp the bad guy to death while singing the 'Eton Boating Song'), but I think it was one of the more enjoyable things I did post-*True Identity*.

1992: New York, Writing, the Fabulous Three Crack Gags in NYC

In 1992, I went to New York with James Hendrie to write stand-up. I can't quite believe all this activity happened in the one year. There was obviously something to prove, and I was determined to prove it.

I'd been speaking to Tom Gutteridge (then boss of production company Mentorn) about filming some stand-up. He suggested I go away with a writer and come up with an entire act. I decided to take a month out and go to New York City to reconnect with everyone I'd worked with during *The South Bank Show* and spend the time working up a new hour. New York seemed to be the obvious place to do this. There were so many comedy clubs there – Catch a Rising Star, the Comedy Cellar, Stand Up NY, Carolines on Broadway – and the majority of them did open-mic spots.

Because I'd already been in New York trying out material during the *South Bank Show* week, people knew of me. Certainly, Louis, the manager of Catch a Rising Star, did, and he booked me to perform my *South Bank Show* set on Friday nights (with Theo, the Preacher and the Blues Singer) because he knew it worked. The rest of the week I'd do three shows a night wherever we could get in and workshop whatever we'd written that day.

Although I'd said I'd stay put for a while and focus on family, the reason for this frenetic behaviour on my part was that stand-up was still very important to me. We'd just about received the green light for the *Chef!* TV sitcom but, in my mind, it was vital that people still thought of me as being a comedian – Mr Comedy Pants. Dawn, knowing this was important to me, supported my decision.

I arranged an apartment, and we linked up with Rick Seigel, my tall friend from the Montreal comedy festival. Rick would meet up with us, interfere with our writing and then claim that he'd written all the best stuff. If anything got a laugh during a performance, he'd raise his hand, wave it from side to side and say, 'Folks, I wrote that!'

The mission was to take the stand-up comedy section of my set seriously – to really take it apart, look under the hood, see what we could improve – so that once the show was written I could go back to the UK and get a tour and a TV special out of it. Nothing went to waste. I reconnected with my colleagues at Catch a Rising Star, while Rick got us into Stand Up NY and also a place in Greenwich Village. That was me for the next month – three shows a night, every night, workshopping the material we were writing during the day.

We did other things too: visited record and comic-book shops; bought clothes and books; went out a lot. I took John Shea to see Van Morrison at the Beacon Theatre. John Lee Hooker was a special guest that night, and the place rocked. John was over the moon that we got to go backstage and meet Van the Man and the band. Van's an enigma wrapped in a puzzle surrounded by mystery and covered in breadcrumbs. Like a scotch egg with a guitar. There's no cracking the code. However, saying all that, when he discovered that I was doing a gig downtown in the Village venue, he agreed to bring the band to see my routine.

I was very excited when I showed up at the venue a couple of nights later, but there was no one there, except for two guys in lumberjack shirts. I watched as comic after comic asked them where they were from and if this was their first date. One was from Wisconsin, the other from Arkansas; yes, it was a first date; yes, they did find each other attractive; no, they probably wouldn't sleep together tonight, there was still more getting to know each other to go through. Van and the boys arrived late (they had a show that night), and, by the time they got there, there were a few more people in the place. At least fifteen.

So, I go on and start doing the new material, and it's not going down that well. But it's a work in progress. I've got other stuff to sprinkle round it that I know works, but the new stuff's like pulling teeth – it's just a bit lumpen and overwritten, and I don't know it yet. I'm reading it off cards and fluffing lines. About half-way through this interminably long set – the two lumberjacks on the front row were now kissing each other, but I soldiered on – I hear this very distinctive Northern Irish brogue yelling:

Get off!
[lots of laughter]
Bring back Jim Davidson, all is forgiven . . .
This isn't funny at all.
Now, Charlie Williams, there was a comedian.
I want me money back!
Me: Van, you got in for free.
Van: I *still* want me money back.

He only quietened when I did the Blues Singer's 'Low Down Fingerlickin' Gut Bucket Dirty Hound Dawg'. He liked and understood it. The character had been based, in part, on John Lee Hooker, so there was uproarious laughter during this segment of the show, and then it was over. We told Van we might go to Nell's afterwards and he and the band wanted to come.

An amount of ales were imbibed – and then all of a sudden it was a party, and a great time was had by all. At least I think a great time was had by all. I may have lost several brain cells in the process.

The writing and performing in New York continued. The Catch a Rising Star set was peppered with the new material that had begun to work, but it was mostly stuff I'd done before:

Chat: Being black and British
Preacher: 'My children, my beloved children . . .'
Chat: Being black and British and in New York
Blues Singer
Chat: TV and films; more black and British observations, plus some Jamaican stuff for good measure
Theophilus P. Wildebeeste
Song and off

The shows went well. The new material continued to be a hard slog, though. You have to really trust yourself with new jokes. Sometimes they can work immediately, but what really niggles is when you know it's a great idea, but you haven't got the set-up or the punchline or the storytelling right, and, therefore, the audience just simply refuses to give up the funk. They sit there watching and smelling your fear as you begin the ONE BIT THAT'S NOT QUITE WORKING YET. I remember this whole bit about an enormous housefly in my bedroom banging its head repeatedly against the window, in an attempt to get out. I opened the window, and it still smacked against the glass over and over, until, frustrated, I yelled, 'Your entire head is made of eyes, you knob. Use your frikking eyes!' It never quite got the laugh it deserved – and the moment you get to that part, the audience pounce and rip you to pieces like rabid dogs at the back door of an abattoir. It was hard work. I left NYC at the end of that month . . . bruised.

But it was always going to be difficult. A month is nowhere near long enough to develop a new and excellent, firing-on-all-cylinders comedy set. After Jerry Seinfeld retired his old material, it took him at least eighteen months to develop his first new set in decades. I was kidding myself if I thought it was all going to come to fruition easily.

Back home in the UK, however, the big surprise was that when I started doing the best bits of the new gear from the New York tryouts on-stage, they went down a storm! The best jokes had been practised and honed to the bone. I knew the material and was able to deliver it with confidence. This version of the set was shaped and completed by myself and TV comedy writer Jon Canter, who'd joined me at the onset of the nineties. Kim and I had decided that we'd take a break from each other. We hadn't fallen out or anything, but we felt that the two of us needed new stimuli, new people, a new vibe. Best to take a break. So, through Peter Bennett-Jones, I asked around for someone who might collaborate on material for a new show. The compulsion to get out on the road was powerful at this point. It was probably the case that all the years of schlepping from Land's End to John o'Groats had brainwashed me: from north to south, then east to west; from Jollees in Stoke to Blazer's in Windsor. I was just like Junior Walker – a road runner – and just like him, I couldn't stay in one place too long. This is what I did, and everyone knew it.

The Chronicles of Jon Canter

So, I started working with Jon Canter, a Robert Culp lookalike with a handsome smile and neuroses (in a good way) up the wazoo. Recently, Jon sent me an email after I asked him for his thoughts on our relationship. He preferred the hard slog of churning out a few words rather than sitting on a Zoom call with me for ninety minutes – and who can blame him? (He's going to pop up a few times during the next section.) In the nineties Jon often came to our house in Berkshire, where we now lived. We would meet up at PBJ Management in London too. They'd give us coffee and biscuits, and we would talk and laugh until the cows came home.

Jon Canter

Jon Canter: Here we were, forging a new relationship, so naturally enough I was intrigued by his earlier writing relationships, particularly with Kim Fuller. He'd written so much with Kim, creating characters like Theophilus P. Wildebeeste, Mr Nettleford, the Bluesman and Deakus that were fixtures in Lenny's act. Lenny and Kim had obviously been joined at the hip, which is why Lenny and I took to calling Kim Lenny's 'first wife' – which, of course, meant I was his second.

I've never worked with Kim directly, but I've been to meetings with him and he's a fountain of ideas. In fact, he's a charismatic guy who gives off a lot of energy. So, actually, he's a bit like Lenny. More like Lenny than me, in fact. But there's a price to pay for reliability. Working with Kim was more exciting than working with me. When Lenny talked about Kim, I got the sense that they'd fallen out, got back together, fallen out, got back together ... which had made for a more intense relationship than the one Lenny had with me. With all due respect to me, 'all due respect' is not that sexy. Kim was the comedy love of Len's writing life. But that didn't mean they were destined to get married or stay married for ever.

Jon had a phenomenal work ethic: he was on time for every meeting, always with a plan of action, the structure and subtext of jokes carefully thought through. He taught me a lot about laying out stand-up routines on the page. We wanted each 'bit' to have its own narrative structure – beginning/middle/end – that built to a climax of hilarity. We wrote long and then cut back to the bone. Sometimes we'd write nine pages on a subject; three useable jokes might survive from that, and the rest would have to be dumped. Luckily, we had created a page called 'the Smorgags-bord' – basically, a loose affiliation of jokes that could be done at the top of a show in a rapid-fire, non-sequitur way; quick jabs to warm them up. Like a smorgasbord but with jokes instead of pickled herring. It seemed to work. Jon helped to reshape the New York material into a show I recorded for Central Television called *Lenny Go Home*.

Jon: The point of the Smor-gags-bord was to relax Lenny and whet the audience's appetite for the main event, the show itself. It was meant to last around five minutes. But it never did. Lenny had been a professional comedian for half his life. This was a man who could really look after himself, where talking to an audience was concerned. He'd grown up doing working men's clubs. He'd dealt with drunks, racists, idiots, men sitting there with their arms folded because they didn't want to be there but had been made to come by their wives . . . he was battle-hardened. He was ready.

So, he had loads of things to say to an audience, things he'd said thousands of times before, things that weren't even in that script but were part of his armoury, weapons he could produce whenever they were needed. For example, he might say to someone in the front row: 'Good evening, my friend, are you in showbiz?' 'No? Then get your foot off my stage!'

Glasses/big women/guy with beard/guy with bushy eyebrows . . . these gags had been road-tested for fifteen years or more. They never let him down. But these weren't just gags, they were opening gambits. So, he'd say hello to the guy 'wearing a suit just in case you've got to go to a meeting'. Then what? His name's Terry. So Lenny would say something like, 'Your name's Terry? Would you say that's held you back?' And Lenny would be off. There was nothing more enjoyable for him than chatting to Terry, the guy in the suit, who turns out to work in computer software, because Lenny has a computer, and he's got some problems with it, and maybe Terry can help?

The joy of this for Lenny is three-fold. Bantering with the audience is something he loves to do. Secondly, he's very good at it, because he's had a lot of practice. Thirdly – and this is the best bit! – *he doesn't have to remember anything*. None of this is material from the script. This is chat, this is in the moment, this is comedy jazz; this is just him and Terry at the Barbican Theatre in York, chatting together like old mates. And the audience knows that and loves it. This is the joy for them. They know that what he's saying to Terry in front of them, right here, right now, has never been said before and will never be said again. And that makes it special, unique. Isn't that what going to the theatre is supposed to be about? The communal sharing of unrepeatable moments?

But then the Smorgagsbord ends. And we have this transition bit: 'Can you get a decent curry round here? I love going out for curries with my guy friends . . . the conversations are so sophisticated . . . "There's going to be a map of India on that bowl tomorrow . . ." "Waiter, I'll have a Johnny Cash special. 'Ring of Fire', ha ha ha ha . . ." And black guys always want the hottest curry. I've got this mate called Carlton . . . he's got to have the chicken tikka plutonium . . .'

There we are, then. The show proper has started. The Smorgagsbord has been cleared away. The main course has arrived. And my feeling was always one of anti-climax. Because the serious business has now begun, and who wants serious business at a comedy show?

Now Lenny's doing the material he did last night in Leeds and will do tomorrow in Newcastle. This is the material he and I have worked on for months and honed and honed. The pressure's on. Lenny's got a hundred minutes of material in his head. Will he be word perfect? Will he get it in the right order? Will he deliver it precisely in the way that works best for the material? He's no longer making it up as he goes along. It's like the comedy jazz bit is over and here we are watching the serious comedy classical music, starting with 'The Curry Sonata' by Lenworth Henry (1958–). Time to stop mucking about, which is a shame, because mucking about is fabulous fun – not just for him but for the audience.

Jon and I had bizarre conversations about a world called 'Comedy Land' or just 'The Land'. We liked the idea of there being a place where all the funniosities and japesters and jackanapes and jesters lived and, depending on how funny they were, some of them were placed in the town centre, next to their own statue; some of them were next to the municipal buildings; some near the overpass. Some acts were far away on the very outskirts of the territory, looking for a way in; others were two hundred miles away, nowhere near where the action was happening. We wanted to be in the town centre, just by the car park – at least with a Google maps postcode programmed in. We'd make endless lists of subject matter, like:

Crime
Jail
Black people on TV
Relationships
Sex
Kids
Alcohol

Short titles, like a track list on an album, so that you could tell what it was from the top of the tin. We'd meet up and riff, then Jon would disappear and come back with pages and pages of material from which to choose. I often wondered if he had some Disney critters helping him behind the scenes when he fell asleep over the keyboard:

Rat in waistcoat: Come on, everybody. Jon's asleep, let's get to typin'.

Badger in slacks: How many willy jokes should we put in here?

Weasel in *Peaky Blinders* cap: As many as it takes – he's gotta hand something in by morning.

Rat: What about his mum?

Badger: He's rinsed that subject matter out.

Weasel: Innit, though? What about his brothers and sisters?

Badger: Ditto.

Mongoose in Doc Martens: Black people throughout history? Y'know, like when the first guys landed on the moon, were black people already there? Runaway slaves going, 'Aw shit! They found us.'

Rat: Not bad – work up some more of those.

Beagle in a trilby: I've got a really good double entendre here.

Rat: Bugger me! A talkin' dog!

Jon and I would work like this, and then, come tour time, Jon would come on the road for the first ten or twelve shows, and we'd edit the material as we went along. By the time we got to show ten, we were up and running, all dead weight gone.

Jon: The late and great Peter Bogdanovich was the director of *The Last Picture Show* – an immortal classic of American cinema. But Bogdanovich is immortal to me and Lenny for a different reason.

I've got a long face. There's just nothing I can do about it. I got it from my dad's family. I've also got serious eyebrows – I can look pretty stern – and a ferocious work ethic, also inherited from my dad. So, you don't, if you're Lenny Henry, necessarily want to be stuck in an office with me for several hours, trying to come up with funny stuff. Not least because, even when you do come up with funny stuff, I won't necessarily laugh at it. This is serious work; this is what I do for a living. I distrust fun.

I noticed right from the start that Lenny was naturally more amused by stuff than me. He's fierce but if he likes something, he expresses it, he gets it out there. In other words, he *laughs*. If he was doing a tryout at a small club, say the 99 Club in Leicester Square – an underground club that really does feel like the coalface of comedy – he'd laugh at the comedians who were on before him, which I rarely did, being too preoccupied with our own material and whether this was a crowd that were likely to enjoy it. Similarly, the other comedians in the dressing room, waiting to go on, would hardly ever laugh at the comedian currently on-stage. They might nod and go, 'That's good.' Or look sad and go, 'That's very good – why isn't that in MY act?' But Lenny had the extroversion and the generosity of spirit to laugh out loud. (His laugh, incidentally, resembles the cry of a seagull, something that's amused me for years, since I often work on our material from an office in my house in Suffolk, two hundred yards from the North Sea. Many's the time a seagull has landed on a nearby chimney, and made a noise like Len.)

So, being long-faced and serious, I didn't always laugh when Lenny said something funny. But I always had the decency to say, 'Yes, that's good,' which is better than nothing.

But what about when Lenny said something *unfunny*? Or I said something unfunny? We absolutely needed a private language to deal with that moment. Which is where Bogdanovich came in.

One of the ways to say something's unfunny, without hurting each other's feelings, was to say that it started well but then got bogged down. That was always a great thing to say, especially if one of us was reading out a page of script, which might take two minutes, and the other one was sat there listening but not (especially in my case) laughing.

So, instead of saying, 'That started well but got bogged down,' we'd say, 'It was a bit Peter Bogged-downovich.' That made insulting each other's bad jokes not just less painful but actually enjoyable. If Lenny said something I'd written was 'a bit Peter', I'd always be amused rather than offended. Because it's amusing in itself. And we came up with it. It's ours.

In 1992 Jon and I did an hour-long comedy film for the BBC Christmas schedule called . . .

Lenny Henry: In Dreams

This was a high-concept show that featured me talking to my 'shrink' about my weirdest dreams and nightmares. It was directed by James Hendrie and was probably one of the oddest shows I've ever done: stuff about press intrusion, showing up semi-naked in the high street, having a driving lesson with a sightless teacher. I'd quite like a psychiatrist to watch it now. I don't know what the audience made of it. It felt like we were stretching ourselves, and that's always worth doing.

Jon: Almost the first thing Lenny asked me, as we sat in his office getting to know each other, was whether I had any ideas for films. There's only one answer to that, as any freelance writer will tell you. You never say you don't have any ideas. It's professional and social death. It's like asking a milkman if he has any milk. So I made up an idea on the spot. My idea was that it would be fun to write a comedy film about the relationship between a gangster and his psychiatrist, which was possibly ahead of its time, since *Analyze This* came out a few years later. Lenny immediately picked up his phone and rang a producer he knew. He pitched my idea, a minute after I had it, which scared the shit out of me, because I had no idea what the story was. All I had was 'gangster/psychiatrist'. I had two words, at most. But Lenny was on fire, telling this person that we'd work up some pages and send them to him/her, which of course we never did. No matter. I immediately thought of Lenny as fearless.

8

CRUCIAL YEARS

Mum's Seventieth Birthday Extravaganza!

Mum used to talk about life and love and family as being a garden, which you must tend regularly or everything will die. Well, if that's the case, being in show business could make you the most neglectful gardener on earth. The kind of gardener who'd leave a message on your mobile like, 'Uh, yeah, sorry – I can't take care of your garden as I'm away this week. Can you do it? Or everything will die . . .' That seemed to be the constant mantra of my life. There were good moments, bad moments, and then severe neglect of the garden at pivotal moments when I should really have stayed my ass home.

These are all things, little things, that can be overcome. But what you can't overcome, no matter who you are, are feelings of low self-esteem, shame, worry and concern. This was confirmed for me when my mum got ill.

She was always a big, tough woman, but recently she'd been carrying too much weight, and it was getting her down. She was diabetic and suffered from asthma and glaucoma. To be honest, it was a struggle almost from the time I got back from making *True Identity*. I was going to see her every Sunday, or as often as I could, but my once towering pillar of strength was fading with every visit. She would drift in and out of good health, as if her well-being were a boat without a sail and subject to whichever way the wind was blowing.

Her seventieth birthday, in 1992, was classic. Mum approached us. She was to be seventy years old – and there was going to be a party. We all looked at each other. It was the first we'd heard of it. She wanted a celebration of her life on earth. Some kind of acknowledgement that she had done well: none of us were in jail or dead or hooked on drugs. She'd raised us right – she had lovely grandchildren and even some delightful great-grandchildren. All of whom did as they were told, by not jumping up and down on her couch or leaving the toilet seat up when she'd told them otherwise. She wanted to celebrate seventy years of surviving the hostile environment. Even though she didn't put it like that, that's how I saw it. She'd come to this country in 1957 and found herself immersed in bigotry and prejudice, and she'd come out the other end. And things had come good. She wanted to put the flags out for her triumph against the forces of evil – poverty, racism and misogyny in all their forms. We all wanted to do whatever we could to make it an unforgettable evening. She deserved that.

ONE DAY MUM MADE A BIG POINT OF GATHERING US ALL TOGETHER IN HER FRONT ROOM.

I WANT A BIG PARTY WHEN I'M SEVENTY.

OH YEAH?

YES, MAN. WID FLOWERS AND CAKE AND A GOSPEL CHOIR AND EVERY TING...

SHE'D BECOME A BORN-AGAIN CHRISTIAN BIG STYLE BY NOW.

OK. SOUNDS GOOD.

AND EVERYBODY FROM THE FAMILY, GRANDCHILDREN, GREAT-GRANDCHILDREN, GREAT-GREAT-GREAT-GREAT-GREAT-GRANDCHILDREN-- EVERYBODY PRESENT.

SO YOU WANT A BIT OF A DO FOR YOUR 70TH?

YES, MAN. SOMEWHERE WID GOOD FOOD AND A PLEASANT ATMOSPHERE, WITHOUT THE CIGARETTE SMELL OR THE ALCOHOL BUSINESS.

RIGHT. AND THIS IS TO CELEBRATE REACHING A GRAND OLD AGE?

FOR ME 70TH.

ALRIGHTY THEN. ORGANISE AN EXTRAVAGANT BIRTHDAY EXTRAVAGANZA WITH A THOUSAND GRAND-CHILDREN AND POSSIBLY A GOSPEL CHOIR. OK.

SO THAT WAS THAT--WE ALL RAN AROUND LIKE HEADLESS CHICKENS, ATTEMPTING TO ORGANISE A BIG BIRTHDAY BASH FOR A JAMAICAN LADY OF A CERTAIN AGE WITH INCREDIBLY HIGH EXPECTATIONS.

WE MANAGED TO BOOK DUDLEY TOWN HALL. BEV SORTED A GOSPEL CHOIR AND THE FOOD; KAY, SEYMOUR, PAUL, HYLTON AND MYSELF ALL MUCKED IN WITH RESOURCES, TIME, HEAVY LIFTING, YOU NAME IT.

IT WAS A GREAT NIGHT-- EPIC--BUT THE BEST PART OF THE EVENING WAS THE BEGINNING, WHEN MUM ENTERED THE HALL.

ALL THIS...FOR ME?

It was worth all the hassle, nervous breakdowns, taxis, people carriers, crazy-ass Jamaican chef shenanigans and wardrobe malfunctions just to see that smile.

Mum's 70th

But between then and her passing in 1998, her health would get progressively worse. She would go from home to hospital to respite care; then have carers, then more carers. Mum's rapidly declining health became my main worry for the latter half of the nineties.

Charlie Books

When my daughter was little, I read to her before bedtime as often as I could.

Eventually, she would read to me.

But the most noticeable thing about the whole book-at-bedtime experience was just how few books there were that featured black or brown protagonists. There were NO little black girls having adventures in enchanted woods, or discovering foreign spies in the village, or going on quests to find dragons or a giant eye hovering over a volcano. She enjoyed all the Narnia stories and the Nitwits and the Hobbit, but I couldn't help thinking that she'd explode if there was just one picture-book story in which she could identify herself.

One of my good friends at the time was a caricaturist and writer called Chris Burke. I'd met him through my music manager, Erskine Thompson. Chris had painted the cover of a reggae greatest hits album – it was a grungy depiction of black youts at a dance. I loved it and subsequently asked him to do two tour posters for publicity purposes. He painted a lovely poster for *Stand Up . . . Get Down* and then another one for *Rock the House*. Chris and I got on well, and so when I told him that I was up for writing some handmade stories for Billie, he said it was a great idea and to send him whatever I'd done so far.

I hadn't really put my mind to it, but I started to jot down ideas and various scenarios. I did a story about Bill being abducted by aliens and having a great time, a cowboy story and a few others.

Chris and I would meet up, and I'd be sat there in the pub going, 'Yeah, and then the tractor beam shines down and she's whisked away in the light by this enormous celeriac-shaped spaceship.'

Chris: Celeriac?
Me: Yeah, all nobbly and stuff, with hair coming out at odd intervals.
Chris: Yeah.
Me: Yeah, and when she gets up there, there's a breakdance competition.
Chris: Breakdance?
Me: Yeah, 'cos it's like a mothership connection – these guys are funky, so there's a dance-off, and she wins, yeah!
Chris: OK. Can I have another pint of stout?
Me: Hang on, I haven't told you about the polar bears yet!

This resulted in some pencil sketches on paper, folded up into quarters, that I could read and show to Billie for the next few evenings. She loved them.

I really liked them too – and the actual creative activity was fun. Also, I liked working with Chris. I suggested we approach some publishers and show them our ideas. We did, and suddenly there was a two-book deal on the table, and Chris and I had to come up with something a bit more robust than just 'small child abducted by aliens'.

So, we did two *Charlie* books. Charlie was a little mixed-race girl with huge Medusa-like curls who got into adventures at the supermarket or in the sandpit at the local park, or anywhere that hinted at mystery and adventure, behind a closed door or adjacent to a giant tree. The books were called *Charlie and the Big Chill*, which came out in 1995, and *Charlie, Queen of the Desert*, which appeared in 1997. They were lovely, short bursts of creative energy, featuring great illustrations by Chris. However, due to my work-load at the time, and Mum becoming more and more ill as the years passed, there was no chance of keeping 'children's book author' on my ever-increasing list of roles. There was simply no time.

Crucial Films

It's the early nineties and, in the midst of birthdays and multiple acting, stand-up, comedy and documentary projects, there was a prevailing idea that, with the advent of Crucial Films, we should do something to make a big splash. Create an event. Perhaps organise something to let people know that we were here not just to create employment opportunities for Lenny Henry (although that was an important plank in our list of 'reasons for existing'), but also to be a prominent voice in the diversity and inclusion debate.

I was very aware of the lack of writers of colour within the comedy sphere. This was the early nineties, and there still wasn't a new comedy group teeming with black and brown talent producing a prime-time TV show. I was like, 'Damn. Somebody should do something.' Usually, when someone says, 'Somebody should do something,' it means that they have to do it. So Polly McDonald and I talked about organising an initiative for writers of alternate class, race and gender. We didn't want the usual predominantly white, middle-class, Oxbridge, mostly male group. We wanted marginalised groups of writers and creators to come and have several days of lectures, TV-watching and general chats with people like Jim Moir, head of BBC Light Entertainment, John Lloyd, producer of *Not the Nine O'Clock News*, *Spitting Image* and *Blackadder*, Richard Curtis and more. In the end, it felt like everyone came down to talk to our writers' group, and some great stuff came out of it.

The producers of what was to become *The Real McCoy* were there, and they were able to source writers from our new talent pool. Also, I'd told my brother Paul to get involved, and he'd signed up. Paul is my youngest brother: handsome, funny – a charmer. He'd spent all his school days wondering why the words slid off the pages when he tried to read them. Like so many kids, he was told he was thick and went undiagnosed for dyslexia for many years.

Paul was a tearaway growing up: always down the park playing cards and smoking cigarettes when he should have been indoors doing his homework. Mum used to chat foolishness about 'That bwoy will be the living death of me one day – he's always out, he never comes in, he smells of cigarettes and he always have money? What kind of child is this?' He drove her to distraction, and it was inevitable that he would follow me and Sharon down to London. But he had no qualifications; all he had was his charm, wit and size. He was a big bloke and so was able to get security jobs on the doors of various nightclubs. He quickly made lots of friends and hung out with me when he could.

I'd always thought Paul was funny. I'd seen him make people laugh at a funeral, so I knew he had the thing. So, when it became clear that our 'Step Forward' initiative was going to happen, I let him know, and he jumped at the opportunity.

In the final couple of days of our week together, we split the group up into smaller groups and asked them to come up with ideas for a fictional show with a multiracial cast, and then to write a sketch. Richard Curtis oversaw one group, James Hendrie another; Kim Fuller and Annie Caulfield also sat in. The sketches were all handed in at the end of the first day, and the supervisors had to read them and create a hierarchy of funny for the next day. We'd invited some actors, like Victor Romero Evans, to read our favoured sketches. We didn't know who'd written what. All the sketches were handed in anonymously.

It was a long day. Some of the sketches went on for too long, some were devoid of originality, some were too original! It was crazy, but in the end the winning sketch was about a Jamaican football pundit who marvelled at John Barnes and the things he could do mid-game that no one else could, such as:

> put in every rhatid bulb in the floodlights
> give out all the oranges at half-time
> make the football kits for both teams, by hand – no sewing
>   machine neither

Victor performed this sketch with such gusto that we could barely get our breath. It was hilarious. And Paul had written it – he won best sketch of the week and got a job as a regular contributor to a new show called *The Real McCoy*. I was so proud of him. Still am.

Paul

Music

Music was always important to me – as was a suppressed longing for a music career. It wasn't that I was a great singer; I just loved being in a studio, making music. But there's a problem with being a character comic: if you come up with characters who sing, you feel like maybe you could, given the right material, be a singer of some kind, right? I think what I wanted was a legit music career, alongside my comedy one. But to get anywhere near to breaking the surface and reaching the shore as a comic, I needed laser focus. Anything else would be a distraction.

But music and comedy go hand in hand. Most of the comics who came up in the eighties had that desire to be in front of a big crowd and, like their favourite bands, tear it up. But the live comedy experience is very different to the live music one. Comedians don't really tolerate audience participation, they don't want punters shouting out punchlines or attempting to recite whole routines alongside them. Comics want to get up and perform *for* you, not *with* you.

I recently went with my friend Larry to see Bruce Springsteen on Broadway. I'd only ever seen Broooooooce at Wembley Stadium, so the sight of him performing in a 1,500-seat theatre was almost too much to bear. On-stage, he possesses a firework display of charisma. The sheer level of personality and skill involved in telling his autobiographical tales, and then factoring in his songs and musicianship, was off the chart. But. But, but, but, BUT. Springsteen wasn't the only Broooooooce in the house that night. There was a whole bunch of OTHER Bruces in that audience waiting to deliver their all. Every time the man opened his gob to sing a song, literally everybody, even the ushers, joined in. In the end, if you can't beat 'em, join 'em: '*BOOOOOOORR-RRN IN THE YOU-ESS-AYYY!*'

But comics don't want the audience joining in with the jokes. If we reheat old material, the second we start the routine, some wiseass yells out, 'HEARD IT!'

I'd always been into music, from the very earliest days of buying tunes from the bargain box at Graduate Records, up Dudley. They always had a lucky-dip bunch of singles at 10p: 'You never know, there might be something halfway decent in there.' There never was!

Music, particularly soul music, was what I loved the most. It's probably the case with all comedy performers that the thing to which you've devoted your life might not be the thing you love best; it might be the thing you do because you can't do the thing you love best. I was certainly not musically gifted. I couldn't play an instrument. I could sing a bit, but wasn't good enough to impersonate someone like Stevie Wonder (Gary Wilmot could do a killer Stevie). Singing impressionists were the gold standard in my eyes. Sammy Davis Jr's mimicry of Billy Eckstine, Nat King Cole, Frank Sinatra and Dean Martin was nothing short of miraculous. No recording career for me.

Or so I thought.

From the moment I did singing impressions on *Three of a Kind*, people kept saying – despite my voice having a limited range – that I should make a record. I'd already had a couple of attempts at making music back in the day with 'Boiled Beef and Carrots' and 'Mole in the Hole'. Because of my funkateer/clubber status, I was a bit sniffy about comedians making 'comedy' records. I wasn't a fan of 'My Boomerang Won't Come Back' or 'Shaddap You Face'. If you're going to make a tune, it should be funky and state of the art, and it should say something.

Sue Thompson, Roberta Green,
Erskine Thompson and Nigel Planer

I got a music manager in the early eighties. A very cool guy, Erskine Thompson used to do A&R work for various record companies around London. He was a skinny black DJ with a high forehead and a downbeat sense of humour; he would send me records when I was on tour in Blackpool. He linked me up with Jo Dworniak and Duncan Bridgeman from I-Level. They made that great record that went: '*Let's dance together in a minefield.*' They had a unique sound, and Jo's bass-playing was loud, bendy and off the hook. I made demos and attempted to write songs with them. And, strangely enough, some tunes did emerge. Jo and Duncan took their time and made it fun. They also brought in other people to help create a funky vibe, like Danny Cummings (the charming percussionist from Wham!'s 'I'm Your Man' video), who came in for a few days and made a huge contribution. He was great on harmonies and hooks – truth be told, they should have been making records with him, rather than me. I felt as though I was in the way when Danny got on the mic. What a singer! What a drummer! A mind-blowing combination.

Erskine found other musical collaborators for me to jam with. There was a charming black guy called Paul Robinson, who used to write with Maxi Priest. I'd travel across London to see him, and Paul would be playing from the minute I arrived to the minute I left. I often suspected he didn't need me there. There was also a multi-instrumentalist and songwriter who'd played with everyone. I'd arrive at his house first thing in the morning, and he'd be smoking a large spliff the size of a semi-rolled Persian carpet.

'Mornin', dude. You wanna egg sandwich? I'm havin' one.'

'Yeah, sure. Bit early for that, innit [meaning the spliff]?'

'Nah, man – gotta beat the rush.'

He'd go in and make the sandwich, and we'd start. After a while, this guy would do a couple of lines of Peruvian marchin' powder – 'Crank me up for the old late-morning buzz . . .' Then he'd eat a bowl of Crunchy Nut flakes. Then he'd have another spliff. Then honk up two more lines . . . This would go on all day. I honestly couldn't keep up with the guy and always kept my nose out of his business, like some prim Jamaican auntie: 'Oh no, young man, you keep those tings away from me. I am a deesant young lady of a certain h'age.' This guy scored big gigs too – I don't know how he didn't just explode when he got on-stage. Still, he was enthusiastic and loved the music, and that's what counted.

He was the real thing. We made several demos that I thought were quite good, but none of them got any traction. I just couldn't sing or write well enough to pull them off. All the songwriters I worked with were excellent, whereas I felt like musical kryptonite most of the time.

Erskine paired me off with really fine producers and writers and musos who must have wondered what the bloke from the telly who said 'Katanga, my friends' was doing in their gaff. Often my knowledge of funk and soul would get me through, but the moment I started singing, they'd humour me, knowing that I didn't have the natural singing talent of a Maxi Priest or a Teddy Pendergrass, or even Charlie Drake! I was an impressionist more than anything – copying Luther Vandross was a bit easier than trying to out-sing him. We all knew that I was being a bit of a dilettante. Shame, really. I would have loved to have had a hit record. But it was clear – stick to the comedy, son: it bought your mum a house.

So I did.

But I didn't stop singing in character. I'd created the Blues Singer on various tours, with jokes from Harry Enfield and Kim Fuller. Harry used to come round the house and sit in the garden doing the Blues Singer voice and improvising funny dialogue: 'Uh, good evenin' to yuh. My name is Low Down Stinkin' Hound Dawg the Third, Fourth and Fifth, ya'all . . . I sold my soul to the devil . . . he took everythang. Never even got a receipt. You can't buy a house in Mississippi without a soul . . . that's what the real estate agent told me anyway. It was hard to understand what he saying through the white hood and everythang . . . but I managed . . .'

Kim wrote the best jokes for Low Down in the end, also the best song, 'Adultery Blues', which was featured in *Live and Unleashed*. Whatever we did after that just couldn't compare.

I made many attempts from the late eighties right through to the end of the nineties to make music, but with no real success. There was a moment with Trevor Horn of Frankie Goes to Hollywood fame. He'd heard some of my demos and asked for a meeting at Sarm West studios in west London. Trevor was very impressive, all shoulder-length hair, specs and sharp casuals. I was awestruck by him and stayed quiet for the majority of the meeting. We were on the roof – the sun was slowly making its descent in the west, like one of those giant coins on the TV show *Tipping Point*. Trevor said something like, 'I've heard all your demos. Some of 'em sound all right.'

Me: That's . . . that's great, Trevor. Thank you!

Trevor: Thing is, though – is this what you really want to do? Be in the music business? You're established in the entertainment business – anyone can see that.

Me: Yeah, I know.

Trevor: But the music business is different. Are you prepared for the long haul? There'll be long tours, songwriting, hours and hours and hours of travel, promotion, marketing, interviews, showcases – you'd be starting from scratch. Is that what you really want?

Me: Ummm . . .

Trevor: I've just signed a kid – amazing young man. He's of Nigerian–Brazilian descent. He's got a voice to die for – he sings like an angel, lovely tone. Weird name. And he writes his own songs. I promise you he's going to be a star, and he's younger than you – like, in his early twenties.

Me: Uh huh.

Trevor: This is his shot, working with me – and he really wants
it. He's called Seal, for God's sake . . . [I laugh for a moment,
then stop. He's serious: the dude's called Seal for real.] He's
there when I arrive at the studio and he's the last one to leave.
He's writing songs almost every day and practising his singing
almost every night. The kid's determined. Are you prepared to
put in that much effort? I mean, you're near the top of the tree
with comedy, but how long do you think it'll take you to get up
there with music? It could take the rest of your life and, trust me,
there's loads of people with more musicality and better singing
voices than you jockeying for position. So you've got to really ask
yourself: 'Is this the moment I jump ship from being a successful
comedian to being a beginner vocalist?' With the slightest
possibility that I could make you a hit record . . .?

Me: Ummm . . .

At that moment, I knew I didn't have the stamina for starting a brand-new career from scratch. No matter how much I
loved pretending to be Teddy Pendergrass or Prince, I genuinely
couldn't see myself as a serious musician – so I stopped playing
at it and stuck to the comedy.

With all that agreed and tidied away in my head like Stickle
Bricks in a biscuit tin – 'Comedy is the way forward' – Kate Bush
then called and asked me to come and sing on her new album,
The Red Shoes. I wasn't sure why she wanted me to come down
to the studio, but I knew that if I didn't do it, I'd regret that decision for the rest of my life, so I said, 'Yes! Of course.' And at her
request, I arrived at her house to start work.

She was a brilliant host. I hadn't eaten, so she made me scram-
bled eggs and toast and a big mug of tea. She talked about how

much this album meant to her, and played me 'Moments of Pleasure', which made me cry. Then she played the track that I would be helping out with that afternoon, 'Why Should I Love You?' I was thinking, 'It's a good album track: not just Kate Bush(y), there's something quite Minneapolis(y) about it too . . . something . . .'

'OH MY GOD! IS THIS PRINCE SINGING AND PLAYING GUITAR??????'

She smiled, said, 'Yeah,' then made another cup of tea.

That was probably one of the best music experiences I've ever had, bar none. What an afternoon. I mean, Prince didn't actually show up, but his killer guitar stylings and backing vocals were there, and lovely Kate was there, steering the whole thing, smoking fags, drinking coffee – and being absolutely fantabulous. No pressure, none of that macho, 'Huh! Think you can sing, eh?' type of behaviour. She just assumed that it'd be cool and, when she was happy, we stopped. I was blown away by the way she worked. She liked to improv with different types of voice: light, gruff, soft, loud. There was one point when she said, 'Shall we do some WHUMS? Come on, it'll be fun.'

And then we sang 'WHUM!' all over the last bit of the track. Boss, boss, boss times.

Mandela Days

I was fortunate to be asked to take part in the first Nelson Mandela tribute concert: Mandela at 70! It was to be held at Wembley Stadium on 11 June 1988. BBC2 were to screen the entire thing, along with many more networks around the world.

During 1984, the anthem of 'Free Nelson Mandela' by the Specials had been released and, in my case, had fostered interest in the imprisoned ANC leader. How strange that a hit record can make people turn their attention to something they had previously ignored. I knew about Mandela, but there was something about that record – *'Twenty-one years in captivity / shoes too small to fit his feet'* – that made me pay attention whenever it came on the radio.

I was approached by Dali Tambo, founder of Artists Against Apartheid, and the folks from the BBC to be a part of Mandela Day. That I would do it was never in question. I found myself reading up about Mandela, what he had sacrificed and why. And then, before we knew it, the Nelson Mandela 70th Birthday Tribute was upon us. A BBC journalist called the first Mandela concert 'The biggest and most spectacular pop-political event of all time; a more political version of Live Aid with the aim of raising consciousness rather than just money.' I co-hosted with Whoopi Goldberg and we were part of the amazing the running order: Sting, George Michael, Richard Gere, the Eurythmics and many more. I spent quite a lot of time getting into full white-face make-up, sculpted nose, tight pants, shiny shoes and sparkly

gloves – the full gear. When the compère announced, 'And now
. . . MICHAEL JACKSON . . .' the crowd went batshit crazy.

And then there was the sound of 72,000 people going, 'Oh, for
f**k's sake, it's Lenny!' under their breath. I've never heard such
unanimous disappointment in my life.

I went on later as Tina Turner and, before walking on-stage,
Billy Connolly told me that I looked like a Brazilian hooker he'd
once met. Whitney Houston and Stevie Wonder were top of the
bill. What a night! And Nelson wasn't even there. Apparently, he
watched it on the telly in Robben Island and said, 'Well, we've
got to do this again, lads! That was quality!'

And a couple of years later, after Mandela was released, they
did do it again. After I'd returned from Los Angeles and basically started my career again, I was asked to do a second concert,
but this time with the great man himself in attendance. The concert would take place at Wembley Stadium once more. Mandela
began the show with a forty-five-minute speech, eight minutes of
which involved a standing ovation. He spoke about finally being
free, political sanctions against South Africa and the abolition of
apartheid – an incredibly powerful opening.

This time I co-hosted with Denzel Washington, and the whole
event is up there among the high points of my life. Afterwards,
we all got to meet the man himself. There was a party in north
London and, when I arrived, I was ushered in by Dali Tambo,
past what looked suspiciously like the queue for the curried goat
and rice. I was whisked past everybody and introduced as the
'doofus who did Michael Jackson in the first concert'. Nelson
smiled and ushered me over to have my picture taken. He was on
good form and told me he'd enjoyed the concert but could have
done with less Lou Reed (who sang a twenty-eight-minute version of 'Last Great American Whale') and more Tracy Chapman

Dad and granddad

and Natalie Cole. He was lovely. Several flashes of light, and we were done.

For quite a long time that photograph hung over my daughter's bed. We had her convinced that this was a picture of 'Dad and his granddad'. She believed us for ages.

Mum Was Getting Sick

From 1991 onwards, Mum began to fall prey to illness; whether it was shortness of breath due to asthma, her deteriorating eyesight due to glaucoma, or her heart condition, she seemed to be fighting for her health every single day. It felt like every time we saw her, something else was wrong. During this time she would always say things like, 'I'll speak to you soon, if the Lord sees fit to keep me alive.' She really did think she was being tested. During this period, she became a born-again Christian. Having fallen off the heavenly wagon when she first arrived in the UK, she found it within herself to become born again. She'd been in hospital having a serious procedure, when a nun came to visit and held her hand throughout a particularly painful recovery. This woman was so kind that Mum was made to reconsider her faith and, after a period of contemplation, she presented herself at the local Pentecostal church. This came as a big shock to me – the mum who'd raised me at Victoria Terrace and Douglas Road did not feel like your typical Christian. She cursed and drank and smoked cigarettes. She hit me with the buckle end of the belt, also in my face with a cooking pot. When she became a born-again Christian, I was sceptical, thought it might be just a phase. But this rekindling of faith was real. She stuck at it, and I believe it sustained her through many years of being sick and in and out of hospital. Even though she was suffering from a relentless number of ailments, her belief that God had her back would somehow pull her through.

In between trips to the doctor and the hospital for various

treatments, Mum was becoming a very capable advocate for her church. She'd go out collecting donations at local pubs and clubs with a couple of her fellow parishioners. Even after she lost both her legs, she would go out in her wheelchair and give testimony, visit sick pensioners, do what she felt had to be done. I became a big fan in those last few years – she was doing all the things she wanted to do. She was ordained as a lay preacher, and the photographs of her on that momentous day are joyous. She's got a big smile on her face and is wearing her church crown – we were all very proud. She still questioned God about her various aches and pains, but eventually she just accepted her lot in life, through losing first one leg, then the other, and finally having a stroke which robbed her (and us) of her speech. She was eventually at peace.

Mum getting sick

Of course, while all this was happening, I was being a dad, husband, comedian, actor, writer and producer. Simultaneously. Like one of those insane plate spinners at the circus, but blindfolded and riding a unicycle. At some point, the floor was going to be strewn with broken crockery, and it would all be my fault.

Meanwhile, Back at Crucial Films . . .

I first had the idea for *Chef!* at the end of my time in Hollywood. While I was stuck in Los Angeles, a kind person would organise for me to read all the Sunday papers from the UK. And as I read, it became very apparent to me that chefs, particularly the high-end ones, were behaving appallingly and getting away with it because their food was beyond extraordinary. I was reading stories about Marco Pierre White ordering people out of his restaurant for putting salt on their food without tasting it first; Nico Ladenis lambasting a table of female customers because they'd hung their handbags on the backs of their chairs, which meant the waiters had to take a two-mile detour to serve the customers next to them. Gordon Ramsay wasn't quite doing his ultra sweary shtick yet, but he wasn't far off. I was fascinated, and saw that over-emotional man-babies in charge of Michelin-starred restaurants could get big laughs. So I sent producer Charlie Hanson my notes regarding this outrageously rude chef called Gareth Blackstock.

We had managed to get some development resources from the BBC. But, this being the early nineties, there was a problem in persuading the head of comedy, the late Geoffrey Perkins, that we could make the hotshot, really rude, yet articulate Gareth Blackstock likeable. I wanted Gareth to be scandalously smart and one of the best chefs in Europe, if not the world. But I also wanted him to be arrogant. In our research, Peter Tilbury (creator of *Shelley*, co-writer of *Birds of a Feather*) and I had met a lot of chefs, and our consensus was that most of these guys must be crazy. So, a slightly unlikeable bastard figure was at the centre of the piece, and we were immovable on that. But Geoffrey wasn't having it.

Geoff: Why d'you wanna play this arsehole, Len? It's like you'd be working with one hand behind your back.

Me: I wanna do it because Peter's writing really nails these guys. He understands the effort it takes to be the best. He's spoken to a lot of them and this is what it's like in a real, Michelin-star kitchen. We've never seen this before. It's a good premise and situation.

Geoff: But I don't really like him. I mean, it's funny, but you're at the centre of it all. Why do you wanna play this guy?

Me: The writing's good. It will stretch me as an actor.

We were at a restaurant in west London. We'd had lunch, including desserts and some wine – Geoffrey liked a long wine-filled lunch. So we pitched *Chef!* and various other sitcoms too. I had an idea about a drunken, grand actor and his loyal, scrofulous man servant, played by myself and Rik Mayall (shades of *The Dresser*); there were a couple of sketch-show pitches and a few other things. Geoffrey would consider, sip his wine and knock the idea back for whatever reason; he had a brilliant comedy mind, so the fact that he was a tough gatekeeper too shouldn't come as a surprise. He was one of the best and also one of the nicest people in the universe. He worked on *Spitting Image*, Harry Enfield's TV shows, *Have I Got News for You*, *Father Ted*, *The Catherine Tate Show* . . . He was a champion for comedy on the telly and was one of the driving forces behind Channel 4's first incarnation of *Saturday Live*. If he thought something was a bit iffy about your pitch, you listened. We made notes about *Chef!* and other things, then paid the bill and stood up, rather shakily, to leave.

Then, two seats behind Geoffrey, a TV exec-type woman who'd been lying down, almost unconscious, for our whole afternoon session sat up and slurred elegantly, 'Oh come on, Geoffrey, green-light something, ya bastard!' And then she lay back down, possibly for another ninety-minute power nap.

Eventually, Geoff did green-light *Chef!* Woo hoo!

The Making of *Chef!*, 1993 to 1996

After two years of shenanigans, rewrites, many bottles of wine and eating at nice restaurants – research – we finally got to make the show. Not having the resources for a big writers' room meant we were totally dependent on Peter Tilbury's work ethic and brilliance, and it absolutely paid off.

We shot on film (to avoid that naff video look that most sitcoms favoured at the time), and then, in a weirdo fit of weirdness, I asked if we could shoot with several film cameras in the studio sequences. This involved a lot of faff – we needed video playback keyed into the film camera's workings so that the audience could watch events unfold via monitors. However, there was a noticeable flicker throughout the shots, which was distracting. Also, film cameramen aren't really used to shooting in a TV environment. They're used to filming on location or in a purpose-built studio, with a red light and bell system for complete silence, sound-proofing and a bar nearby.

Shooting film in a TV studio depends on capturing the moments carefully in front of a live audience. Like filming a play as it happens: you can do retakes, but if the cast are on fire and doing their thing, often you just move on. When you shoot film, however, you're dealing with a lot of artists who want to protect their work as much as possible. So we'd be mid-scene, with Roger Griffiths doing or saying incredibly funny things as Everton – he's on a roll – and then you'd hear the cameraman go, 'Well, this is no good for me. I can see a lamp stand.'

Or (tuts loudly), 'Why is his face like that?'

Or, 'This is terrible, he's not lit. Why is he standing in shadow?'

Or, 'Sorry! Forgot to change a lens.'

It was a real problem, and created a great deal of tension on-set. Fortunately, on the first season we had Remi Adefarasin as our director of photography. Remi is an award-winning cinematographer who has worked on films like *About a Boy*, *Match Point* and *Elizabeth: The Golden Age*. I don't know how we secured his services, but when I met him for the first time, I was blown away. Remi, a person of colour, is a genius at lighting black skin on film. I couldn't believe it when he walked on-set. Polly had really done her homework and made sure that our set was diverse, with enough of a gender and ethnic mix to make it feel not just vibrant but like the places we all came from. The cast was diverse too, with the wonderful Caroline Lee-Johnson and guests such as Albert Roux, Kevin Allen, Trevor Peacock and, all the way from Jamaica in season three, Oliver Samuels!

It was still tough to shoot those first two seasons. The single-camera scenes that were pre-filmed before we went into the studio were relatively simple to shoot, but because our esteemed director, Lord John Birkin, was so fastidious about mapping out every single scene via an almost Renaissance approach to storyboarding, our scenes would take a long time to shoot. While the camera crew tended to improvise based on the pre-visualised scenes, John wanted them to stick to the storyboards – so there was conflict. In a way, I admired him: he was the director, the guy calling the shots, so he was fighting for what he believed was right. But the days were long, and I got more and more exhausted as the shoot went on. The chef, Gareth Blackstock, was an incredibly articulate character – which was one of the reasons I wanted to play him. For each moment, he found the perfect bon mot in an instant – unlike me, who usually thought of a comeback to some audience member's heckle as we pulled into Membury services to buy a Ginster's pasty much later. Gareth had wit and a delivery to which I could only aspire. But this took some learning, and I'd spend hours every night committing pages and pages to memory, and the effort was taking its toll.

The location-based material for *Chef!* was shot at the height of summer, in a working kitchen with real flames and heat. Food would be pre-prepared, and we'd rehearse pretend prep around it – some of us better than others. Roger Griffiths is actually a chef, so he looked like the real thing, but the rest of us needed skilful editing. When my family watched *Chef!*, they'd look at a pair of expert brown hands chopping onions with lightning speed and yell, almost as one, 'THAT'S NOT YOU, LEN!' The upshot of the heat from the stoves, the exterior heat of the summer and the pressure of all the line-learning meant that there were days when the performance took a while to rise. I would know the lines but, because of sweat and tiredness, they would simply refuse to pop out of my mouth in the lovely comedy-jokes fashion I was used to.

This exhaustion came to a head during the filming of the 'England Expects' episode, where Gareth and Everton sourced English ingredients for their participation in a Paris-based cookery competition. John Birkin had set up a complicated tracking shot, which would begin with my hands on a pheasant and then pull back and follow me to the left and right in lovely sweeping movements, as Everton began to reveal the fact that he had forgotten a key ingredient and we might have to go out and source it in Paris 'or somefin', Chef, d'you know what I mean, sorta fing?' I, as Gareth, am furious and castigate him for not doing his job properly.

That was the spine of the scene, but John B wanted to shoot it like a movie, all in one shot, with no coverage (close-ups or mid-shots). And therein lay the problem. If there's a mistake, you can't just pick it up on a close-up or mid-shot; you have to keep going back to the beginning and start all over again.

Eight takes later, it was very hot in the room, and I was the one who kept fluffing his dialogue. The crew were obviously excellent throughout this, hitting their marks every time after several run-throughs without the cast. Now I was cocking it up left, right and centre. I felt immense pressure to succeed, while also feeling a kind of shame that I was letting the side down. However, once I'd seen Polly's pained expression out of the corner of my eye during the fourteenth take, I stopped and asked John if I could take a mini-break, went to the bathroom and splashed cold water on my face. I did deep breathing. I tried to stop myself from bursting into tears. Then I went back onto the set and we persevered – and, eventually, John did do some carefully placed cutaways so he could use the best of the other takes. Polly had probably had a quick word in his shell, like. So it all worked out in the end, but that's what you get when you work with unique talent: a determination to protect the work by any means necessary.

The last season was shot on video, mostly in the studio. I was never really happy with the look of it, but it was easier to shoot, and I imagine the financial implications were a touch easier to bear.

Keep Going, Len! (1995)

From 1991 to 1998 Crucial Films was quietly achieving its goals via the hard work and dedication of Polly and our ever-growing team. We made six short films with the BBC called *Funky Black Shorts*. We opened the floodgates when we announced that we were looking for young, new black filmmakers to contribute to the series. A group of associate producers was booked to read every single entry and eventually a selection was made. I wrote a short film and handed it in under a pseudonym. It was called 'The Godsend' and it was about a working-class black male housekeeper (played by Treva Etienne) who secures a job working for a wealthy couple with a baby. The husband is away all the time at work in the City, while the wife (overwhelmed by baby and trying to be the perfect homemaker for her husband) confesses that she is losing it. The housekeeper insists on helping with everything: the baby, the cooking, the cleaning, the windows, getting the car started and more. Eventually, the husband suspects there is more going on than just a lamb casserole and he fires Treva's character, who then goes back to his tower block, to be greeted by his wife, played by Jo Martin, holding the fort with the babies, mess and chaos. She tells him, 'You're out all the time, doing God knows what on the road. I'm here trying to do all this on my own. What use are you? What's the point of you?' It was the first thing I ever directed.

Other films in this collection included 'Hard Shoulder', written and directed by Avril E. Russell, which featured Caroline

Lee-Johnson breaking down on a dark country road and being menaced by a nameless driver. Another that stood out was 'I Bring You Frankincense', written by Jonte and directed by Ngozi Onwurah, about a little black kid playing *you know who* in the school nativity play.

Another *Lenny Henry Show* . . .

In the mid-nineties the BBC gave me a Saturday-night slot for a new take on *The Lenny Henry Show*. Kevin Lygo (these days head of ITV) was our executive producer, and a mixture of old- and new-school writers (my brother Paul Henry, Carlton Dixon, Annie Caulfield, Jon Canter, Kim Fuller) and a new script editor (Geoff Atkinson) were brought in to figure out what this show would be. Geoff is a genial, driven comedy creator. I'd worked with him on the original *Lenny Henry Show* and was struck by just how much material he could produce in a very short space of time, much of it very usable. Geoff has a weird sensibility in his work; he likes oddness and looping conversations that defy logic. Not all of his stuff was to my taste but, when he hit the right buttons, it was jackpot time. He could be hilarious, and was on many occasions. Plus, he was punctual.

I wasn't really working with Kim at this point for a number of reasons, and so the reunion with him was bittersweet. However, some of the best bits of the show stemmed from improvisations between Felix Dexter and me, with Kim and Geoff poking and prodding us into surreal directions. Geoff and Kim would then write up the pieces, and Felix and I would remind ourselves of what we were talking about and then go out and perform for the audience. We played two academics, called Jeremy and Kenneth. I was Jeremy, a mature student who'd been mentored by Felix's Kenneth through my PhD studies. Jeremy was rather silly but clever; Kenneth a one-upmanship merchant who couldn't help reveal that he'd marked me down on my PhD papers. This was very different territory to our usual subject matter. Felix was brilliant because his head was in an unusual space. He was only interested in the ten best ways to be excellently funny in this sketch, and would push and push and push until he got where he wanted to be. He was a pedant about syntax, was brilliant at voices and was genuinely funny, but he annoyed me during the improvisations, mainly because he was so fast and way ahead of all of us. He'd already decided in which direction the sketch should go and hadn't bothered to give any clues during the performance. I think I was mad at him sometimes because he was so good. I felt as though I was being schooled every time we sat down to jam.

We also played two gay fashionistas who were in a relationship. Their TV show was called *GARMS*, and they presented the very best in affordable couture to their followers on a cable channel near you. During this semi-improvised piece, Felix and I had a row. The thing is, I had not got into my career via multiple courses on structured improvisation. I just had loads of energy and did silly voices and things like that. Whereas Felix absolutely knew the rules of comedy improvisation, and his brain whirred like a finely tuned Porsche engine as he navigated the twists and turns of whatever premise we were attempting that day . . . leaving me way, way back in the dust, lying there wondering why I wasn't being quite as funny as I used to be in 1974. God bless him, he was bloody funny.

I'd just completed a tour written by Jon Canter and myself, in which the stand-up material centred on the black British experience as seen through my eyes – a thirty-something brotha of Jamaican heritage hailing from the Black Country. Here's Jon to tell us about it:

Jon: When I started working with Lenny, he was basically the only black person on TV, apart from Trevor McDonald and Floella Benjamin, neither of whom was a stand-up comedian.

I always felt it was as much a burden as a privilege for him to be somehow the Voice of Black Britain. It wasn't anything to do with pride in his background. It was to do with responsibility. It felt to me that Billy Connolly, for example, didn't have to worry about what his comedy said about Scots people, so he was free, he was liberated; he could afford not to worry about offending anyone.

One of the paradoxes of this was Lenny's audience. When he played a gig in the Midlands, the audience would be predominantly black. But a lot of the time, most of the audience was white, simply because of the demographics.

So he came up with a great idea for the Smorgagsbord. Almost as soon as he came on-stage, after saying, 'Hello, York/ Yeovil/Sunderland/Bath/Galway/Adelaide,' he'd say, 'Black people in the house say "*HOOOOOOO!*"' And they would. All seventy-nine of them, or forty-two of them, or whatever, would say '*HOOO!*' very loudly, and make the other one thousand nine hundred people in the audience laugh, a laugh which Lenny rode by saying, 'Come on, let's take the white people outside, we'll deal with them there!' which also got a huge laugh. This was a routine that never failed.

But then, in the four-hundred-seat Theatre Royal in Winchester, Lenny said, 'Black people in the house say "*HOOOOOO!*"' And there was complete silence. And that wasn't because the black people in the house were shy. It was because they were non-existent. No black people were in the audience for Lenny Henry, live at the Theatre Royal in Winchester.

So, less than a minute into the show, Lenny turned to me in my usual position, sitting in the wings with the script on my lap, and said, 'Can I go home now, Jack?'

As an exercise, I did a word search for 'black' on my computer when we'd completed and tried out the show before touring, and there were 275 mentions of the word 'black' in the script. It wasn't that I was being militant or anything, it's just that I wanted the audience to know that I'd been thinking about these things. Also, I wanted the show to be a deeper dive into the black experience, rather than the usual shallow skim followed by several knob gags and a song. So that's what I was doing on-stage. And, similar to my time in Blackpool with David Copperfield, my predominantly white audiences were very choosy about what they liked and didn't like. Everything got laughs (I was a different Lenny now, remember) but it felt a bit like I was haranguing them, forcing them to see that I was black, and, in retrospect, I find myself thinking, 'But they knew you were black, Len. What you goin' on about it for?'

It's just how I felt at the time. I guess we were going for a tougher stance on black issues, parenting, the police, jail, crime, etc. I liked the show – and because this was Jon and not Kim, I was doing more stand-up stuff than characters. I think Deakus and Theo were still in the show, but there were now long stretches of me just talking to the audience in stand-up Lenny mode.

So, this version of me, the black and proud Len, was who was doing stand-up on the new iteration of *The Lenny Henry Show*. This attitude also bled into the sketch material, which seemed beefed up with a more topical edge. There were immediate problems once the shows began recording. Alan Yentob, the controller of BBC1, had given us an 8 p.m. Saturday-night slot, but then, on the day of transmission, he rang me in the car and said they were moving the show to later in the evening as it was a bit 'racy' and 'in your face'.

I remember being cross about this (we all were), because if we'd known we were going to be on later in the evening, that would have affected our approach to the material: we could have done a more adult show. As it was, I think the later slot helped the show – it still felt no holds barred. We performed affection-ate parodies of Morris Day and the Time, Jodeci and the Mighty Arrow. We did characters called the Stroppy Ragga Girls and a Scouse lowlife called Squeako. I sang with Chaka Khan and, as a result, got invited to her birthday party and sat with Prince for the entire evening, trying not to read the word 'Slave' that had been painted onto his cheek.

We did some pre-filming for a series item called 'Nathan Gunn'. He was a Blaxploitation-style private eye in the London of the swinging sixties, solving a murder mystery – which meant lots of sixties movies parodies, sizzling funk guitar courtesy of ex-Steel Pulse alumnus Mykaell Riley, and fabulous costumes for me. Literally, I looked like a pimp. I don't know why a private detective whose job is to stay in the shadows, trying to follow people unnoticed, would choose to wear a pink cowboy hat and matching suit with extra-wide lapels, orange shirt and seven-inch platform-soled shoes. But there you are. It felt funny to us. We were in the *Airplane/Police Academy* wheelhouse with this mini-series – the jokes were very much of this variety:

Nathan: I've dragged up a couple of witnesses . . .

    (Cut to: two obviously male witnesses, dressed like Ru Paul at Mardi Gras, stood next to Nathan.)

    A pause.

Nathan soldiers on with his explanation . . .

There was a lot of fun to be had during the Nathan Gunn filming, and one of the main reasons was my sidekick (a dopey copper working the London beat as Nathan's liaison), an actor called Jonty Stephens, who would not stop cracking gags, acting the fool, making faces and improvising all the way through. He would be very camp one moment, and the next make requests for silence on-set while he retreated into a *blue bubble of theatre, darling*, to enhance his performance. Then he would be incredibly butch in his attitude, standing with his legs impossibly far apart. He would do whatever he could to break us up on-set. Just before a take, he'd do a bang-on impersonation of Eric Morecambe. He'd adopt a familiar E.M. pose and say something like, 'And I cleaned that up!' Or, 'What do you think of it so far?' Then he'd hold up a live chihuahua or a piece of fruit and say, 'Ruggish.'

After a couple of episodes went out, I was called into the BBC and told that I'd been asked to appear on a programme called *Bite Back*. This was a viewer-centric show hosted by Trevor Phillips, where the viewers could come into the studio and complain about, question and assess the preceding week's programmes. It had a reputation for being quite tough at times, and I didn't want to go anywhere near it. I knew Trevor; he was the second black broadcaster called Trevor with his own show that I was aware of at the time, and I thought he was a decent bloke. After a bit of jiggery-pokery, I decided to give in and make an appearance on the show.

It was really odd – we'd been accused of 'reverse racism' and of 'being too black', and so on. This was a very white audience – lovely people, but all dominant culture. Trevor and I were the only brothas in the studio that day. It felt weird. I could tell Trevor was enjoying the supposedly offensive clips from the show that got screened – and, no offence to that show's particular audience, but this was my lived experience as a human being of colour, living and working in Britain at the time. *The Lenny Henry Show* had a pretty decent audience for what it was. It didn't feel as though we were being overly offensive in the writers' room or when we watched the show back for editing purposes. I wasn't being openly racist or anti-white. I didn't do that (still don't), so it felt like I was being hauled over the coals just for being black and on television.

Another viewer-centric show, *Points of View*, was better than *Bite Back*. This was a show hosted by Terry Wogan and, later, Anne Robinson. It also featured clips of the previous week's programmes, and then had letters from viewers either complaining or yelling 'hoorah' from the highest rooftops in celebration of their favourite show. On that programme *the producers* had to assess the complaint and write a measured and usually contrite letter in response to whatever caveat had been presented by the viewer.

I felt that this particular version of *The Lenny Henry Show* had an edge to it. We'd intended for the show to be almost a *Saturday Night Live*-style celebration of black British life, while employing everything I'd learnt from my own show and *Three of a Kind*. The general consensus was, '*Nice try, Len, but no cigar . . .*'

Mum

I was seeing Mum as often as I could – still most Sundays. In 1993 she had had a leg removed due to diabetes-based complications with a wound that wouldn't heal. This was devastating to the entire family. Mum had always been mobile and, although a big woman, was really fit – she walked everywhere. But suddenly she had to struggle with a prosthetic leg, which wasn't doing what it was supposed to do because of her size. It caused great pain whenever she tried to walk on it. She spent a lot of time sitting down or in a wheelchair. She comfort-ate a lot during this time. We arranged for carers to come round and look after her. I remember going round one weekend, and on the stove was Saturday soup, which involves simmering a whole sheep for most of the day and, later on, adding hard food (dumpling, green banana, dasheen, cho cho, pumpkin, plus spices and herbs). Mum looked very pleased with herself.

Me: Did you make the Saturday soup?
Mum: I teach the carer how to make it. Them can't cook, y'know, so I have to step in wid me one foot.

The carer had done a great job. In fact, whenever a new carer came on board, Mum would take the time and patience to teach them the basic tenets of Jamaican cookery – which, by the way, she NEVER taught me. I think those tenets are:

Mum: Take whatever you want to cook. Dash it into the fryin' pan. Fry it. Dash in the herbs and spices and everyting. Dash in the boil water. Dash in the potato. Boil water. Dash in the hard food. Make sure you season everyting good. Dash in whatever else you want.

Wait till it cook.

If it don't taste good, dash in more tings – herbs, spice, special sauce, jerk seasoning – whatever you have in the house.

Eat it.

She was the Jamaican Mary Berry!

But despite her ability to take care of those who were supposed to be taking care of her, things were not good. Her illnesses were increasing in severity, and all the sibs had opinions on what to do about it. There was a camp that said we should make the effort to be with Mum as often as we could, but let the carers take the strain off when necessary. There was another group who wanted to put Mum in a nice retirement community/care home, where she could be monitored twenty-four hours a day by professionals.

Mum had a lot of say in all this because, although she was in a wheelchair, she still had her smarts and common sense. She wanted to be in her own house, eating her own food, sleeping in her own bed for as long as she possibly could. She didn't trust hospitals. Whenever she went into intensive care, she'd lie there and bleat out, 'What am I doin' in this place wid all these OLD people?' We loved her, but this part of our lives was hard. Mum was really being tested and in a lot of pain. Sometimes the carers would be late, and at other times they might not show up at all. We just wanted Mum to be happy and well; none of us wanted her to suffer any more.

However, events conspired against us. In December 1994, due to diabetes, Mum's other leg was amputated too. At this point, we siblings were overwhelmed with stress and concern for her. What were we to do? Bev was seeing her three times a day, bringing her meals, cleaning the house, making sure she was bathed, her hair done and skin moisturised. Kay performed similar duties, press-ganging her husband Malcolm into laundry duties. Hylton visited as often as he could, so did Seymour. I visited on Sundays, sometimes *en famille*, sometimes with just Billie in tow. Sometimes it'd just be me, and when that happened we'd always talk for a long time about a lot of issues from the past: stuff we'd never really discussed – perceived slights and problems – got talked out. We spoke about how often and how hard she would beat me when I was a child. I asked, 'Was it because you didn't love me or something?' And she told me it wasn't about not loving me. It was about trying to protect me. She was trying to give me a shield to deal with the outside world. She was tough with me so that when the world was tough on me, I could handle it. This was Mum's thinking: she treated me rough when I was growing up so that when I was in the outside world, no matter how low I felt, I'd been lower.

As I got older I'd ponder on what Mum had sacrificed to raise all of us; how difficult it had been for her being separated from the rest of the family in Jamaica. I realised just how solid my relationship with the family was, and just how much they'd supported me spiritually. Which meant that any worries I'd had about being neglected, about myself being an untended garden, were unfounded.

When you're a child in a West Indian family, you'd hear the words, 'Come out the room! Big People talking!' We'd leave that room and then listen at the door as the adults talked freely about the really important things that concerned them. It took for ever, but gradually I became a young adult – still not Big People in Jamaican eyes: 'Twenty-five? Pah! Still a yout. Come out the room, Big People talkin'!'; and then an adult (thirty-five: nearly there, but still nowhere near Big People status yet). Suddenly, Mum and I were able to discuss grown-up matters on a level playing field. There was mutual respect, empathy and kindness as we chatted about how difficult her life had been, raising us in England in such a hostile environment – as well as myriad issues that had previously been deemed as 'Big People Talk' but which were now ours to explore freely: what my birth father Bertie was actually like, why she'd fallen for him, what Papa really said when she told him she was having me, and why they'd stayed together after she'd had me. Wasn't he angry? Was that why he was always so distant whenever we were around each other?

We talked about love and being married, and how compromises had to be made to keep families together. I talked about how hard it was to keep all the plates spinning all the time, and she told me to 'Stop the noise. Look at you earnin' all that money and complainin' about yu big house and everyting. You are blessed. Never forget that. You've helped this family so much. So shut yu mout.'

That was me told.

Once I was able to comprehend just what she'd been through – once I could, in turn, tell her some of the things I'd had to deal with on my bizarre journey through show business – I could finally sit with her as her son, hold her hand and say, 'I love you.' And she would say, 'I love you too . . .' That meant so much to me.

I used to feel that I wasn't doing the dutiful son bit properly because everyone else was more present than I was. I was fighting to maintain a career, doing *Chef!* while making *Funky Black Shorts*, the African American humour documentary for *The South Bank Show* and the *Loud* tour of Australia. The nineties were non-stop.

Red Nose Day, 1993

Comic Relief was a constant presence too. In 1993 we'd generated eighteen million pounds. Everyone was determined to keep going. There were more people to help, grants to be sorted out, trustee meetings to attend. Throughout all that, Mum's health continued to worsen. Mentally, I've always tended to ignore the down moments – there's always the feeling that whatever this chapter might be, there'll be another one along in a minute. *'Just ride it out, Len; do your best to get through it.'* But there were gaps in my judgement – decisions I made, things said and done; even though one tries not to regret them, you can't help feeling a sting when you look back upon them. I do regret not spending more time with my family, and with my mum when she was going through this painful experience. I did feel that the other sibs were lumbered with having to provide constant back-up while I gallivanted off to Australia or was on the road in the UK, seemingly having a great time. I didn't feel I was, but I felt that that's what people were thinking: 'What kind of son visits his poorly mum once a week when he can fit it in? What kind of son is that?'

Meanwhile, work was fine. No matter what it was like or who was in it, work was always fine. *Crucial Tales* got green-lit and made. This was a season of six thirty-minute films about the black experience in the UK, made by writers and performers of colour. I was very proud of this series, albeit a little disappointed when we had to cut the episodes down from six to four due to the BBC's budgetary restraints.

The episodes were directed by Kolton Lee, Ngozi Onwurah, Avril E. Russell and Danny Thompson; they were written by Jonte, Rohan Leslie, Avril E. Russell and Bryan Waters. There was an early appearance by Idris Elba in one of them. This felt like a proper step forward for us – having the resources to curate diverse talent, making a four-part anthology series featuring black and brown protagonists. It felt revolutionary since we also had a diverse group of people working behind the scenes. Everyone worked their conkers off. This was what being a black-led indie production company was all about. I was proud of everyone there – Polly McDonald, Simon McCleave, John Brennan and everyone else. We were pushing through the sticky development mire and actually getting things made.

Red Nose Day, 1995

What a difference a day makes – £22 million raised! Everyone was hyper-emotional. All the things we'd set out to do were happening. This was cause for celebration, whooping and hollering, dancing and barking at the moon.

Then Mum had a stroke. It was February 1995.

I felt things slipping away from me.

But work hardened my heart and kept me moving; it seemed that work took priority over everything. I was being dubbed 'Len the Workaholic' by family and friends. And it was true – to an extent. I understood work and its structures, the ins and outs. But *real life* – family and normalcy – seemed impossible to negotiate, like a blindfolded kid trying to do a Rubik's cube with one hand tied behind his back, on a skateboard, in the middle of the M25 at rush hour.

The worst aspect of the stroke was that Mum, who was always full of chat and gossip and stories and scandal (even when she became born-again she'd have a twinkle in her eye while discussing someone who was no better than they ought to be), suddenly had no speech. She couldn't talk or answer back or argue – and that was a huge loss.

I'd go see her, and Billie would immediately want to go and play 'Horses' in the back garden. Mum and I would sit holding hands, watching the show-jumping display. She'd smile and raise the odd eyebrow, and I'd have to imagine the conversation we'd be having if she could talk:

Mum: Hmm mmmmm – what a way she have, h'energy!

Me: She certainly does that–

Mum: What you feedin' her? It look to me like you givin' her too much sugar!

Me: Mum!

Mum: Well, only people who can run an' jump so high like that is them h'illegal athletes in the Olympics or take the stereo-oids.

Me: Just 'steroids'; they pronounce it 'steroids'.

Mum: What me did just say? Steroids. Anyhow, she look like she's hopped up on someting h'illegal.

Me: Well, if sweets were illegal, you'd be right.

Mum: Humph. She fit and full of energy, though, that's for sure . . .

Me: That is for sure. You all right, Mama?

Mum: Chuh, man, mi all right. If the Lord see fit to keep me alive over the weekend, I'll be all right, y'know? Yu want some'n to eat?

Me: Mum, I'm fine. I'm not keen on the food in this place.

Mum: What you talkin' about ? I teach the janitor to cook stew chicken, rice an' peas. He'll be here in fifteen minutes with some orange squash.

Me: Er . . . I'll stay, then!

That's what it felt like in my head every time I went to visit her. Because our conversations were one-sided, with the odd sigh or eyebrow raised to signal Mum's engagement, I found myself wondering how we were all going to get through this. How was I supposed to negotiate and navigate real life, real relationships, real responsibilities – to friends, family, parent – when the show-biz stuff was so shiny and attractive and doable, or manageable, and just over there?

The family unified to help with Mum. We'd found her constant care, rather than just home care. It became clear that she needed to be somewhere where they'd keep an eye on her. I tried to make sure that I visited more often, but things were picking up at Crucial Films. We'd got the green light for *Neverwhere*, created by me and Neil Gaiman, written by Neil and produced by Clive Brill. This was a big deal – and we needed to figure out how to best serve the unusual story and aesthetic vibe on a BBC sci-fi budget. The first thing that got decided was that the show would be shot on digital video, rather than 16mm film.

Neverwhere, 1996

Digital video was cheaper, so that decision was made from the off. Dewi Humphreys, who'd worked on *Chef!*, came from a camera-operating background. He was the loveliest of collaborators, full of ideas. We assembled a groovy, diverse and willing cast and crew. Initial designs were by Neil Gaiman's amigo Dave McKean (who'd designed all the *Sandman* covers for DC up to that point). I asked Brian Eno if he'd create the music for the show, and he agreed.

The show was a tough nut to crack: there was a great deal of shooting in the cold, rain and snow. Members of the crew had T-shirts made that said 'Never Warm' and 'Never Again'. But Neil's enthusiasm and innovative genius, plus everyone's gung-ho attitude, meant that – for all its rock 'n' roll, goth-influenced, kick, bollock and scramble nature – it actually turned out pretty good. Yes, it could have looked better – better sets, better special effects – but Neil and I often say that the people who could have made something like *Neverwhere* on the scale it was intended had not been BORN yet: they are young and read comics and graphic novels and know about first-person gaming and world building. Gaiman's novels are written for a cine- and comics-literate audience used to seeing his fantastical ideas conveyed through cataclysmic panels of light and shade, bolstered by, at times, surreal line-work from some of the industry's most interesting and talented artists. Back then, TV didn't stand a chance, no matter how well intentioned we were.

Just to be clear: I was and am incredibly proud of what our little production company produced in association with Neil. His ideas are magical, weird, sexy, funny and smart. Despite wobbly sets and some odd costume choices, I felt we conveyed the world very well. I stand by the show. I remember Polly had asked our editor, Bryan Oates, if he could put together a sizzle reel of the series to show the BBC's commissioners. Bryan went to town and made a twenty-minute cut-down version of the best bits from the series, complete with movie trailer-style music, shocks, laughs, thrills and spills. When we showed it to BBC executive Chris Parr, he was absolutely gobsmacked. He couldn't believe what we'd achieved.

Neil reminded me recently that, although the reviewers who watched the whole series before they pronounced judgement were kind, the general consensus was that we hadn't fulfilled the premise of the show. In my defence, I always thought our intentions for the series were undermined by a lack of resources and time and the utilisation of video rather than film stock. I reiterate: for me, watching the show was like receiving the Victoria Cross every week for services to fantasy, magic and weirdness. I loved it, and seeing people like Clive Russell, Trevor Peacock and Peter Capaldi giving it their Shakespearean best warmed the cockles of my heart and made me proud of all of us. In my mind, we had cleaved to Neil's vision to the best of our ability.

Having poked my oar in on *Neverwhere*, I then pulled away from production company duties and focused on the *Lenny Henry at Large* tour, which would cover all of the UK and, eventually, Australia and New Zealand.

Red Nose Day, 1997:
Small Change, Big Difference

Whatever was going on in my private life, Comic Relief activity would lift me up. In 1995 we raised twenty-two million pounds, in '97 we surpassed that and raised twenty-seven million. As an organisation we were growing; there were more and more people in the offices. The board meetings took longer as there were so many grant applications to discuss, people to consider hiring and discussions re. corporate sponsorship with which to engage. I continued to be on hand for the odd trustee meeting or creative session. Richard Curtis was always on it, full of ideas for 'What's next? How do we get people to understand this bit? What's a really cool way to achieve this?' He never seemed to stop. Comic Relief rolled on, and the funds raised went higher and higher. We just kept expanding and growing.

I had a good relationship with the CEO, Kevin Cahill. I was always welcome in the office and was able to pop in and draw false moustaches on all the pictures of me in the building. Kev would enthuse me with everything that was going on, and I'd be revved up, ready to engage with the next stage of the journey. The hard work was happening behind the scenes with the fundraisers, the creatives running the night of TV, the filmmakers in Bristol who made all the appeal films, and the writers, directors and musicians who gave their time for free in order to raise money for charities in the developing nations and the UK. It was a humongous task every two years, but whatever happened – whatever the flak or pushback or mealy-mouthed moaning we received from whichever paper accusing us of abnegating our responsibility to the UK by focusing so much on developing nations – our team was (and is) so adept at handling the chatter that we barely felt it. There will always be moments when we have to take time to repair, fix or sort out some reputational issue. These things can occur in any organisation. The commitment to doing the right thing is so powerful that even in the face of the deepest recession or governmental pushback, Comic Relief finds a way forward, raises crazy money and makes us all incredibly proud.

Coltrane and Curtis during filming for the *Cracker* special
for Comic Relief 1997

Australia, 1998

I was on tour again. I'd only just done something called *Larger Than Life* in 1996. I remember Adrian Edmondson asking me why I was out on tour again so soon. I didn't know. I told myself that I was compelled to keep moving, jumping through hoops in order to earn a crust, pay the mortgage, afford the car, the life-style. The need to be on the road and to hone my craft possessed me – it still does. I loved my wife, my daughter and my home. But something drove me to be on tour constantly, to make things constantly, to be out there constantly. All my life I'd done this, leaving the people closest to me behind.

Lenny: Good evening. Yep, yep, yep: make some noise. Fantastic. Thank you very much for . . . OK, let's get the serious stuff out of the way: there are fire exits here and here, so if there's a fire, stay in your seats, and the fire will exit through them!

Let me talk to my people. (Addresses the front row.) Hey! There's a guy here wearing a suit just in case you gotta go to a meeting. Wow! You're wearing man-made fibres! I love the way man-made fibres sound like characters from *Neighbours*: 'Mom, can Rayon and me go to Terylene's house? Nylon's gonna be there.'

Thank you very much for coming out tonight. I'm so glad you're here. I'll tell you why: I got burgled recently. They didn't break into my house; they broke into my shed, took the lawn mower. One of the ones you sit on. Nobody saw a thing. Unbelievable. What's the matter with English people? There's a guy speeding down the M4 on a John Deere ride-on mower and nobody says a damn thing?

Best thing was, after I reported it to the police I got a phone call from victim support. They wanted to know if I needed any counselling, any help. I said, 'Could somebody come and mow my lawn?'

I've been watching a lot of telly recently, and I get so angry! Where are the black people? When my parents came to this country there were no black people on TV either – and this was in the days of the black-and-white television. They should have called it 'white-and-white television'. If a black person did come on, viewers thought there was something wrong with the set. They'd ring up the TV shop: 'Hello – there's a black person on my television. Can you come and get him off?' The only black people you saw on television in the sixties were the Black and White Minstrels – and they were white! Lovely white dancers with black shoe polish all over their faces and these huge white lips! (Mimes drawing them into place.) Hmmm, accurate! My mum would be this close to the screen: 'Well, it's nice to see some black people on TV for a change. But look at them lips. They must be from one of the small islands!'

It all seems fairly inoffensive now, but at the time, for some people, it felt like a lot of blackness to be taking in. How odd that I was so intent on doing this stuff about the lived black experience, while simultaneously living a middle-class life in Berkshire with my wife and kid, in a neighbourhood where I was one of about six black people. I should have been doing material about shopping in antique shops, eating pastries on a regular basis and having reiki.

The show was being generally well received, however, so I thanked the comedy gods for that. My Australian tour promoter, Maggie Gerrand, came to see me in Birmingham. She immediately put her hat in the ring for a tour of Australia and New Zealand. I said 'yes'. But then, disaster of disasters: Mum's deteriorating health had reached an all-time low. She was very sick and in hospital.

Looking back at this scenario, I can't help disliking myself and the way I reacted in that moment. My mum's really poorly, and my response is: *'What will my Australian tour promoter think if I don't fulfil my commitment?'*

There were tense discussions with the doctor in charge of my mum's case. He was a decent bloke – very patient with me and the rest of us. I think I babbled about 'needing to know whether I could go to Australia or not' in quite a forceful way. He must have seen some kind of desperation in my eyes because he held me by the shoulder and said that Mum was OK for a while and that I *could* go on tour; not to worry – they'd look after her. I was relieved but also very nervous about the prospect of being away while Mum was poorly. However, I trusted the doctor's advice implicitly and knew she'd be in good hands.

Jon Canter and I had worked hard on assembling the show – basically a remix of a previous show called *Large*, this one was called *Larger Than Life* – and we'd made Antipodean-friendly cuts and revisions because we knew that the show was going to transfer to Australia. The show had been toured and was well practised. It was going to be good. I could feel it.

I also felt the guilt and shame of running away from the situation at hand. What was that all about? Why couldn't I just stay and work through the vigil, be at Mum's side, just be there? I still don't know and still question my behaviour at that time. (I just watched a wonderful episode of *This Is Us*, where Jack, at his mother's funeral, battles with his guilt over the memory of neglecting her years earlier. I was very moved by this, for obvious reasons.) But I went to Australia.

The Australia–New Zealand
Larger Than Life Tour

There was a lot of work to do on arrival. This was the first time I'd been to Australia since *Live and Unleashed*. I had to do warm-up gigs, a great deal of press and publicity, TV talk shows and radio. The blessing was that there was a good reaction and, due to all the marketing and promotion, I managed to build an audience and sold out almost immediately.

There is much about Australia that is pleasant, though, at times, there was overt racism to be dealt with. I seemed to get on with most people because I was 'the bloke off the telly'. But when my brother Paul came over to see me, if he went out during the day, or in the early evening before the show to have a drink in a bar, he would get majorly stared at by almost every bloke in the place.

Me: How 'stared at'? What kind of staring?
Paul: You know – kind of 'I want to kill you, but there's too many witnesses' kinda staring.

I was really sad that he'd had to put up with that. I'd never had any of that racist bullshit to deal with while in Oz; people were generally fine with me. However, there were a couple of moments when I felt like Malcolm X at a Klan buffet.

I got yelled at by a taxi driver on the way to a TV interview. I was with the PR person, and we were late. He was trying to find the destination; the PR person was looking for the address in her handbag. I had a schedule in my hand and started to tell the guy the address, when he turned on me and yelled at the top of his voice, 'I WAS TALKIN' TO THE LADY!'

Right in my face. Spittle and everything.

There was another incident where I felt sick to my stomach at what happened. It was after a show. I'd showered and changed and had been told that there was a huge line of people wanting merchandise and autograph books signed. I came out and was greeted by a lovely cheer from the waiting crowd. There was a rope between me and all the people; everything was copacetic. I sat down at a table with a glass of red wine and a sharpie and signed like a maniac – but the line just didn't seem to go down. I kept going, but after I'd been meeting and greeting and signing for nearly an hour, way at the back, a tall white guy, with his girl-friend, leaned out of the queue and yelled at the top of his voice, 'Come on, Lenny, hurry up, you black c*nt!' He laughed and looked around, as if to say, 'Am I right, everybody?'

Everyone in the line moved six feet away from this dude, like he'd just invented social distancing. I was shaking. I hadn't been called that kind of thing since school. I hated that it had happened in front of everyone, after a good show. I hated that it had hap-pened to me. Maggie took my arm and led me away quickly to the people carrier – she didn't want me in this toxic situation any longer. As I walked away, I turned to see the guy who'd shouted arguing with his girlfriend. She was dark-skinned (darker than me), probably Indian or Sri Lankan. It looked like she was break-ing up with him there and then. He was crying by the time we got out the door. Serves him right.

The tour rolled on: we visited Melbourne, Sydney, Perth, Brisbane, Tasmania and, halfway through, we hit Canberra. It's the eighth-largest city in Oz and has government buildings, embassies, the Royal Mint and the Australian Defence Force Academy – and every time I've been there, it's been empty. If the Specials had gone there, they would have taken one look and said, 'Nah, man, we was wrong about Coventry – *this* is a ghost town, too rhatid . . .'

I'd walked around the town and bought books, comics and records. I'd soaked up the atmosphere of the city and made some notes about things I could say (about its emptiness, the official buildings, the lack of punters, the fact that everywhere seemed to close at 4.30 p.m.). The show was bostin', as we used to say in Dudley. My brain was poppin' and I felt like I was in the place to be – the act flowed through me almost as if I wasn't there. Cool beans.

At half-time I sat in the near dark in the dressing room, doing a meditation called 'heard things'. You sit in silence, no distractions, no music, just you and yourself . . . you let yourself drift into that half-space . . . you float there. It's called 'heard things' because you have to close your eyes and mentally tick off noises from the exterior (outside your window) to the interior (outside the room) to where you are (in the room). I went to a truly deep place and was really hearing things: trucks going by, distant voices, someone crying – which sounded a bit like me, but I wasn't crying . . . and . . . was that my mum's voice?

A gentle tap on the door. It's Maggie telling me that Part Two is about to begin. I go to the bathroom, wash my hands, get a cold water from the fridge, drink some. Then I body-swerve the interval cheese and ham sandwich that's just *lying* there waiting to be munched on, and I head to the side of the stage, focusing on the peace I'd just earned – well, until that last weird bit.

The second half goes even better than the first, and there's a standing ovation. I even initiate a post-show self-talk as I walk back to the dressing room.

Me: Yay for me!

Me2: You see, Len, things *can* go right for you if you let them.

Me: All right, all right, I'm enjoying myself – that was a good show.

Me2: Well, just *remember* that!

Me: I will! Bloody hell, man, stop going on about it. You're gettin' on me nerves now!

I got back to the dressing room, thinking I'd have a shower and then maybe we'd have a post-show meal and a glass of wine and maybe a sticky toffee pudding . . . but then Maggie's at the door, and she's white as a sheet. She's actually whiter than that. And her eyes are wet, and I don't know why. And then she says something, but I don't really hear her, because I've caught the gist and now my eyes are wet.

Mum died tonight.

My mum's gone. She's dead.

I took a breath – I was hysterical.

I rang Bev and told her that I'd call her when I got back to the hotel. As soon as I reached the hotel room, I rang her and we cried with each other. I spoke to everyone who was there – but I didn't really break down until I spoke to Kay's husband, Malcolm. As soon as he got on the phone, I said something like, 'Malcolm, you've been there for Mum. I just wish I coulda bin there as—' then I let out this wolf howl, this roar of anguish at Mum being gone from the universe. Malcolm just kept saying, 'I know, Len. I know – I know, chap, let it out . . . let it all out.' I have never felt so far away from my family. It drove things home to me: I'd been neglectful these last few years, neglectful of true friends and my close family. I had prioritised being out on the road and show business above everything else.

I was angry with myself.

I wanted to go home.

At last.

At five that morning I got a flight and went straight to Bev's house. I sat in an armchair and helped to organise Mum's funeral. This was a real family affair: everyone came to Bev's and drank tea and ate ackee and saltfish and fried dumplin'; we wrangled small babies, toddlers and kids, and talked about how to give Mum the best send-off anyone had ever had.

And we did it. Between us, we organised a legendary funeral for Mum. The church was so packed there had to be an overspill area, with speakers so that they could hear the service too.

Bertie, my birth father, was there. He met Dawn and Billie for the first time and didn't say or do anything untoward. I was glad; in the circumstances I wouldn't have known what to do if he had said something hurtful or stupid. Judy and Brian Green and Neil Haftel from the Lockshen Gang were there. Greg was there. I sat with Dawn and Billie and Sharon; Dawn and Sharon wept and wept. Auntie Pearl, Mum's sister, got up and started to riff around the idea of 'putting tings right in your garden. Yu see, when you have a garden, and it's choked wid weeds and I ain't talkin' about no ordinary garden, yu know? I'm talkin' bout the garden of your soul – when yu garden is choked up wid weeds an pests an everyting . . . yu mus' h'attend to dese tings.' Even here, Sharon and I looked at each other and smiled. This was great, and it was funny. As Pearl chuntered on, Sharon whispered to me from the side of her mouth, 'Get the hook.' I laughed and tried to turn it into a random 'Hallelujah'.

I had to get up and make a speech, and, through tears that just wouldn't stop, I spoke about Mum's beginnings in Jamaica; about how, after Seymour had been attacked by children from a

nearby village, Mum rode there on a donkey like Clint Eastwood
and laid down the law to the entire town: 'Anybody touch *one* of
my children again, they wi' have to deal with me!' Then she rode
the heck outta there . . . at two and a half miles per hour.

I spoke about how she used to cook for 150 people, even when
it was just the five of us round the table. I made jokes about her
laugh, and also about how she mispronounced words like 'film'
and 'certificate'. She'd say, 'I want to watch the John Wayne flim.'
And, 'Where's my birt cerfi-ticket?' I remembered how she used
to give us beatings *and* tell us off at the same time, while hitting
us ON. EVERY. SINGLE. SYLLABLE: 'Didn't. I. Tell. You.
Not. To. Go. In. My. Purse?' I talked about just how much she'd
changed as a person in her later years, becoming a born-again
Christian and giving herself to the service of others.

I've no idea how, but I was able to find some humour during
my speech, and somehow this made me feel happy. I'd written
the eulogy based on my own personal experience and the things
I'd learnt. A methodology for the future, perhaps?

We walked down to the grave-side, and there were more hymns
– all these people treading on this carefully tended final resting
place, singing hymns, yelling 'hallelujah' and joining in with yet
another fire and brimstone sermon. This time outside in the cold.

Then, Mum was buried by all of us. In Caribbean culture
members of the family take it in turns to shovel the dirt into the
grave until that work is done. There were guys stood to one side
with one of those mini-JCBs, thinking, 'Well, we'll just bugger
off home, then. You don't need us.'

And then back to the hotel for the reception and the food – the
endless variations of Jamaican food – things that Mum used to
like and make every week, things we took for granted when she
was alive: her soup, her rice and peas, her roasted red snapper, her

gungo peas and rice, the stew chicken, the red pea soup, the Saturday soup, the curry goat and rice. All washed down with the alcohol from the cash-only bar, and the free multi-fruited squash.

For a funeral in Dudley, it was an amazing turnout. People came from everywhere to pay their respects to Mum. I realised that she was much more than the matriarch of our family – she was a community icon. Everyone knew her; she had made wedding cakes and dresses, thrown rent parties. She had won money at bingo and given half of it away when she heard people's hard-luck stories. In her new role as lay preacher, she had gone out with youngsters from the church, collecting money for charities. She went to conventions and travelled far and wide to do so. People liked her, respected her, were saddened by her passing. But they couldn't have been sadder than we were. Mum was gone, man. What were we going to do?

It was like she'd been driving along in a huge people carrier, with us in the back, and then suddenly just disappeared – and taken the steering wheel with her. How would we all survive this? I had no idea. I just felt as though I was floating, drifting, out of control now, spiralling. Sinking.

Mum's death had a huge effect on all of us. We were all devastated. Someone had dropped an atom bomb directly into the midst of our family and . . . BOOM! This is what it felt like to us.

9

PICKING UP THE PIECES

I was just lost. I tried to recover from the shock of it all. Why was I even shocked? She'd been sick for years. I was bereft. There was a huge Mum-shaped hole in the place where she used to be, and I just did not know how to exist without her. When I flew back to Australia to resume my tour, each night began with me shivering, out of control, teeth chattering. I put my back out somehow and was in horrific pain. A local doctor put me on the strongest painkillers he had. One night I went on-stage and apparently did one of the best shows I've ever done in my life. I can't remember it at all.

When I returned from Australia I began grief counselling, which went on for a while, then transitioned into cognitive therapy and continued for at least the next four years.

I managed to write a show with Lennie Barker and Kim called *Have You Seen This Man?*, which was an excuse to mourn Mum while being funny about her. Seemed like a good idea. Simon McBurney came on board as a kind of spirit guide and helped us put the show together. It began with film footage of the *Windrush* arriving, and then segued into a number of passengers talking about what it might be like when they finally arrived in H'ingland! It was a tribute to Mum, and every performance moved me away from grief and further towards some kind of acceptance.

However, my selfish need to succeed through constant working, and the vast hole left behind by my mother's passing, was taking its toll on my family life. I made some bad decisions, and this had repercussions all round.

Simon provided me with a kind of North Star to cling to:

Simon McBurney: Lenny, your mum had just died and you were going through things very much in the public eye. I remember you during rehearsals questioning every aspect of your life: your blackness, your career, your politics.

The past is not dead. It is not even past. Confronting it takes courage. And so we talked, we laughed, we cried and we walked the streets, clutching headphones and a microphone and asking people in Shepherd Market, 'Where are you from?' 'What does it mean to be British?' It wasn't about treading a familiar road but hacking out a whole new path, a path you're still on. Speaking out, not just about and for yourself but about the experience of a whole generation. Confronting a path of history which stretches backwards and forwards in time, and concerns ALL of us, because it is ALL our history. Alive as a snake. And, well, if we don't do that, we are all lost.

You had this Seamus Heaney poem in your head about using your art to dig deeper into your reasons for living. My advice at the time regarding surviving all the things you were experiencing was to keep digging: a new thing will grow from this.

He was right. Now was a time for an extended period of repair, rest and rehabilitation. I decided that there should be no more Crucial Films. Although we were doing reasonably well and were in the black – thanks to Polly's judicious handling of our affairs – being part of a production company in the midst of mourning and turmoil felt too much. I needed to spend more time with my family. So that was that: no more Crucial – and by this time, we had grown; we had personnel covering drama, series, serials, films *and* comedy. We'd had a pretty good run, and I was sad to see everyone go, but it had to happen. There were times when I was very much wrapped up in my own world of hyperkinetic busyness and not really paying attention to what was going on around me. Producers are supposed to be on point, all the time, 24/7. I was not. I spoke to Polly about the whole Crucial Films experience and she reminded me of the stresses of helping to produce Lenny Henry-related projects, as well as the diversity and inclusive nature of the non-Lenny Henry projects:

Polly McDonald: Obviously the big issue at the time was access. It was such a pleasure to work with you, sometimes. [I laughed at the 'sometimes'.] This is going to sound a bit patronising, but your ability to concentrate and really think things through at times was really impressive and terribly encouraging. You weren't around very much, and one thing that did frustrate me was that if we were in a meeting with one other person, you'd be fantastic and thoughtful, intelligent and contributing loads of really smart stuff. But if there were more people in the room, it was like you'd opened the fridge door, the light had come on, and you felt like you had to do a tight twenty-minute stand-up set. People would let you get away with it because you were a famous person and they kind of expected it, but it was frustrating that other people couldn't see the side of you that I knew. It wasn't the end of the world but, ultimately, you were underselling yourself. And despite how it ended, Crucial Films was important – there was a good vibe there, people enjoyed working with us. BBC executive Jane Tranter was incredibly supportive at the end and sent me a note to say how sad she was that we were no more. I was proud of what we achieved in the end: seven years – it's a whole life cycle.

Polly's right: after Crucial I felt like I was swimming along in the middle, settling into a holding pattern, treading water. There'd been dark clouds hanging over my head for a while, but although work had its place, I needed to prioritise family. There was a lot of thinking going on, a lot of talking therapy, and it helped. (Comedians love therapy: you've paid for this person to listen and, by God, they will!) I think I got a lot out of it. Moving forwards, I was doing lots of odd little jobs: children's television, voiceovers . . . I was ticking over. I wasn't a particularly happy camper at this point in my life. Was all this grief worth it?

The Year 2000

At the beginning of the new millennium we decided we should take a three-month family sabbatical in order to take a breath and recalibrate. Dawn, Billie and I decamped to Bali, New Zealand and Los Angeles, and connected with friends, family and foreign shores. It was a much-needed tonic.

But I was still grieving for Mum – it had been only a couple of years since she had died. The pain of her leaving was still on me like a sticky overcoat.

In Pieces

It was when I was feeling glum at my house one day that Clive Tulloh, my trusted friend and colleague who was an executive producer for Tiger Aspect productions, asked me what I was interested in doing next, and I blurted out that I just wanted to make people laugh again. This wasn't me craving success or money; it was me seeing that going back to comedy sketches would be a positive thing. It might cheer me up.

I was not to think of it as grabbing the brass ring or breaking through the waves and swimming to shore.

Just think of it as the day job. Go to work. Do your job. Come home.

'Let's make a comedy show again. Can we call it *In Pieces*?'

So that's what we did.

Clive – the executive producer of *In Pieces* – encouraged me to get more involved in the ideas-generation process. He'd hired a young co-executive producer called Lucy Robinson. She was smart and had a large Rolodex (remember them?) of new and happening writers that she wanted me to meet. We talked about my intentions for the show; although there would be a pilot episode, I wanted it to be not only funny but also stylish. No laugh track – the material should stand on its own two feet. (We lost that battle. When the BBC's head of comedy saw it he said immediately, 'Needs a studio audience.' He just thought it was a shame not to play it to a real audience. I gave up arguing in the end. I didn't care what they did as long as the show looked like a MOVIE!)

We came up with some ideas. My baby brother, Paul, had an idea about a Jamaican guy he'd seen at a funeral, who was trying to chat up the widow of the deceased. He kept emphasising the '-tion' bits of words, like 'delibera-*shon*' and 'expecta-*shon*'. When Paul did it, I imagined a disapproving black community around this guy. If he was just following this poor woman around and bothering her, it could feel as though he was just a dirty old man, a stalker. But if he was part of the community and everyone knew him, it might be different. We called him Donovan Bogarde, and his object of desire? Mrs Johnson . . .

We had a guy called 'Black Man, innit?', who went up for the unlikeliest job interviews, and when it was explained to him that he just wasn't suitable for the job because he was not an expert in baking, OR an award-winning artist, OR an eight-year-old female actor, he would kick off and accuse them of racism: 'It's 'cos I'm a black man, innit? Yeah, yeah – when we was slaves, rowing you from here to there and pickin' cotton, it was fine. But now, when it's about playin' the lead in *Annie* – you runnin' your mind games, innit???' He'd badger them until he got the job.

There was a series of quite complicated flatulence-based sketches, where Omid Djalili and I would be in a variety of situations from the movies – classic gangster flick, *Alien*-type movie, Spanish Inquisition, American Civil War, and so on. The only thing our characters would have to do was keep quiet – no noise at the high-stakes cinematic turning point in the story – but then one of us, whether through fear or just constipation, would fart. The other one would laugh and laugh and laugh uproariously, until we were captured or killed by the bad guys.

The other movie homage was called 'Fights'. These were silent movies – no dialogue, just two people taking a dislike to each other over something incredibly trivial and then slowly building up to an epic movie battle using whatever instruments of pain that came to hand. We made one in a pet shop, where the various puppies, mice and hedgehogs were used as weapons. We also set one in a coroner's room where Omid played a doctor examining a dead body, and I played the annoying detective chief inspector who is careless with his doughnut and his coffee and accidentally drops them into the chest cavity.

There was also a nativity play, where Tony Gardner and I played two shepherds who were late for the adoration of the Magi and annoyed the Lord God so much they ended up being struck by lightning.

I played spies, cops, detectives, pet shop owners, geezers, crooks and know-alls – the lot. I enjoyed myself immensely. The pilot went out at Christmas 2000, and we were nominated for the Golden Rose of Montreux award. It had been almost twenty years since *Three of a Kind* had won the Silver Rose of Montreux and the international press prize for best light entertainment programme. To win the Golden Rose all these years later would be a huge honour and the tying-off of a loop.

I was very nervous about it all – it had been a long time since my name had been in the awards circuit for anything – but I got a call from Clive asking, 'If I could get you out to Montreux, would you get on a plane?'

I said, 'I'm on my way.'

On arrival, I was whisked, in my purple Ozwald Boateng suit, to the venue and then to my seat, where Paul Jackson was next to me – almost in tribute to us winning the Silver Rose twenty years earlier.

Clive was there too, smiling away. We sat through the ceremony and, sure enough, when they got to the Golden Rose category, I heard my name announced. I almost stopped breathing. There's an expression – people say they are 'beside themselves' when something remarkable happens. Well, this was a true out-of-body experience! I walked up onto the stage and collected my award – the Golden Rose of frickin' Montreux. And it weighs a ton!

What surfacing looks like

I thanked everybody involved with the show: all the writers; the very talented director, Matt Lipsey; my co-actors – everybody who had anything to do with it. I told them it had been a long journey to get there. Last but not least, I thanked my family – who were at home in the living room, thinking I was in the shed in the back garden.

Then I lifted the award in the air. I'd finally broken through the surface!

I returned home the next day, bedazzled, still in shock, but somewhere on the road to happiness. The end of an era, but the beginning of a new life.

EPILOGUE

Or so I thought at the time.

I had answered the question of the first book's title: *Who Am I?* I had surfaced and was finally who I am.

While researching this book, I was surfing the net and came across an article about me as a kid, when I was working at a local factory – this was just after I'd made a splash at the Queen Mary Ballroom, but just before the *New Faces* appearance in 1975. A bloke, who was a local agent, was dissing me in the article because I was inexperienced and didn't really know how to play to a tough, grizzled working men's club audience.

First things first: dude, I was fifteen when I did that gig.

It took me at least ten years to get even halfway decent and consistent as a performer. On many occasions, I was spared the loss of dignity suffered by most show business turns because of my appearances on *Tiswas* and *Blankety Blank* and things like that. There was something else going on besides the 'Can he do an hour and get an ovation at the end of it?' kind of vibe. People gave me a pass at times because I was young and they'd seen me on the telly. I worked with Larry Grayson and Don Maclean and the Grumbleweeds and Vera Lynn and Stan Boardman and Keith Harris and Orville and Gerry and the Pacemakers and Tommy Cooper, and I was somehow able to keep my head mostly above water. I was willing to learn in order to get to the next step in the journey.

I loved this career – where I didn't have to get up at five in the morning and get the bus to the factory and work till five every single day of my life, as my father did. I loved that I got to have rehearsals and laugh all day, and then go out and maybe see a movie or a comic or a play – and then get up the next morning and repeat the whole process again.

I think I improved despite having no real ability. I couldn't really sing or dance. I'd forget the middle bit of jokes. I'd fall over or knock props over (in front of Princess Anne!). I don't know how I was allowed to grace a stage, but they kept letting me have another go – just to see what happened.

I am so humbled and grateful for those chances to improve: those grown-up performers who took it upon themselves to take me to one side and ask who was writing for me and whether I shouldn't think about upgrading the material; the people who made me question who I was and what I was doing in terms of my identity as a black Briton.

From the mid-eighties onwards, everyone just assumed that I was a veteran club act who knew what was going on. I didn't.

Geoff Posner told me, in 1984, that it was important that I speak between the sketches because I was the only black person on television with their own show. I was twenty-five years old and had this extraordinary and valuable platform – it would have been insane not to let me speak my truths (whatever they were) on national television.

Reading this back, the constant references to rising and falling and swimming and almost drowning feel never-ending.

But the point, I guess, is that I was always learning, always trying to improve.

Ever tried. Ever failed. No matter. Try again.
Fail again. Fail better.
　Samuel Beckett

Seems to have been written for me. I Failed Upwards – but I kept going because what was the alternative? I guess what I've learnt (and this has taken years) is that you can't just work *all the time* . . . you need to take time out, stop, smell the ackee and saltfish. Otherwise, you'll burn out, and that's no good to anyone. Work hard but, for God's sake, play hard too. The playing always feeds back into what you're doing at work, especially if you're a creative.

The main thing I've learnt is that the work never really goes away.

It'll be there when you get back.

So go spend time with your family.

Take a sabbatical.

Learn how to play chess.

Take piano lessons.

Plant some yams, onions, sweet potatoes and cabbages in the backyard, for a laugh.

There are many things I want to do. But the one thing I can't do now is take my mother back to Jamaica and see the expression on her face as people watch her walking down the street and yell, 'Hey, H'inglish woman! Yu have money?'

I would have loved to have seen that – but I never took her. I let the work take over.

Silly sod.

DOWN IN THE BASEMENT
WITH OTHELLO

The early noughties had seen me appear in four sketch shows. FOUR! My plan for the future was not to do any more. They're a young man's game. You need strong legs, a cast-iron constitution and skin as thick as an elephant's to endure the rigours of sketch comedy. And I had endured: two seasons of *The Cheapest Show on the Telly*; three, plus a Christmas special, of *Three of a Kind*; two seasons of the 1980s *Lenny Henry Show,* plus two Chrimbo specials. Then I'd returned in the nineties with a wilder, crazier, more Afro-Caribbean-tastic sketch show produced by Kevin Lygo and Geoff Atkinson. In 2000, I'd won the Golden Rose of Montreux for yet another sketch show called *Lenny Henry in Pieces* – two series of that and I was back doing an old-school, tribute-band version of the original *Lenny Henry Show*. I had no idea what I was doing, in spite of all that effort to get away from sketch shows.

I felt deflated, like a balloon the day after a banging party. What was to become of me?

I drifted, did the odd thing, and then I spent a lot of time doing stuff for BBC Radio 4.

Radio people want you to do things, a plethora of things: I was invited to write plays, present documentaries, create sitcoms. I was blessed. I enjoyed it. I was suddenly in a place where my creativity was celebrated.

One particular radio show – called *What's So Great About . . .* – challenged me in many ways. The idea was that I undertook to

329

try out a variety of occupations or popular music choices and report back to the listener to see if their own reactions were confirmed. We investigated Bob Dylan (great songs, not sure about the voice); mathematics (ugh); The Pogues (great songs, loads of energy, not sure about the voice); motivational speaking (there's something in this). And, finally – Shakespeare.

The latter programme was originally called 'Lenny and Will'. I was the guy who'd seen one or two Shakespeare plays on the telly – and even studied them for my BA Hons – but didn't really get into them. To me, it was all posh blokes with a speech impediment and a cabbage down their tights. I remembered reading *Romeo and Juliet* aloud at school, with Ronnie Barton playing Romeo and me as Juliet. There was lots of laughing as we mangled Shakespeare's love rhymes in our Dudley accent.

So this present-day foray into the world of Shakespearean acting was all set to leave me cold. Then one day Judi Dench came to see us and spoke, very movingly, about her various Shakespearean adventures. She spoke reverently about performing Lady Macbeth, playing counter to Ian McKellen's Scottish king. I watched the play on video several times and was struck by her style of speech – absolutely in rhythm and metre, spot on – but somehow, she made it seem like conversation. She was a devastatingly wonderful verse-speaker and read two sonnets for us, which had me captivated. Judi Dench rocked.

There was also the fateful phone call with Barrie Rutter of Northern Broadsides theatre company. He rang from his home-town of Hull, to make a plea for Shakespeare that we can all understand, Shakespeare in our own voices, Shakespeare that rides the conversational rhythms like a disobedient pony. He performed Henry V's prologue at length down the phone:

O for a Muse of fire, that would ascend
The brightest heaven of invention,
A kingdom for a stage, princes to act
And monarchs to behold the swelling scene!

He burned through the text, making the consonants pop and the vowels roll off the tongue. And it was all spoken with a deep and percussive Hull accent. It worked too.

We invited Barrie down to London shortly afterwards for a second programme – a follow up to 'Lenny and Will' – which would be about me slowly falling for the idea of taking part in a play.

I'd always hated the idea of doing theatre. I knew lots of people who'd done it – Alexei Sayle had played Trinculo in *The Tempest* and, by all accounts, enjoyed the experience. I'd also seen Rik Mayall tear apart the Olivier stage at the National Theatre in *The Government Inspector* by Nikolai Gogol. God, he was funny in that play. I was very jealous, but nothing in me actually wanted to emulate him. It seemed like such hard work for so little return.

It wasn't that I didn't like plays; it was more that I didn't know how I fitted into them. Up until 2009, I'd been the kind of guy who loved my job as an entertainer and didn't give a second thought to turning down a play for a number of reasons:

- They want me to be in it for too long.
- They want me to join a repertory company and move to Leeds.
- I'd have to learn four plays in eight weeks.
- They want to give me two quid and a toffee apple.

I just didn't fancy it. Mainly because I was scared.

Learning a play is hard – what happens if you forget where you are, or oversleep in the dressing room, or put on the wrong wig, or just simply forget to go in one night. A play is a relent-less beast – once you commit, that's it. So I gave all offers the big body swerve – my agent sent very nice responses to all approaches from theatreland:

- Lenny's on tour at the moment
- Lenny isn't taking any offers right now – he's writing a new show
- Lenny's doing a TV series with Kay Mellor/Lucy Gannon/ Chris Chibnall
- Lenny is on a slimming holiday in Spain
- Lenny is spending time with his family
- Lenny is no longer with us . . . please give a donation to the Entertainment Artists Benevolent Fund . . .

Though there were loads of excuses for not doing a play – I'm not proud of the fact that my worry was memory failure, fear and the lack of serious bucks, but that's how I felt. Fear obviously taking pole position.

I don't know if you have one, but I have an inner critic (every-one out there is just waiting for you to fail at whatever you choose to do), who, at the trickiest moments, chooses to show up in my head and yell very loudly, 'Hey! Doofus! You can't do this!' and 'No way in the world are you gonna pull this off' and 'You're shit. Just give up.'

Honestly, I know it's just going on stage and saying stuff like you mean it, but going on with all that needless and painful chat-ter in your head day after day? It's all a bit much. So fear was a major issue – I could deal with it when I was doing stand-up but that's different. Who am I hurting if I forget a line during one of my own gigs. I'll just say something else or make a stupid joke about my lips not working properly or having false teeth or old age creeping in. I can always improvise if I bugger something up when I'm doing my own shit. But when I'm in a play, I can't do that. I can't just go off at a tangent in the middle of a Molière play and start riffling through women's handbags on the front row – 'Whoa! What's this, young lady?', etc.

However, I was a different Len now. Disaffected by the disappointments of being a road comic in the early twenty-first century, I decided to put my back into being a working actor. I wanted to be open to the idea of accepting a role in a play.

Barrie Rutter came down from up North to give me a masterclass in Shakespearean acting. We would rehearse a speech from *Othello* in the basement of the BBC. My Executive Producer, Simon Elmes, would record it all for posterity as Barrie pushed and pulled, rocked and rolled, coerced and cajoled me into giving something that resembled a performance. To say I was nervous about all this is to put it mildly – I was terrified.

This speech, though, was a doozy: Othello has recovered from his temporary madness to find his once beloved wife Desdemona and her maid Emilia both dead on the bed. He is trying to make sense of it all. He is calm as guards enter and posture, as if they're about to take him into custody. . . He speaks to them:

> *Soft you. A word or two before you go.*
> *I have done the state some service, and they know't.*
> *No more of that. I pray you in your letters,*
> *When you shall these unlucky deeds relate,*
> *Speak of me as I am. Nothing extenuate,*
> *Nor set down aught in malice.*

> *Then must you speak*

Of one that loved not wisely, but too well;
Of one not easily jealous, but being wrought,
Perplexed in the extreme; of one whose hand,
Like the base Judean, threw a pearl away
Richer than all his tribe; of one whose subdued eyes,
Albeit unused to the melting mood,
Drops tears as fast as the Arabian trees
Their medicinable gum. Set you down this.
And say besides, that in Aleppo once,
Where a malignant and a turbanned Turk
Beat a Venetian and traduced the state,
I took by th' throat the circumcisèd dog,
And smote him, thus.
He stabs himself.

Now there's a lot going on here – odd language, strange and foreign references – but there's also beautiful poetry – 'nothing extenuate', 'a malignant and a turbanned turk', 'drops tears as fast as the Arabian trees their medicinable gum'. I made an effort to learn it as well as I could the night before. It seemed impossible. How do you learn such a complicated way of speaking? Fine for Paterson Joseph and Judi Dench to insist that I get the words in my gob – but this just felt undoable. No one speaks like this unless they're in a Shakespeare play. No one's going on about turbanned Turks down your local pub. This was going to take some doing.

I got to Broadcasting House early the next day. We weren't due to start until 10 a.m., but I was there in the local cafe, running my lines and drinking coffee and hoping I could remember it all. It didn't feel as though I knew it at all – where is my memory? Why can't I remember this? Argggghhhh!

I went in past the security guys and their jokes about me looking like Ainsley Harriot, and I managed to find Simon downstairs. He was all set up and ready to record. Barrie Rutter had arrived and was just having a cup of tea in the canteen.

He was soon there and certainly looked the part of actor/manager. Barrie had been running Northern Broadsides since the early nineties; he was an artistic director who took it upon himself to preside over all aspects of managing a theatre company, from casting to choosing costumes to advising on music to directing the actors. He pretty much did everything. Barrie has an air about him – he's very alpha and isn't scared to tell you if something's not working:

Oy! That's rubbish.
Do summat with yer hands
Generals don't walk like that, y'daft bugger

And stuff like that. But it didn't feel as though he was undermining you – more like he was elevating you, trying to get your head in the game. He behaved as though we were actually rehearsing the play – for real. And it was exhilarating! He made me chew the words, spit them out, roll my tongue around them, hit certain beats and then lay out for a moment. It was rock and roll – it was a poetry slam, it was acting, proper acting. I could feel something happening to me. My hands had weight – he made me do less with them and, as a result, they would settle into a relaxed place by my sides. Then, when I wanted to gesture, it would be a powerful movement that meant something. I'd never realised how much I used my hands until Barrie told me to 'Stop waving yer hands about like a big dozy pillock!' As we walked around, Simon with his big boom microphone recording our every word,

I found myself silently wishing this rehearsal could go on for ever. I'd never rehearsed anything, whether it was a sketch or a song or a monologue, for this long. With comedy, you'd usually run something a bit, learn it, perform it and then forget it. But with this Shakespearean stuff, it was like injecting the words into your system for the foreseeable future. This wasn't a case of learning a Delbert Wilkins monologue, deciding when the manic laugh went in or where the killer punchline was – this was about caressing the words and then pumping them out, then whispering, then standing, then reaching – this was a real workout. It was all about retaining the muscle memory of the performance: where and how and why you were standing a certain way; facing a certain direction actually contributed to the long-term memory of the piece.

I loved every aspect of that morning. Barrie made it easy for me to understand the acquisition of the text. 'You don't bugger about round a table. Aye, y'read it first to get a sense of it, but the sooner y'can gerrup and start doin' it the better!' And then he'd go off and grab another brew and a biscuit.

And the more we did it, the better it got.

I hadn't realised, up to that point, just how restrained I was as an actor. Even though I was known for having boundless energy, jumping up and down with my tongue out like Animal from *The Muppets* – actually, I'm quite shy in the spaces in between. Don't get me wrong, I loved to dance and sing and all that, but generally, when I'm not on stage, I'm this other guy. Quieter maybe.

Anyway, when you're doing a play like *Othello*, all that goes out the window. Being shy and restrained is only useful for some elements of the play. Other moments require a majesty and stature and volume, and you've got to give it some.

So, right about now, consider me enchanted. I've done the same speech at least forty times, with Simon recording and quietly asking me to repeat the odd moment, and Barrie walking around me, coaching, pushing, encouraging me every step of the way, until I felt confident to let go at last. To let go of the idea of me 'not being the kind of guy who acted on stage in a play', let go of that whole 'Anyway, you don't get any cash if you do a play', let go of that 'I'll be staying in digs again. A gas meter next to the bed, beans on toast in the morning and mug of tea with six sugars and a bus ride to the theatre.'

I had to let go of all these preconceptions because, after one morning of rehearsals, I WANTED TO DO THIS PLAY. I can't explain it better than that. I had gone from being a light entertainment 'turn', hell-bent on sticking to the status quo of touring, gigging and the odd telly appearance – to the idea of being somewhere for a considerable length of time and doing two things and two things only: rehearsing a play . . . and then performing it for an audience.

We got to the end of rehearsals, and I said these fateful words to Barrie Rutter: 'Do you think I can do this Barrie?' And he replied: 'Course you can!' And that was it – as Barrie has told me repeatedly – 'after that it was just a case of dates and diaries'. I had other commitments; I couldn't run away from them and join a theatre company. But, in the end, I was able to begin a rigorous regime of verse-speaking lessons with Bardy Thomas, gym workouts and the odd meeting with Barrie in London, before schlepping all the way up to Leeds to begin work at the West Yorkshire Playhouse (latterly the Leeds Playhouse).

The Playhouse is a community theatre in many ways. It has a main theatre space and a smaller auditorium. They have a large rehearsal space underneath the main theatre and a big canteen area where (at least when we were there) the local community come in and do daily activities. I loved it there.

The first day involved a read-through of the entire play with all the cast around a set of tables. There were production staff and theatre staff dotted around too. Lots of cups of tea and coffee, glasses of water, biscuits, throat sweets – whatever it took to make us all relax and put our backs into the matter at hand.

The Table read: Barrie was playing the Duke, Desdemona's dad, so he was in amongst us, not just sat in the director's chair but kind of split between authority and working-actor mode.

I was nervous because Simon was there, recording a special edition of Radio 4's 'Lenny and Will', part three – I've got a part in a Shakespeare play, now what?

Conrad Nelson was playing Iago, Jessica Harris was Desdemona, Matt Connor was Roderigo and Richard Standing was Cassio. And there were many others. I was the most inexperienced person at the table by far, but they all made me feel welcome. They'd all done hundreds of plays – this was my first, and somehow they had all vowed to carry me along with them, to encourage and nurture me and get me across the line.

As we read, I could feel my voice striving for something – some authority, some deep resonant power. But it wouldn't do that at first; I sounded like me but with a cold. Why would that happen at the read through? We hadn't even started yet – and I sounded like Jimmy Clitheroe? Bloody hell, this was impossible!

Finally, we got to the end. And that was it – we'd read it. There was a round of applause from everyone around the table. I looked at Barrie and he smiled and then stood up to give a speech. It went a bit like this: